To Paul,
Whose worship leadership inspired me

To Sammy,
Whose partnership affirmed me

To Jan,
Whose insights challenged me

Deborah Moore Clark

O Come, Let Us Bow Down and Worship

A Spiritual Guide for Leadership

SMYTH & HELWYS
PUBLISHING, INCORPORATED MACON, GEORGIA

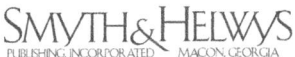

Smyth & Helwys Publishing, Inc.
6316 Peake Road
Macon, Georgia 31210-3960
1-800-747-3016
©2003 by Smyth & Helwys Publishing
All rights reserved.

Library of Congress Cataloging-in-Publication Data

Clark, Deborah Moore, 1952-
O come, let us bow down and worship / Deborah Moore Clark.
p. cm.
Includes bibliographical references.
ISBN 978-1-57312-364-8
1. Worship—Biblical teaching. I. Title.
BS680.W78C53 2003
264'.061—dc21

2002152736

Table of Contents

Preface 3

Chapter 1 7
Why Worship?

Chapter 2 15
Scriptural Models for Worship

Chapter 3 53
What Is Worship? Characteristics and Descriptions

Chapter 4 75
Worship Is Not . . .

Chapter 5 89
Components of Christian Worship

Chapter 6 135
Inclusive Language, Inclusive Worship

Chapter 7 153
A Matter of Style

Chapter 8 175
Worship Reform—How?

Chapter 9 191
The Planning Process

Chapter 10 207
A Team Approach to Planning

Chapter 11 227
The Consequences of Authentic Worship

Bibliography 235

Appendix 1 243
Sources and Authors of Marginal Quotations

Appendix 2 251
Recommended Reading

Preface

For many years now, the study of worship has been an active interest of mine, both for personal and professional reasons. I hope the following glimpse into my personal pilgrimage will tell how this is so. Although my Christian heritage is rich, I have not always been as interested in the dynamic of worship as I might have been.

The eldest daughter of a Southern Baptist pastor, I received many opportunities for involvement in church life. I literally grew up in the church. During the first decades of my youth—the 1950s and 1960s—the church played an important role in my social life and in the social lives of people like me who lived in an essentially rural area on the verge of great growth. During my impressionable years, church, school, and family activities were the mainstay of my existence. Since those childhood days, the church has remained a focal point of my life.

While I was growing up, my parents made sure I regularly attended the usual assortment of church activities—worship, Bible study, missions activities, and related recreational-social events. Like many other young people of my time, I was fortunate to be privately schooled in piano and organ lessons, encouraged to practice, and asked to use my musical talents at church.

As with other ministers' families, money was often tight, so I began working at part-time jobs during my teen years to help with the usual expenses teenage daughters incur and to save for college. When I was seventeen years old I found work as an organist and adult choir director in a small United Church of Christ where I served until leaving home for college.

Through that experience and two other similar positions following it during college, I began to feel God's specific call to music ministry.

Not long after college graduation—at some undetermined point—I began to realize my poverty when it came to understanding and leading in worship. By this time, I was serving my third church as organist and choir director, planning and leading music in worship on a regular basis. It dawned upon me that I was going through the motions where worship was concerned, not realizing the importance of my contribution as a worship leader—or worshiper. Now, please don't misunderstand. Church participation at that time was probably one of the most important aspects of my life. My faith in God was strong and my appetite for Bible study was keen. I enjoyed my work as a part-time staff member. I was saving money to go to seminary. But somehow, amid all this religious activity, I realized I was missing something. For the first time, I saw that my understanding of worship was shallow, and my contribution to worship, although meaningful, was much less than my best effort.

The epiphany was quick and illuminating. God spoke in that still small voice inaudible to human ears but discernible to human hearts. As a result of the Spirit's convicting encounter, I began to read and study, first about church music ministry, then about worship. Looking back upon the experience, mysterious and confounding as it was, I realize that in a serendipitous moment God's Spirit touched mine and a new prophet was born. Like Isaiah's encounter with God in the temple, in an instant, the Holy One seemed to call me out, challenging and leading me to reform my attitudes, my ideas, my behavior, and most of all, my leadership concerning worship. The years since this quiet but life-changing happening have been rich in the discovery of worship's wonder and magnitude. Part of what I share in the following pages are the discoveries of this pilgrimage. But the journey is not complete.

I write with the hope that you who read will reflect, question, and find the inspiration so graciously given me to look further. I share with questions still unanswered, but with a prophetic urgency to teach. I reason that others who faithfully attend worship every week—those who teach Sunday school, those who serve as diaconal ministers, those who volunteer in the many aspects of church life, and those who lead worship week after week—may also not fully realize the power and the mystery of the throne they approach in worship. While I could never say for certain whether another person truly worships or not, I reason that many others who lead and attend worship faithfully may also be worshiping—like I did—without full knowledge of all they do or of what is expected of them.

This conviction that many worshipers are just like me underpins my effort in writing this book. I want to share what I have learned about the richness of worship. I want to stretch myself to learn more. I want to help the family of God, of which I am a part, to worship more fully. But more importantly, I want to honor God with my worship and my writing, individually through my own efforts, and also within the community of faith where I serve and worship.

Many books about worship have already been written. Many, if not most, may be more scholarly than this manuscript. This book, however, is designed to be an *interactive* text—a practical manual or study guide—for stimulating discussion and creativity in worship planning and leadership. It may be used in individual study, but it works best for group study.

Who This Book Is For

This book is for pastors, ministers of music and other church staff ministers, liturgists, worship committees, worship study or focus groups, seminary students, worship workshop participants, and any other people actively engaged in learning about, planning, and leading corporate worship within Christian churches of the free church traditions *and beyond.* Readers may also include individual worshipers as well as small groups within worshiping communities who desire to learn more about worship and to look critically at their own corporate worship practice.

Certainly, no reader who uses this book will ever agree with everything written here. But what is more important than approval or rejection is for this text to stimulate a process of critical thinking and honest questioning about this taken-for-granted, yet remarkable event called worship. I hope the use and re-use of this manual will inspire additional study and learning about worship practice and participation.

How to Use This Book

Students and teachers alike can use this manual to facilitate both worship workshop learning and teaching. The format suggests some possible uses, emphasizing the book's purpose as an interactive study guide. Questions to ponder end each chapter or major subsection. These questions are tools for interaction with the text included to stimulate critical thinking, honest discussion, and perhaps even a debate or two. I do not know the answers to all the questions. The idea is to get the reader—the worship leader, the workshop participant, the worshiper—to think openly, honestly, and critically about his or her own attitudes about worship and worship practice. Some of the questions, without apology, are meant to be challenging and are posed to provoke conversation, struggle, and critical thinking.

An annotated bibliography appends the text (see Appendix 2.) This short recommended reading list is included for those who wish to dig deeper into the subjects discussed within the study guide. The list is small but diverse, representing my best recommendations to readers wanting more.

Biblical quotations throughout the text come from the New Revised Standard Version (NRSV) unless otherwise noted. In a deliberant attempt to be inclusive, I have chosen non-gendered language for God and human beings. Where quotations have been included that follow a more traditional, male-gendered approach to language, these have been altered for inclusiveness.

In sum, I hope the text and the format will serve as resources for opening wide the door of creativity—in thinking, in planning, and ultimately, in worship practice—as those who use it honestly and critically will become catalysts within their communities of faith for worship reform. The process, without a doubt, has challenged and nourished me.

Deborah Moore Clark
Charlotte, North Carolina

On the whole, I do not find Christians, outside of the catacombs, sufficiently sensible of conditions. Does anyone have the foggiest idea what sort of power we so blithely invoke? Or, as I suspect, does no one believe a word of it?

—Annie Dillard

CHAPTER 1

Why Worship?

That [God] seeks worshipers is unparalleled for nowhere in the entire corpus of Holy Scripture do we read of God's seeking anything else from a child of God. God desires worship above all else.

—Kent Hughes

Some critics of worship may ask boldly, why worship at all? Many Christians, by the irregularity of their worship, testify to their belief that worship is merely an optional activity. Others, bored by the Sunday event, find themselves wondering, why bother? In this brief introductory chapter, several reasons why we must worship are explored. If these reasons fail to convince you of worship's necessity, then I urge you to stretch your mind and imagination about worship as you read and interact with the chapters that follow. If you are already convinced of the need for worship, I encourage you also to read on. Bring with you attitudes open to expanding and enriching your thinking and practice of life's most important event—worship.

To Obey the Scriptural Command

From beginning to end, the Bible makes reference to worship and communion with God. Implicit within the story of Eden is the Creator's communal relationship with man and woman. From Abraham to Micah, the Hebrew Bible attests to the necessity of worship. Abraham provides a model for worship on Mount Moriah. Moses, instructed by God, provides guidelines for living and worship in the wilderness and promised land. "Exodus devotes 25 chapters to the construction of the Tabernacle, the locus of divine worship. Leviticus amounts to a 27-chapter liturgical manual."[1] Judges, kings, and the children of Israel struggled to develop and preserve monotheistic worship of the One Holy God. The Psalms—recording the songs of David and Hebrew worship—declare lyrically, *Worship the LORD in holy splendor* (Ps 29:2b) and *Extol the LORD our God; worship at [God's] footstool. Holy is [God]!* (Ps 99:5). Pre-exilic prophets condemn ritualism lacking ethical and spiritual content. Post-exilic prophets emphasize balance between inward and outward devotion.

Jesus, steeped in synagogue worship from early childhood, teaches frequently about worship and a right relationship between ritual and lifestyle. The apostle Paul deals repeatedly with abuses in early Christian worship practice, admonishing Christlikeness in worshipers. Finally, one of the last commands recorded in the New Testament was given to John by the angel who says, *Worship God!* (Rev 22:9). We worship because God expects it. We worship because Jesus worshiped. The Bible tells us so.

To Maintain Our Proper Relationship with God

We are not so very different from the children of Israel, repeatedly promising to serve the Lord of Hosts, then forgetting our promises. Like Israel, we voice again and again, *All the words that the LORD has spoken we will do* (Ex 24:3b). *All that the LORD has spoken we will do, and we will be obedient* (24:7b). But scarcely after the words have fallen from our lips, we build graven images, forgetting our vows. We promise and forget, we promise and err, we promise and wander, we promise and stray, we promise and fail, and on and on the cycle goes. Over and over, we do what is evil in the sight of the Lord, forgetting the Lord and worshiping earthly idols.[2] But God, like a forgiving and

We keep doing these things over and over again on Sunday morning because we know that if we didn't we might lose our love. In fact, those times when we don't feel like it, when we really feel no deep attachment or desire to worship the Beloved, are the times we ought to be sure and worship . . . . We come feeling our relationship with God is weak and shallow; then, in the ritual, the singing, the words of Scripture, the familiar friends and setting, we go forth strengthened, having grown in our love.

—WILLIAM H. WILLIMON

loving husband, woos us back time and time again as we forsake our vows and play the harlot.³

Because we are prone to wander, we need the regular reminder of worship to keep us committed. Troy W. Petty described this need when he wrote, "Life in covenant with God rests upon repeated incidents of worship and renewal. Worship serves to remind us of who God is, what [God] has done, and what [God] is yet doing on our behalf. Renewal of our faith is needed because of our inability or failure to live up to God's demands."⁴

O to grace how great a debtor
daily I'm constrained to be!
Let thy grace, Lord, like a fetter,
bind my wandering heart to thee:
Prone to wander, Lord, I feel it,
Prone to leave the God I love;
Here's my heart, Lord, take and seal it,
Seal it for thy courts above.

—ROBERT ROBINSON, 1758

Worship reminds us who we are, who we are not, and who we may become. Worship woos us back into a right relationship with the Holy One. If we forsake this opportunity, we fail to live responsibly in relationship with God.

Because God Is

Frank E. Gaebelein wrote, "We worship God not because we feel like it, but because [God] *is* God and worship is [God's] due and our necessity."⁵ Freelance writer Karen Moderow made a similar point when she wrote, "Worship is like a circle. We worship the Lord because [God] deserves to be praised for who [God] is—apart from our feelings or circumstances."⁶ Moderow's simile ("like a circle") helps us visualize worship as a never-ending, ongoing process of praise. This negates the notion of worship as a once-a-week, one-hour event. Rather, worship is a process reflected in our Sunday praise and our Monday living. God, the Great I Am, deserves and

God said to Moses, "I AM WHO I AM." [God] said further, "Thus you shall say to the Israelites, I AM has sent me to you." God also said to Moses, "Thus you shall say to the Israelites, 'The LORD, the God of your ancestors, the God of Abraham, the God of Isaac, and the God of Jacob, has sent me to you': This is my name forever, and this my title for all generations."

—GENESIS 3:14-15

desires our worship in the strains of our songs, in the expressions of our faces, in the tones of our voices, in our manners and motions, in our telephone conversations and prayers, in our frustration and joy, and in our sadness and glee. Ideally, all of life is worship. What offering shall we give the Alpha and Omega?

To Form the Community

We live in a culture that views worship as a private thing—private devotion, individual fulfillment, a one-hour fix to meet personal needs. This me-centered approach treats worship more like a buffet, cafeteria line, or food court where people gather to eat but more or less dine separately, eating only what they want. This modern-day emphasis focuses on individual tastes, likes and dislikes, appeal and preferences. But this is not what worship is about. Worship is more like a great banquet—a feast, festival, or family reunion—where more than a great hall or table is shared. A common meal is shared, and as through the sharing and feasting on common foods, community forms.

All praise and thanks to God, Who reigns in highest heaven, To [Maker] and to Son And Spirit now be given. The one eternal god, Whom heaven and earth adore, The God who was, and is, And shall be evermore.

—MARTIN RINKART, 1636; TRANS. CATHERINE WINKWORTH, 1858; ADAPTED 1985

In worship, the Maker gathers up worshiping individuals, transforming them into a new whole—a community—existing to worship and serve God. In her classic book *Worship*, Evelyn Underhill asserts, "Christian worship is never a solitary undertaking. Both on its visible and invisible sides, it has a thoroughly social and organic character. The worshiper, however lonely in appearance, comes before God as a member of a great family; part of the Communion of Saints, living and dead."[7] Steeped in history and tradition and undergirded by two thousand years of spiritual culture, Christian worship has persisted and survived, and it cannot be understood apart from these influences. The community of faith, seen in this light, takes on enormous proportion. The spiritual community of God includes those saints departed, all saints living, and those yet to be born.

Christian worship is at once personal and social, yet essentially corporate. According to Underhill, each aspect of worship's twofold character completes, reinforces, and checks the other.[8] In worship, individuals are fused into a spiritual community with all others gathered with them—those in their particular house of worship and those gathered in all other sanctuaries in all places.

Underhill assigns deeper meaning to the church's corporate worship than "... merely a collection of services, offices, and sacraments. Deeply considered, it is the sacrificial life of Christ Himself; the Word indwelling His Church...."[9] Using phrases like *Corpus Christi*, "mystical body," and "supernatural organism," Underhill describes the church transformed by corporate worship. Names such as these and the Body of Christ convey great weight and responsibility.

A group of individuals gather for worship. Through worship, the Creator God gathers up the individuals, molding them together into a spiritual community. And although the newly formed group is a diverse collection of personalities with varying interests, talents, and abilities, this new body becomes one in Christ. This supernatural gathering, knitting minds, wills, and souls into the unified body of Christ, happens only in worship. Nowhere else. This gathering of individuals into community takes place for a purpose.

Once formed through worship, the Christ community faces the challenge of great responsibility and must ask itself: What service shall we perform in God's name? What acts shall we perform as Christ's body? In what joint projects shall we, the Body of Christ, engage to express our collective faith? How are we as a community empowered through worship? What does it mean to leave the sanctuary a changed and united people?

The Christian community is not a mere phenomenon, however distinguished. It is an event. Otherwise it is not the Christian community.... The fact remains that it is not itself a foundation or institution. In correspondence with the hidden being of Jesus Christ Himself, it is an earthly-historical event, and as such it is the earthly-historical form of His existence.

—KARL BARTH

Both personal and corporate worship are necessary. The two are intertwined. At the heart of corporate worship is the private preparation and worship of each person in the pew. As worshipers worship side-by-side, the test of true worship—a changed heart—remains individual and personal. The Redeemer judges this condition personally with each worshiper. But the drama does not stop there. While the one-on-one encounter is going on in the hearts of individual worshipers, God is also working to collect and transform those gathered into a community who will be called upon to extend their worship by practicing corporate acts of social responsibility, generosity, and ministry in the world about them. In this sense, the changed heart of a

. . . the corporate worship of the Church is not simply that of an assembly of individuals who believe the same things, and therefore unite in doing the same things. It is real in its own right; an action transcending and embracing all the separate souls taking part in it.

—EVELYN UNDERHILL

community of faith is also judged. What will be the community's corporate response to its encounter with God in worship? Worship begins with individual contrite hearts but ends with a newly formed mystical community of faith. We worship to form this community.

Because We Are Loved

William Willimon, in his book *What's Right with the Church,* discusses at some length the extravagance of worship. He writes, "Worship . . . has a scandalously gratuitous quality to it. People seem to do it for the sheer fun of it."[10] Comparing worship to being in love, Willimon describes the unmeasured and fanciful behaviors of lovers—singing, laughing, writing poetry, crying, shouting, dancing, sending roses, hugging, kissing, and so on. Brilliantly, Willimon illuminates the analogy with this profound conclusion.

> So here we are at the heart of it all. Here is the scandal of Sunday morning behavior. We love because we have been loved (1 John 4:19). Our alleged excessiveness in worship is the excess produced by love. The church's worship on Sunday is a way of being in love . . . if you have been loved, you already know something of how lovers need to return love. You are already on the way to understanding irrational, nonutilitarian, gratuitous, delightfully useless behavior like Christian worship.[11]

Questions to Ponder

1. What reasons motivate you to worship? How did you arrive at this point?

2. Do you find yourself asking, why bother to worship? What motivates your questions?

3. How may pleasure, selfishness, greed, and misplaced priorities serve as modern idols? Can you think of others? List them.

4. What idols interfere with your worship of God?

5. Does worship woo you back into a right relationship with God? In what ways does this happen? If not, what gets in the way?

6. Does worship woo your church back into a right relationship with God? In what ways does this happen? If not, what gets in the way?

7. What connection do you make between Sunday worship and weekday living? How do you express this connection?

8. What connection does your church make between Sunday worship and weekday service? How is this connection expressed in the life of your congregation?

9. How does your own worship continue through the week?

10. How does your church's worship continue through the week?

11. How, when, and where do you fail to worship God? In an act of confession, commit these times to God.

12. Recall a time when you were in love. Describe your feelings, thoughts, and behaviors. How is your worship of the Holy One similar? How is it different? How is your church's corporate worship similar? How is it different?

13. Whom do you love? How do you express this love? Make a list of your various expressions.

14. In what ways do you express your love toward God? In what ways does your church express its love toward God?

NOTES

[1] Kent Hughes, *Disciplines of a Godly Man*, quoted by Davis Duggins, senior editor of *Moody* in "In Spirit and in Truth," *Moody* 96/6 (1996): 28.

[2] This paraphrase loosely follows the repeating refrain within Scripture: *The Israelites did what was evil in the sight of the LORD, forgetting the LORD their God, and worshiping the Baals and the Asherahs* (Judg 3:7). The cyclical scenario of the children of Israel promising to obey God, forgetting their promise, doing evil deeds, and receiving God's merciful forgiveness is a recurring theme within Hebrew Scripture.

[3] Israel's unfaithfulness and God's redeeming love are described metaphorically as harlot and husband in the book of Hosea.

[4] Troy W. Petty, "Worship and Renewal," *The Religious Herald* 155/23 (1982): 12.

[5] Frank E. Gaebelein, "Heeding the Whole Counsel of God," *Christianity Today* 25/17 (1981): 29.

[6] Karen Moderow, "Breaking Through the Sunday Blues," *Moody* 96/6 (1996): 31.

[7] Evelyn Underhill, *Worship* (New York: Crossroad, 1985), 81.

[8] Underhill, *Worship*, 84.

[9] Ibid., 86.

[10] William H. Willimon, *What's Right with the Church* (San Francisco: Harper, 1985), 115.

[11] Ibid., 117.

CHAPTER 2

Scriptural Models for Worship

While the Scriptures do not provide orders of service for us to follow, a number of Scripture passages do provide insight into ancient worship practice. For instance, the New Testament pages appear to be replete with hymn fragments that may have come to us directly from the worship of the early church. Scholars do not agree on which New Testament passages are or are not hymn fragments. Nor do they agree on the criteria for identifying hymns within the pages of the New Testament. Despite this disagreement, there appear to be numerous New Testament passages that may be identified as hymn fragments—bits and pieces of liturgy sung by the early church in worship. According to Ralph P. Martin, these fragments fall into four categories:

1. The Lukan canticles
2. Hymns in the Apocalypse
3. Jewish-Christian fragments and exclamations like *Amen, Hallelujah, Marana tha,* and *Abba*
4. Distinctively Christian forms: sacramental, meditative, confessional, and christological hymns

Among the latter, passages such as Ephesians 5:14, Titus 3:4-7, 1 Timothy 6:11-16, 2 Timothy 2:11-13, 1 Timothy 3:16, Hebrews 1:3-4, Colossians 1:15-20, Philippians 2:6-11, and the Prologue of John's Gospel found at John 1:1-18 may provide windows into the cultic practice of the early church and synagogue.[1]

Scattered elsewhere within the apostolic writings are references to hymn singing, to observances of the Lord's Supper, and to prayers and offerings. But before this, the Old Testament relays stories of ancient Hebrew worship: people and communities who built temples, offered sacrifices, gave offerings, and prayed, sang, and danced before the Lord in worship.

Despite all these references, we still do not have a concrete order of service, no model worship service like the Model Prayer. But these glimpses into the past do provide a way to glean what may be acceptable to offer the Holy One in worship. In this chapter, I examine a number of Scripture passages, and in expository style I offer them as fragmentary models for our worship practice today.

A Classic Model: Isaiah 6:1-12

> In the year that King Uzziah died, I saw the Lord sitting on a throne, high and lofty; and the hem of his robe filled the temple. Seraphs were in attendance above him; each had six wings: with two they covered their faces, and with two they covered their feet, and with two they flew. And one called another and said: "Holy, holy, holy is the LORD of hosts; the whole earth is full of his glory." The pivots on the thresholds shook at the voices of those who called, and the house filled with smoke. And I said: "Woe is me! I am lost, for I am a man of unclean lips, and I live among a people of unclean lips; yet my eyes have seen the King, the LORD of hosts!"
>
> Then one of the seraphs flew to me, holding a live coal that had been taken from the altar with a pair of tongs. The seraph touched my mouth with it and said: "Now that this has touched your lips, your guilt has departed and your sin is blotted out." Then I heard the voice of the Lord saying, "Whom shall I send, and who will go for us?" And I said, "Here am I; send me!" And he said, "Go and say to this people: 'Keep listening but do not comprehend; keep looking, but do not understand.' Make the mind of this people dull, and stop their ears, and shut their eyes, so that they may not look with their eyes, and listen with their ears, and comprehend with their minds, and turn and be healed."
>
> Then I said, "How long, O Lord?" And he said: "Until cities lie waste without inhabitant, and houses without people, and the land is utterly desolate; until the LORD sends everyone far away, and vast is the emptiness in the midst of the land." (Isaiah 6:1-12)

Isaiah 6 recounts the vision of the prophet Isaiah in the temple. Isaiah has gone to the temple for succor and strength. God is revealed to Isaiah and the encounter fills Isaiah with awe. He confesses, "Woe is me!" and acknowledges his sin. We read that Isaiah is forgiven of his sin and receives cleansing for future service. Isaiah worships following his encounter with God.

The Isaiah 6 account is the best model for Christian worship I know. Isaiah's encounter is worship at its best because it is worship that is God-centered, God-focused, and exalting to the Holy One. An outline of the passage reveals a step-by-step progression through Isaiah's worship experience. This progression suggests a possible framework on which to arrange the elements of our worship.

Reference	**Action**	
Isaiah 6:1-4	Commendation (Praise)	*Holy, holy, holy!*
Isaiah 6:5	Confession and Contrition	*Woe is me!*
Isaiah 6:6-7	Cleansing	*Sin blotted out.*
Isaiah 6:8a	Calling	*Who will go?*
Isaiah 6:8b	Commitment	*Here am I, send me.*
Isaiah 6:9-10	Commissioning	*And God said, Go!*
Isaiah 6:11-12	Clarification	*How long, Lord?*

Commendation (Praise), vv. 1-4. True and transforming worship begins with praise. Isaiah begins his worship adventure with praise following his encounter with the Holy One. Isaiah's vision of God can be described as both awesome and mysterious. In the encounter, the prophet sees the *Lord . . . high and lifted up* (Isa 6:1) and hears the declaration of God's holiness exclaimed by the seraphim: *Holy, holy, holy is the* LORD *of hosts; the whole earth is full of his glory* (Isa 6:3b).

Two writers in particular come close to capturing a glimpse of God's holiness in their respective works. Poet, novelist, and mystic Evelyn Underhill discusses the nature of worship in her classic book *Worship* (1936). She asserts that worship, the essence of all religion, is a witness to Transcendence. She continues that God—the Wholly Other, the prevenient cause of worship—elicits adoration, and she finds summary in the *Sanctus:* Holy, holy, holy![2] Underhill acknowledges a supernatural, all-encompassing, increate sense of God. Isaiah's encounter is similar. The prophet Isaiah's temple experience opens his eyes to a new vision of the unsearchable God. Once we, like Isaiah, begin to see God in this other light, our creaturely response to God's majesty easily becomes an exclamation of awe, and it is then and perhaps only then that we may begin to know God is truly worthy of worship and praise.

Likewise, modern-day writer Annie Dillard deals with God's holiness in her book *Holy the Firm* (1977). In her own unique style, which relates life to spirit, creation to Creator, and mundane to eternal, Dillard asserts that God's absoluteness—beneath all, beyond all, and in all, both indiscernible and incomprehensible to mankind—is God: Holy the Firm.[3] Dillard interprets life spiritually, metaphysically, and philosophically through a complex weaving of story, vision, and insight, yet her message is clear: all of life is spiritual and of God. Dillard, like Underhill and like Isaiah, also seems to capture a real sense of the holiness of God. Once sensed, God's otherness can bring about the profoundest of all praise, ecstatic and spontaneous, emotive and free, yet humble.

That fateful day in the temple, Isaiah witnessed God's supreme holiness as images of God's power and might were revealed to him, yet not fully disclosed. Isaiah relates *the house was filled with smoke* (Isa 6:4b) as God's presence was both revealed and hidden from his human eyes and understanding. Through this encounter, Isaiah recognized, perhaps for the first time, the utter majesty of Immortal God. This awareness caused him to worship and the experience ultimately changed his life. It is no wonder Isaiah cried out in spontaneous response: *Woe is me!* Nor is it hard to imagine that as his confessional cry was voiced, Isaiah may have fallen to his knees or on his face before the throne of God's presence. How can we do less?

Most people need assistance in making confessions. Culture conditions us to disguise our weaknesses, cover our faults, reject guilt, and remain silent about our sins. Worship demands a dramatic turn around from that—confession at all costs. Not surprisingly, help is needed.

—C. WELTON GADDY

Confession and Contrition, v. 5. Isaiah's encounter with the vastness of the Living God causes him suddenly to feel exposed. In an Adam and Eve kind of nakedness, the prophet exclaims, *Woe is me!* (Isa 6:5a). Immediately, he confesses his miserable state as "undone" (KJV), "lost" (NRSV), or "ruined" (NIV).

In an exegesis of the Isaiah passage in *The Interpreter's Bible*, Old Testament scholar and Princeton professor R. B. Y. Scott asserts that Isaiah realizes his "human lips are not fit to join in the ritual song. He realizes that he and all his people, even though they may have fulfilled the cultic requirements of the earthly temple, are debarred from the highest worship by the moral uncleanness of their nature."[4]

It is Isaiah's awareness, then, of himself, of his personal sin and human condition, that leads him to repentance and opens him to authentic worship, and ultimately, to God's leading. From this new and contrite position, the Most High is able to offer Isaiah cleansing, and Isaiah is able to worship, perhaps for the first time. Theologian G. G. D. Kilpatrick, in his exposition of this passage in Buttrick's *The Interpreter's Bible,* ably summarizes Isaiah's confessional experience:

> *Woe is me! . . . a man of unclean lips, . . . for mine eyes have seen the King, the* LORD *of hosts.* It was that realization of sin, that overwhelming sense of unworthiness, which was the first step in the making of a prophet. God can do something with those who see what they are and know their need of cleansing. [The Holy One] can do nothing for the [person] who can stand before what is holy and not feel himself [or herself] unclean.[5]

A real encounter with the Living God inspires spontaneous praise. And out of the awareness inspiring the praise there may come—to the honest and humble worshiper—an almost instinctive contrition. Here lies the test of true worship: the contrite heart, the changed life, the humbled spirit, open and ready for God's leading.

Cleansing, vv. 6-7. Isaiah is forgiven of his sin and receives cleansing for future service. The Redeemer's dealings with Isaiah discount any "broken bottle theology."[6] From Isaiah's testimony we can be assured when God forgives, God cleanses; and when God cleanses, God makes useable. God's forgiveness is absolute and sure. No forgiven life may be deemed second-class, ruined, or beyond repair. There are no broken vessels beyond repair, no useless lives unfit for God's service. Only forgiven vessels remain, ready for fulfillment and use.

The references in verse 6 to a "burning coal" (RSV) or "live coal" (NIV, NRSV) are metaphorical, symbolic of the cleansing effect of fire. Forgiven, grace received, Isaiah is ready to move ahead.

Calling, v. 8a. The Holy One asks, *Whom shall I send, and who will go for us?* The call of Immortal God is issued to Isaiah, and to all like him who know God's forgiving grace. G. G. D. Kilpatrick raises an important question concerning God's call: "This is a phrase generally associated with the vocation of the ministry. But why should it be limited to one profession in life?" Kilpatrick continues, answering his rhetorical question: "A [layperson] may receive and answer a call just as truly as any minister. It is possible for a [person] facing the opportunity of some honest labor or great profession and ready to give his [or her] life to it to hear, as Isaiah did, a summons, and to answer as he did, *Here am I; send me.*"[7]

The point is this: Isaiah's worship experience made him receptive to God's call. Through authentic worship, Isaiah's experience and resulting receptivity can also be ours. Our calling need not be sudden or dramatic, although it may be. More normally, perhaps, our calling may grow out of a sense of awareness of what might be possible given our individual gifts and capacities. The call of God is as individual as each person is unique. God's leading is dynamic. While it is concerned with large decisions regarding life ministry and vocation, it may also focus on the smaller, but no less important tasks of daily projects and responsibilities. In sum, the call of God is part of a daily, ongoing process. Its primary concern is dedication of life. Because Isaiah worshiped—because he had praised, confessed, and received the cleansing grace of God's forgiveness—he was able to hear God's call and respond affirmatively.

Commitment, v. 6:8b. Isaiah has seen the Holy One and regarded his own human estate. He has repented and received God's forgiveness and cleansing. Next he hears God's call to service. What follows is the dedication of a redeemed life: *Here am I; send me!* Page Kelley in his commentary of Isaiah wrote:

> The climax to Isaiah's vision comes in v. 8. The touch of the burning coal had made him a new man. To his vision of God, of himself, and of redeeming grace, there was now added a further vision, the vision of [a] world in need of his ministry. . . . He was so overwhelmed with a sense of gratitude that he was willing to place himself completely in God's hands. God had taken care of his past; he could have his future.[8]

The total experience of Isaiah's worship moved him to commit his life to God's calling. He became a new and different person than before the worship event. Perhaps, then, the most valid evidence of the authenticity of our worship are the uses and commitment of the lives changed by it. Seminary professor Franklin M. Segler asserts this idea in *Christian Worship: Its Theology and Practice* when he writes, "Meaningful worship leads to decisive experiences."[9]

Commissioning, vv. 9-10. In a word, the Lord of Hosts answers Isaiah: *Go.* And to that command God gives Isaiah a message to share with all who will hear. Isaiah's worship had purpose and mission. It was not merely an experience for the sake of experience. The Most High purposed for Isaiah a place of service and showed him a vision of what he was called upon to do.

Clarification, vv. 11-12. Good old Isaiah, so human, so like us, hesitates and questions God regarding the length and details of his service: *How long, O Lord?* Can't you just hear Isaiah clamoring for answers: *Details, Lord, details! Please, give me the details!* Thankfully, the clarification comes in verses 11 and 12 to this servant who asks for God's direction. The Alpha and Omega requires our service until the end of time, or until such time as there are no more ears left to hear God's message. Isaiah's worship experience is now complete and God's charge is laid before him.

This autobiographical account of Isaiah's call and worship experience serves as an excellent model for Christian worship. It is a model replete with action: action by the Holy One worshiped and by the worshiper. Within the passage, there is movement and logical progression from one event to the next. Not one event could reasonably be omitted without diminishing the entire experience, which so dramatically moved the prophet Isaiah. What began with encounter was characterized by commendation, confession and contrition, cleansing, calling, commitment, commissioning, and clarification. Is it not fitting that our worship be likewise?

Questions to Ponder

1. Does your church's weekly worship service contain the progressive elements of commendation (praise), confession and contrition, cleansing, calling, commitment, commissioning, and clarification? If not, what elements are missing? Are other elements routinely included that seem extraneous to this progression? What are they?

2. Using a recent order of worship from your church, arrange or rearrange the order of worship to fit the progressive model suggested by the Isaiah 6:1-12 passage. What changes did you make? What discoveries did you make doing this exercise?

3. How do you experience transcendence in worship? How do the architectural designs of your church's worship space affect your sense of transcendence?

4. Is God's otherness essential to worship?

5. How do you worship the Holy God and at the same time Jesus, the One next to you?

6. How often does your worship experience extend beyond symbol and ritual to become authentic, life-changing worship? Identify a time when you really worshiped. What did it include? What was it about that worship that stands out? What happened?

7. Do you ever feel compelled to fall on your knees before the Most High during worship? If not, what prohibits this response?

8. How have you experienced God's call on your life?

9. To what extent have your worship experiences affected your calling? How does your calling affect worship?

10. How do you relate your vocation to the service of God? In what ways is your life's work connected to your service to God?

Abraham and Isaac: Genesis 22:1-19

> After these things God tested Abraham. He said to him, "Abraham!" And he said, "Here I am." He said, "Take your son, your only son Isaac, whom you love, and go to the land of Moriah, and offer him there as a burnt offering on one of the mountains that I shall show you." So Abraham rose early in the morning, saddled his donkey, and took two of his young men with him, and his son Isaac; he cut the wood for the burnt offering, and set out and went to the place in the distance that God had shown him. On the third day Abraham looked up and saw the place far away. "Stay here with the donkey; the boy and I will go over there; we will worship, and then we will come back to you." Abraham took the wood of the burnt offering and laid it on his son Isaac, and he himself carried the fire and the knife. So the two of them walked on together. Isaac said to his father Abraham, "Father!" And he said, "Here I am, my son." He said, "The fire and the wood are here, but where is the lamb for a burnt

offering?" Abraham said, "God himself will provide the lamb for a burnt offering, my son." So the two of them walked on together.

When they came to the place that God had shown him, Abraham built an altar there and laid the wood in order. He bound his son Isaac, and laid him on the altar, on top of the wood. Then Abraham reached out his hand and took the knife to kill his son. But the angel of the LORD called to him from heaven, and said, "Abraham, Abraham!" And he said, "Here I am." He said, "Do not lay your hand on the boy or do anything to him; for now I know that you fear God, since you have not withheld your son, your only son, from me." And Abraham looked up and saw a ram, caught in a thicket by its horns. Abraham went and took the ram and offered it up as a burnt offering instead of his son. So Abraham called that place "The LORD will provide"; as it is said to this day, "On the mount of the LORD it shall be provided."

The angel of the LORD called to Abraham a second time from heaven, and said, "By myself I have sworn, says the LORD: Because you have done this, and have not withheld your son, your only son, I will indeed bless you, and I will make your offspring as numerous as the stars of heaven and as the sand that is on the seashore. And your offspring shall possess the gate of their enemies, and by your offspring shall all the nations of the earth gain blessing for themselves, because you have obeyed my voice." So Abraham returned to his young men, and they arose and went together to Beer-sheba; and Abraham lived at Beer-sheba. (Genesis 22:1-19)

While the Scriptures do not give us specific outlines for designing worship services, several references provide revealing guidelines. The Genesis 22 account of God's test of Abraham over the sacrifice of Isaac is another of those passages. The story of Abraham and Isaac on Mount Moriah is confusing at best and a very painful story that can easily be misread. Within its parameters, however, the biblical student can find helpful clues to important components of Christian worship.

Used simply as a parable—and not a proscriptive text—the passage reveals some helpful elements regarding worship. Verse 5b contains a clear statement of Abraham's intent to worship: *the boy and I will go over there; we will worship, and then we will come back to you.* In response to God's leading,

Abraham declares his intent. What, then, are the components of Abraham's worship experience with the Holy One?

Encounter, v. 1. A fundamental element of the Genesis 22 passage is the fact there is a personal encounter between God and Abraham. Verse 1 tells us God initiated the encounter. The verse states simply and succinctly that *After these things God tested Abraham* and said to him, *Abraham!* God initiates the contact with Abraham, singling him out and calling him by name. Once God gets Abraham's attention, the patriarch responds to the encounter by answering, *Here am I.* After acknowledging God's presence, Abraham immediately makes preparations for worship in obedience to the Maker's call.

Revelation, v. 2. In every worship experience, God seeks to reveal Creator to creation. In this biblical story, God seeks out Abraham and begins the revelation in accordance with Divine timing: "God had promised Abraham (v. 2) that as he obeyed [God] step by step [God] would make known to [Abraham] at the right time the place where the sacrifice was to occur."[10] God's revelation is incomplete at this point, but Abraham's posture is one of expectancy, patience, and obedience.

Obedience, v. 3. Very simply, verse 3 lays out the fact of Abraham's obedience: *So Abraham rose early in the morning,* or more immediately, *Early the next morning Abraham got up and saddled his donkey* (NIV). Abraham heard God's call and responded obediently, perhaps the very next morning.

Separateness, v. 5. Verse 5 offers us a glimpse of Abraham's need to pull away, to separate himself from the mundane, as he prepares for worship by telling his fellow travelers, *Stay here with the donkey; the boy and I will go over there.* Abraham's need to *go yonder* (RSV) expresses the fact that worship for Abraham, at least in this instance, is a very personal matter. Of course, this does not suggest we cannot or must not worship in the presence of others. Corporate worship is extremely important. But to *go yonder* does seem to suggest worship is a personal, one-on-one encounter between God and the individual, even when that individual sits in a pew surrounded by a congregation of others.

Viewed somewhat differently, this *go yonder* phrase also lays suspect the old contention that people need not unite themselves in corporate worship with other believers because they are just as able to worship elsewhere. The golf course is frequently cited as a possible outdoor shrine. The *go yonder* phrase suggests strongly that worshipers, *whether individually or corporately,* need to separate themselves from the world and its daily distractions—away from the pleasures and golf courses of life, away from the secularity of the workplace, and perhaps away from the scoffing of unbelievers. Like Abraham who pulled apart from the workers accompanying him on the journey, we pull away from the world and gather in places of worship, sanctuaries dedicated for sacred purposes. We worship together with fellow believers as we allow God to interact personally with each one of us and all of us.

Expectancy, v. 8. In verse 8, Abraham responds to Isaac's questions concerning the absence of a sacrificial lamb when he answers the child, *[The Holy One] will provide the lamb for a burnt offering, my son.* Abraham's tone is matter-of-fact, yet expectant. He does not reveal to Isaac what he understands to be God's request. But he does reveal through his response that *he expected God to do something.* We see, then, that Abraham's worship experience is flavored with an attitude of expectancy. Do we expect anything to happen as we worship? Do we expect to hear God speak?

The memorable high points of worship seem to come only a few times in life. A lot of us have stopped expecting anything more.

—Davis Duggins

Preparation, v. 9. Verse 9 tells us *Abraham built an altar there and laid the wood in order.* After preparing the altar, Abraham *bound his son Isaac, and laid him on the altar, on top of the wood.* Then, possibly steadying himself for what he was about to do, Abraham *reached out his hand and took the knife to kill his son.* Abraham, believing God was commanding him to sacrifice Isaac as a burnt offering, made practical preparations for the sacrifice.

Over the past fifteen years, I have discovered how important preparation is to vital worship. Perhaps my most amazing discovery has been that *preparation itself* can become a part of the total worship experience, especially as a worship leader. In 1 Thessalonians 5:16-18, the apostle Paul admonishes the church in Thessalonica to *Rejoice always, pray without ceasing, give thanks in all circumstances; for this is the will of God in Christ Jesus for you.* Not only is this excellent advice for the Christian, it is exceptional advice for the worship leader and planner. Be in an attitude of prayer as you make any preparation for worship, no matter how small or insignificant it may seem. This attitude suggests an openness and desire for God's leadership through the Holy Spirit. Where such willingness to God's leadership exists, the Paraclete always will be present giving guidance.

One way to create and maintain this attitude of prayer is to read and study the Scriptures, allowing them to speak. As a minister of music and frequent worship leader, I refer to the Scripture passage chosen for a given worship service during both the long-range and short-term worship planning processes. By the time the worship service is offered, I have read the passage many times. I begin by reading and rereading the passage, studying it to get its fullest revelation. I often consult a commentary or read the passage in several translations or a modern paraphrase. I read it again as I consider the best choral anthem and solo selection. I reread it as I choose the hymns. I read it over again and look for complementary texts in the preparation or composition of responsive readings or antiphonal calls to worship. And so goes the procedure, throughout the planning process. I can testify there have been many times when I have so tuned myself to God's Word and its message for me that I have been strangely aware of God's pervading presence as I worked. I have been utterly amazed to learn how often I worship while I plan for worship. But more than that, and perhaps the greatest discovery of all, is that my ability to lead and my capacity to worship in the service itself are often directly linked to the quality of my preparations, however minute.

Attentiveness, v. 11. Throughout this entire account, it appears God holds Abraham's attention. When God's angelic emissary calls Abraham's name, Abraham answers, *Here I am.* This is the second time Abraham responds to God's beckon. He never loses sight of the Holy One in his worship experience, but remains attentive to God's presence and leading. Abraham separates himself from other things and concentrates on the task at hand. Even as he makes the necessary preparations for his worship response, Abraham remains attentive to God.

How does God get our attention in worship? Must the Holy One compete with other forces and distractions? Abraham's example suggests we must first focus on God before we can worship. Consequently, focusing upon our faith, our personal feelings, or anything else besides the Holy One could inhibit our ability to truly worship God.

Surrender, v. 12. Wilbur C. Lamm argued that Abraham's worship is characterized by obedience, distinguished by preparation, marked by attentiveness, and climaxed by surrender that results in great blessing.[11] Abraham's willingness to sacrifice Isaac reveals a man surrendered to God's leading. Abraham's surrendered will, despite his inevitable anguish, marks the climax of this episode. Recognizing Abraham's surrender, God responds, *for now I know that you fear God, since you have not withheld your son, your only son, from me.*

Franklin M. Segler, author of *Christian Worship: Its Theology and Practice*, supports this point:

> God appeared to Abraham and called him to leave his own country and go to a land of promise. God promised to bless Abraham, to make of him a great nation, and to make his name great (Gen 12:1-30). Abraham responded with faith and obedience and built an altar unto the Lord and worshiped [God] (Gen 12:7). Later Abraham worshipped God when he indicated his willingness to sacrifice his own son, Isaac, to the Lord (22:9-10).[12]

Abraham's unfaltering obedience leads him to new heights in worship. His willingness to sacrifice Isaac reveals his complete surrender to the Holy One. God acknowledges pleasure in Abraham's *offering of willingness* through the commendation that follows his effort: *for now I know that you fear God since you have not withheld your son, your only son, from me.* God's words, *now I know*, give us insight into the purpose of Abraham's test: "'Now I know . . . .' Did [God] not know before? Does God not know all things? The verb used means to 'know by experience,' and so the words may mean that God had now seen Abraham actually do what [God] had known was in [Abraham's] heart. Abraham's actions had confirmed God's confidence in him."[13] In sum, Abraham's actions reflected the surrender of his will.

One may be tempted to ask, however, "Why did this story of what was planned to be a human sacrifice get into the Bible? Because it was desired to show that Abraham's devotion to the God he worshipped was capable of going to the farthest point religion could reach."[14] The *for now I know* revelation of verse 12 also states emphatically the necessity of worship, not only for our sakes, but for God's. Surely God already knows of our love because the Omniscient is the all-knowing God. But our actions, marked by the degree of obedience and surrender in our worship, all serve to confirm God's confidence in that love.

Change, vv. 12-16. I was utterly amazed a number of years ago when a pastor colleague of mine chided me, stating worship leaders had no business teaching anything during a worship service. He maintained worship did not include teaching or learning. I disagreed then and I disagree now. The God of Wisdom had something important to say to Abraham through this worship experience. And Abraham had great lessons to learn from God. God used the worship arena to teach; Abraham learned and his learning effected change.

In his exposition of the passage in *The Interpreter's Bible*, professor-writer Walter Russell Bowie explains within "the story of Abraham and Isaac there is imbedded the fact that once men not only practiced human sacrifice, but did it at what they thought was divine command." Moreover, the "climax is not the sacrifice of Isaac but the word from the Parent of Good that Isaac should not be sacrificed."[15] Harold Tribble, in his book *From Adam to Moses*, reinforces this point:

> Do not bother about criticizing God for asking Abraham to make a sacrifice of his son, for that was so common among the people of that day that Abraham would not think it strange. And one purpose in the whole experience was to teach the lesson that the children of the covenant should not follow the common practice of offering human sacrifices in religious worship.[16]

A relief not only for Abraham and Isaac, but for us all.

These statements do more than merely suggest God teaches through worship what is and is not expected of us. Worship involves the components of God's teaching and the possibility of our learning. Learning through the worship experience brought change to the heart and mind of Abraham.

In verses 12 and 16, God commends Abraham. The patriarch was committed to God before the test, but afterward, he was even more deeply committed. In this account, Abraham's faith and commitment were deepened as a result of his encounter with the Holy One. Abraham's theology was forever affected. Three changes took place: Now Abraham knew the Holy One who did not want human sacrifice, unlike the pagan gods of the day's culture. Now Abraham knew God, the Parent of Good, who took pleasure in the sacrifices of a person's will and obedience. Lastly, Abraham was assured of God's provision. Before the test, Abraham may have harbored some secret doubt as to whether God would provide the sacrificial lamb, but *now* he knew it for a fact.

Abraham bore witness to his new discoveries when he named the altar *The LORD will provide* (Gen 22:14a). Now God's revelation for the hour was complete and Abraham was left with a new and changed understanding of the Holy One he worshiped. This story of Abraham's encounter with God shows us how a worshiper is changed in true worship.

Blessing, v. 17. Verse 17 reads *I will indeed bless you*. Why did God bless Abraham? Bowie suggests "Abraham was not blessed for correctness in conception of God's will; he was blessed because when he thought he knew God's will he was willing to obey it to the limit."[17] Abraham was blessed through the proof of his love and devotion to the Holy One that day. Page Kelley in *A Nation in the Making* concludes, "God's richest blessings are reserved for those who are totally at [God's] disposal."[18]

In conclusion, Abraham's worship experience in the land of Moriah is earmarked with significant elements that translate to Christian worship practice today. The Genesis 22 passage shows how Abraham's worship was begun by encounter, inspired by revelation, characterized by obedience, guarded by separateness, charged with expectancy, distinguished by preparation, marked by attentiveness, climaxed by surrender, evidenced by change, and sealed with blessing. These hallmarks of worship are ours to claim as well.

Questions to Ponder

1. Do you expect anything to happen as you worship? What? Do you expect to hear the Holy One speak? How?

2. Abraham's example suggests we must focus on God and allow God to get our attention before we can worship. How does the Holy One get your attention in worship?

3. What preparations do you make for worshiping? What effects do your preparations have on your worship experience?

4. What loves in your life serve to cloud your focus upon God?

5. Which elements of your church's ritual displace the Holy One to less than first place in worship?

6. Which elements of your church's ritual elevate the Holy One to first place in worship?

7. What components of your church's ritual typically characterize your corporate worship? Are encounter, revelation, obedience, separateness, expectancy, preparation, attentiveness, surrender, change, or blessing among the components present? Is anything missing? Why?

The Priesthood of Believers: Nehemiah 12:27-47

> Now at the dedication of the wall of Jerusalem they sought out the Levites in all their places, to bring them to Jerusalem to celebrate the dedication with rejoicing, with thanksgivings and with

singing, with cymbals, harps, and lyres. The companies of the singers gathered together from the circuit around Jerusalem and from the villages of the Netophathites; also from Beth-gilgal and from the region of Geba and Azmaveth; for the singers had built for themselves villages around Jerusalem. And the priests and the Levites purified themselves; and they purified the people and the gates and the wall.

Then I [Nehemiah] brought the leaders of Judah up onto the wall, and appointed two great companies that gave thanks and went in procession. One went to the right on the wall to the Dung Gate; and after them went Hoshaiah and half the officials of Judah, and Azariah, Ezra, Meshullam, Judah, Benjamin, Shemaiah, and Jeremiah, and some of the young priests with trumpets: Zechariah son of Jonathan son of Shemaiah son of Mattaniah son of Micaiah son of Zaccur son of Asaph; and his kindred, Shemaiah, Azarel, Milalai, Gilalai, Maai, Nethanel, Judah, and Hanani, with the musical instruments of David the man of God; and the scribe Ezra went in front of them. At the Fountain Gate, in front of them, they went straight up by the stairs of the city of David, at the ascent of the wall, above the house of David, to the Water Gate on the east.

The other company of those who gave thanks went to the left, and I followed them with half of the people on the wall, above the Tower of the Ovens, to the Broad Wall, and above the Gate of Ephraim, and by the Old Gate, and by the Fish Gate and the Tower of Hananel and the Tower of the Hundred, to the Sheep Gate; and they came to a halt at the Gate of the Guard. So both companies of those who gave thanks stood in the house of God, and I and half of the officials with me; and the priests Eliakim, Maaseiah, Miniamin, Micaiah, Elioenai, Zechariah, and Hananiah, with trumpets; and Maaseiah, Shemaiah, Eleazar, Uzzi, Jehohanan, Malchijah, Elam, and Ezer. And the singers sang with Jezrahiah as their leader. They offered great sacrifices that day and rejoiced, for God had made them rejoice with great joy; the women and children also rejoiced. The joy of Jerusalem was heard far away.

On that day men were appointed over the chambers for the stores, the contributions, the first fruits, and the tithes, to gather into them the portions required by the law for the priests and for the Levites from the fields belonging to the towns; for Judah rejoiced over the priests and the Levites who ministered. They performed the service of their God and the service of purification, as did the singers and the gatekeepers, according to the command of David and his son Solomon. For in the days of David and Asaph long ago there was a leader of the singers, and there were songs of praise and thanksgiving to God. In the days of Zerubbabel and in the days of Nehemiah all Israel gave the daily portions for the singers and the gatekeepers. They set apart that which was for the descendants of Aaron. (Nehemiah 12:27-47)

The doctrine of the priesthood of all believers may sound like an unlikely model for Christian worship practice, yet the doctrine is replete with meaning for the worshiper. While the doctrine was not formalized until the sixteenth century by Martin Luther and other Protestant reformers, its concepts have deep biblical roots. The Nehemiah 12:27-47 account of the dedication of the wall of Jerusalem gives us a glimpse into a portion of the ancient post-exilic Hebrew cultus, revealing elements within the worship practice and opportunities for participation on all levels by all present. In this worship account, God's covenant people assume their priestly responsibilities and worship with great joy.

Worship Involves a Variety of Elements

An examination of the Nehemiah passage reveals thanksgiving, preparation, praise, music, and sacrifices and offerings.

Thanksgiving. Nehemiah's biblical account of the dedication of the Jerusalem wall shows the ancient city as she makes preparations for and carries out this celebratory event. Verse 27 relays the intent: *to celebrate the dedication with rejoicing, with thanksgivings and with singing, with cymbals, harps, and lyres.* Thanksgiving appears to be the central, motivating force

Thankfulness and prayer belong together. Thanksgiving is the deep inward certainty which moves us with reverent and loving fear to turn with all our strength to the work to which God stirs us, giving thanks and praise from the depths of our hearts.

—Julian of Norwich

behind this cultic celebration of praise and dedication. Two great companies of Judaic leaders gave thanks (v. 31), and the singers and gatekeepers sang songs of praise and thanksgiving to the Holy One (vv. 45-46). Out of their thanksgiving, the whole community prepared to worship.

Preparation. Everything and everybody was made ready for worship. Verse 30 relates this: *And the priests and the Levites purified themselves; and they purified the people and the gates and the wall.* Raymond A. Bowman, in his exegesis of Nehemiah in *The Interpreter's Bible*, clarifies the rite of purification:

> An indispensable part of the ritual was the preliminary purification of the structures and of participants in the ceremony. Those who had been occupied with secular affairs were regarded as ritually unclean and unfit to participate in the ceremony. Priests were always purified before ceremonies, and laymen too had to be "pure" before joining in cultic ritual. The mode of purification may have been fasting, but it is probable that sacrifice also was involved and perhaps sprinkling with blood or with holy water.[19]

Within the Protestant Christian community, there is inconsistent use of formalized rites of purification preceding worship. Within the confessional and creedal traditions these are more noticeable, like the use of holy water, for instance. But we can all think of preparatory rituals and traditions within our own experience. As a child, I remember the weekly routine of making pre-Sunday preparations. Every Saturday night of my childhood, Mama washed and curled my hair, I read my Sunday school lesson, we filled and labeled our offering envelopes, we shined our shoes, and an early bedtime was strictly enforced to guard against any sleepiness or sluggishness on Sunday morning. And today, while the practice is diminishing among younger members of our current culture, many still prepare for worship by dressing in only their *Sunday best* clothes. No doubt you know of other similar rituals.

If pressed, I suppose we can look at these modern-day preparations as Protestant-type rituals of purification and adornment for attending church and worshiping God in today's times. While all these things are decent, orderly things to do, I am left with the uneasy question of what is vastly more important: What about our preparations of heart and mind?

Over the last year, in preparation for writing this book, I have worshiped in many places with many different congregations. I've had opportunity to observe and experience firsthand from the pew how other worshipers prepare for worship. The time allotted for the organ prelude or voluntary is an excellent time to be quiet, center oneself, and focus upon God and the ensuing worship time. Sometimes an overly boisterous organ prelude or talkative parishioners can intrude upon this centering time, but it is worth the effort. I've come to realize how important it is to *be still and know that I am God* before entering the throne room of the Holy One for the purpose of worship. Pew or pulpit, whatever your vantage, experience has taught me to pull aside—like Abraham—and *go yonder* before attempting to worship.

Praise. With the necessary preparations for worship done, the Jerusalem community assembles and begins to offer praise to the Holy One (v. 31). Praise and thanksgiving are inexorably linked. Just think about it. It's really not hard to praise or rejoice whenever we feel thankful, but it's terribly difficult to offer praise in the absence of gratitude. The biblical account speaks freely of the praise offered to God on that joyous day in Jerusalem: *there were songs of praise and thanksgiving to God* (v. 46). In fact, so great was the rejoicing *the joy of Jerusalem was heard far away* (v. 43).

One has only to read the passage through a couple of times to see the large assembly (v. 31), the processions of leaders (vv. 31, 38), the circumamulation about the great walls of Jerusalem (vv. 31-42), and the clamor of voices and instruments tuned in exuberant praise (vv. 27, 35-36, 46). What an exciting assembly! And all the glory was ascribed to God.

Music. As a musician, I know the joy and power of music. I know how easily, and effectively, it may be used to praise the Holy One. The Jerusalem congregation must have known this too, for the crowd was full of joyful voices, musicians, and instruments: *companies of the singers* (v. 28), singers and their leader Jezrahiah (vv. 42, 46), *young priests with trumpets* (v. 35), and musicians *with the musical instruments of David* (v. 36). More than just the choir processed that day, and the music of cymbals, harps, lyres, trumpets, and voices raised a pantheon of praise. Apparently, everyone present got caught up in the excitement of this open-air effort of praise, for *the joy of Jerusalem was heard far away* (v. 43).

Sacrifices and Offerings. Sacrifices and offerings were also a part of Jerusalem's worship event. Verse 43 states, *They offered great sacrifices that day and rejoiced*, and the *contributions, the first fruits, and the tithes* were gathered into storehouses (v. 44). With thankful hearts, they worshiped God, and out of their gladness, they gave. To God these worshipers offered sacrifices and tithes, contributing the best of their harvests and fields. What a fitting close to worship: giving enveloped by joy.

The parallel is simple. No ending to any service of worship could ever be greater than offering or sacrifice: the offering of one's self to God's service; the giving of time, talent, and personality; the generosity of shared wealth and provision. Evelyn Underhill, in her classic book *Worship*, asserts sacrifice is the very heart of worship. She argues Christianity is essentially sacramental since Christ himself served as the major sacrament: "the medium of that Eternal God's self-giving to [humankind]."[20]

Politics without principle, pleasure without conscience, wealth without work, knowledge without character, business without morality, science without humanity, worship without sacrifice.

—MOHANDAS K. GANDHI, ON THINGS THAT WILL DESTROY US

The time of offering and commitment are sacred times within a service of worship. What does your congregation do to enhance and preserve these times of dedication?

Worship Is Participatory, Involving All Worshipers

Corporate, congregational worship is participatory, involving the total priesthood: liturgists, leaders, ministers, musicians, and laypeople alike. Walter Shurden, in his book *The Doctrine of the Priesthood of Believers*, 1987, asserts that "Christian worship is something the priesthood does." Moreover, he continues, "As in worship so in witness, the priesthood is not passive audience but active participant."[21] This point is undergirded by Franklin M. Segler in his 1967 publication, *Christian Worship: Its Theology and Practice*. Segler states,

> The doctrine of the priesthood of believers, suggested by the "holy priesthood" [1 Peter 2:5] of the church, implies that every member of Christ's body is responsible to worship Christ by offering spiritual sacrifices. This doctrine necessitates participation on the part of the entire congregation. Since all are priests, each individual Christian has the privilege and obligation to worship God for himself [or herself] and to serve as a priest unto God for [others].[22]

Nehemiah 12 provides a fabulous example of participatory worship. Everyone got involved, and the hallowed result was nothing short of spectacular. The biblical list is long but impressive: companies of singers (v. 28), singers (vv. 42, 45), priests (v. 30), Levites (v. 30), leaders (v. 31), people (v. 30), musicians and instruments, and priests with trumpets (vv. 35-36), companies of those who gave thanks (v. 38), officials (v. 40), women (v. 43), children (v. 43), gatekeepers (v. 45), and lastly, the leader of the singers (v. 46). Apparently, everyone present took part in the celebration of worship. There was opportunity for everyone to voice praise to the Lord of Hosts.

If you've ever been a part of a worship service where participation is high and people are actively engaged in worshiping God, then you know how moving an experience this witness can be. Conversely, if you've ever been in the midst of a congregation that seemingly sits back and refuses to participate—evidenced through half-hearted singing, critical or disinterested stares, mumbled congregational liturgies, dozing choir members, stifled yawns, restlessness, and scattered attention—you know all too well just how terrible and unworshipful this can be. One can't help wondering when comparing the two, just what does the Holy One make of the difference?

Dedication of the wall of Jerusalem was a special event in the life of this ancient civilization. The special event gave way to extraordinary expressions of joy and thanksgiving. Every person involved

The experience of worship is a collection of the prayers and praise, the confession and conviction, the music and silence of the people of God. Worship is not performance; it is participation. And if you are not present to participate or if you are present and choose not to participate, worship is diminished for all of us.

—SAMUEL F. WILLIAMS, JR.

had special gifts to bring to the dedication service, for each had a voice to raise, an offering to give, a life to dedicate to God. This worship event sprang from thankful hearts. After making the necessary preparations for worship, all the people—acting as priests before their Maker—bore responsibility for worship and offered praise and thanksgiving to God through music, sacrifice, and offerings. How can our participation be less?

Questions to Ponder

1. What preparations do you make for worship?

2. How do you transition from other things—work, leadership in Sunday school, fellowship with friends, rehearsing with the choir, putting in

last-minute study for the sermon presentation, hurrying through traffic—to worship?

3. What practices or influences help you focus on worshiping God?

4. What practices or influences hinder your focus on worshiping God?

5. Is your church's worship highly participatory? How? How not?

6. What elements of your church's worship foster congregational participation? What factors deter congregational participation?

7. Opportunities for offering and commitment are sacred moments within worship when individuals and churches may dedicate themselves anew to God. What does your congregation do to enhance and preserve these hallowed times of dedication? In what way(s) might your church's practice hinder these times?

8. What gifts do you personally bring to worship?

9. As a New Testament parallel to the Nehemiah 12 passage, study 1 Peter 2:1-10. In this pastoral exhortation to the churches in Asia Minor, Christians are reminded of their calling to serve as a "holy" (1 Pet 2:5) or "royal priesthood" (1 Pet 2:9). Accepting this calling, what responsibility do you assume in your church's worship of the Holy One?

The Model Prayer: Matthew 6:9-13

> Pray then in this way: Our Father in heaven, hallowed be your name. Your kingdom come. Your will be done, on earth as it is in heaven. Give us this day our daily bread. And forgive us our debts, as we also have forgiven our debtors. And do not bring us to the time of trial, but rescue us from the evil one. (Matthew 6:9-13)

In the verses that precede the Model Prayer in Matthew's Gospel (6:1-8), we find the Great Teacher illustrating abuses in the practice of personal piety (v. 1), giving (vv. 2-4), and prayer (vv. 5-7) before addressing proper worship behavior based upon right motives. This lesson in motive and worship provides the setting for the Model Prayer in verses 9-13. Jesus begins by saying, *Pray then in this way,* "meaning the words that follow serve as a model for all praying. The Model Prayer contains all the elements that must go into any prayer pleasing to God. Jesus' beautiful teaching model was, in essence, a verbal object lesson."[23] In other words, according to seminary professor and pastor William Powell Tuck, "Jesus wanted the disciples to use his prayer to develop their own praying."[24] While the primary lesson of the Model Prayer is to teach us how to pray, it may also instruct us on how to worship.[25] The underlying premise of this exposition, then, is the suggestion that all worship is prayer and all prayer is worship.

Praise and Adoration, v. 9. The focus of all worship, as in prayer, is God. As the one who offers up prayers to heaven, the worshiper must begin the act of worship acknowledging, adoring, and addressing the Holy One. The Gospel writers record Jesus' practice of calling God by the names *Father, Abba, Daddy.* These human names for the Eternal Godhead suggest intimacy and relationship, while other names for God—Eternal, Uncreated, Infinite God, Absolute God, Divine Essence, Reality, the Holy, the Unseen—capture the essence of God's ethereal nature, the otherness of God's being.[26] By whatever names we address the Holy One, God's holy name must be hallowed in all our praying and in all our worshiping: *Hallowed be your name.*

In prayer and worship, we offer praise to the One whose name is holy, consecrated, sacred, revered, and totally other. Inherently present within this recognition of God's name is a sense of undeniable awe. Because God is the Holy Other, God is totally and completely worthy of worship and adoration. *Hallowed be your name.*

While working with a church youth group a couple of years ago, I frequently heard them exclaim, "Totally awesome!" This youthful ascription of approval and praise is reminiscent of the popular chorus "Awesome God," by Rich Mullins, which proclaims through music and verse, "Our God is an awesome God. [God] reigns from heaven above with wisdom, power and love. Our God is an awesome God."[27] Our praise, prayer, and worship should both acknowledge and magnify the totally awesome and holy name of God so that we may exclaim, with all respect and in all reverence, *Totally Awesome, hallowed be your name.*

God, of course, is not bound by our view, but our picture of God may indeed bind us.

—WILLIAM POWELL TUCK

Submission, v. 10. To pray the words, *Your kingdom come, your will be done, on earth as it is in heaven,* or to worship with this thought in our minds and this desire within our hearts, we must submit our wills to the will of the Parent of Good. For me, and perhaps for many of us, submitting my will to that of another is difficult. I suppose I'm simply a strong-willed child of God. Perhaps all of us who call ourselves human are strong-willed children. And perhaps submitting ourselves to God's will or to Divine leadership is singly the most difficult task of discipleship. As difficult as it may be, however, the act of submission may also be the greatest test of our worship and the most positive proof of our praise. Our worship must reflect the heartfelt desire, *Your will be done.*

Reliance, vv. 11, 13. *Give us this day our daily bread* from verse 11 and *do not bring us to the time of trial, but rescue us from the evil one* from verse 13 are requests that imply absolute reliance and dependence upon God's care and provision. In his exposition of the passage in *The Interpreter's Bible*, George A. Buttrick maintains the petition for *daily bread* in verse 11 represents concern with day-by-day needs, both physical and spiritual, and the petition for deliverance in verse 13 acknowledges and calls upon God as our "holy Ally."[28] In the dependent postures of prayerful petition or humble worship, we trust our lives to God's safekeeping. We reply upon God's provision to undergird life. We depend upon God's help in times of trouble and temptation. Reliance and dependence are prayerful words, worshipful words. For without them, we creatures become self-reliant and bold, and thereby cease to worship Creator God.

Confession and Pardon, v. 12. The elements of confession and pardon within the worship service are strangely lacking within my heritage as a Southern Baptist, the denomination of my youth. This troubles me, for I am a person who constantly needs the freeing privilege of confession and the healing balm of pardon. In preparation for writing this manuscript, I have worshiped with many congregations within many denominations. Among them are United Methodist, Evangelical Lutheran, Moravian, Evangelical Episcopal, Evangelical Presbyterian, Presbyterian USA, Disciples of Christ, Southern Baptist and other Baptists, and nondenominational congregations. This attempt to worship more ecumenically has allowed me to peek into the worship practices of God's holy catholic church. I have found both richness and barrenness there. Having grown up in a denomination that routinely neglects the richness of confession and pardon, I have been blessed by their inclusion in worship elsewhere.[29] How freeing it is to confess one's sins before the throne of God, and how utterly satisfying it is to hear pastor, priest, or minister proclaim, *Almighty God, [with] mercy, has given [Jesus] to die for us and, for his sake, forgives us all our sins. As a called and ordained minister of the church of Christ, and by [this] authority, I therefore declare to you the entire forgiveness of all your sins, in the name of the Father, and of the Son, and of the Holy Spirit.*

Verse 12 of the Model Prayer reads: *Forgive us our debts, as we also have forgiven our debtors.* The passage is replete with important messages about responsibility for giving and receiving forgiveness. But it is enough to say here that the passage reminds us that confession, forgiveness, and pardon are viable and important aspects of every prayer and every act of worship. Thanks be to God!

Questions to Ponder

1. How are praying and worshiping similar? How are the two dissimilar?

2. Does your church's worship practice include a time of confession and pardon. Why? Why not?

3. By what names do you routinely address God? Can you think of new names and descriptive words by which to call God?

4. Does your concept and naming of the Holy One include balance between the familiar and the incomprehensible? Using your list from question 3, circle your names for God that reflect familiarity. Underline those names that reflect God's otherness. Is your list balanced? How might you balance it?

5. What concept of the Holy One does your church's liturgy most frequently suggest? Familiar? Incomprehensible? Balanced?

6. The Model Prayer is framed in corporate language: *our* Father, *our* bread, *our* trespasses, as *we* forgive, lead *us,* deliver *us.* To what extent does your church's liturgy gather the worshipers into this kind of mutuality instead of remaining only a roomful of individuals?

Worship Personified: Jesus Christ

Everything our worship should be is personified in the life and ministry of Jesus Christ. The historical Jesus claimed before religious leaders and a population of curiosity seekers and followers that he was the living example of God's true temple.

In all its parts, [Jesus'] life is a life-giving act of sacrificial worship.

—Evelyn Underhill

While at once supporting and frequenting local synagogue Sabbath observances and festal days, Jesus clearly challenged current norms as he preached and taught about worship that returned to the type of worship the Most High was intending—worship in spirit and truth. Jesus took every opportunity at hand to illustrate how the Immortal God desires worship from all peoples. The life and ministry of Jesus, through its ever-widening circle of love, inclusion, and justice for all people, provides the ultimate example of true and sincere worship. His unparalleled liturgy of life remains our best model for worship.

The True Temple, John 2:13-22

While Jesus' condemnation of the temple is presented in all four Gospels, it is the John 2:13-22 account that places the event at the beginning of Jesus' public ministry. The Johannine account also lends some clarity to the event by including Jesus' interpretive remarks about the destruction and resurrection of the temple in verses 18-22.

For a Jew like Jesus, the temple was a place of sacrifice where worshipers went to seek forgiveness. The temple was a place of worship. God dwelt there. Through his passionate display, which "undermines the sacrificial system at the heart of temple religion," Jesus tried to impart a new truth about God's kingdom.[30] But those in the temple on that day of reckoning, and his disciples as well, failed to realize the full impact of Jesus' prophetic actions and words until months, perhaps years, later. John writes of the temple cleansing from a vantage point some sixty or seventy years following the resurrection, so he—and the other Gospel writers—can see with more clarity than those immediately upon the scene.

Hulitt Gloer, in his essay "A Temple of Flesh and Blood," holds that "the Temple in Jerusalem was but [a] forerunner to another temple—a temple not of wood and stone, but of flesh and blood, the true temple in which God tabernacled among the people."[31] Minds of onlookers and disciples alike were riddled by Jesus' words found in verse 19: *Destroy this temple, and in three days I will raise it up.* John solves the puzzle in verse 21 when he writes: *But [Jesus] was speaking of the temple of his body.*

Following the resurrection account, a new dimension to Jesus' actions begins to take focus. According to Gloer, "It is now clear that Jesus was all that the temple of wood and stone was supposed to be and all that we who are his body, the church, are meant to be—the place where God's 'temple' purposes are realized, where humankind encounters the presence of God and discovers the good news of the eternal relationship offered to all in Jesus."[32]

Raised up as the body of Christ, the church becomes the true temple of God. What does this have to say about worship? Everything. As the church, you and I are vessels designed for worship and communion with the Blessed.

Such a holy purpose calls and ordains us to worship in spirit and truth, attitude and action. As God's temples—places where God's purposes are realized—our worship could never be relegated to mere Sunday morning activity, but must be reinterpreted to include both ritual and lifestyle. Raised up as the body of Christ, you and I—as the church—become the true temple of God.

> *When we dig deep into the core act of our worship, we learn that we've always defined it as the worship Christ gives to the Father. It is a response to God, what God has asked of creation, the body of Christ giving praise to God.*
>
> —JAMES NOTEBAART

Observing the Sabbath

Luke reveals a glimpse into the patterns of Jesus' life. In Luke 4:16, the physician tells that *When [Jesus] came to Nazareth, where he had been brought up, he went to the synagogue on the sabbath day, as was his custom.* The phrase *as was his custom* clearly reveals Jesus regularly attended synagogue worship.

Apparently, Jesus was raised and trained in the synagogue. Following his circumcision and purification, Mary and Joseph presented the infant Jesus to God in the temple at Jerusalem and made sacrifice there (Luke 2:22-38). Seniors Simeon and Anna blessed the child. But more revealing than this incident of parental faithfulness to Jewish law is Jesus' visit to Jerusalem when he was twelve years old. In Luke 2:41-50, the Gospel writer tells of the young boy's interest and preoccupation with temple teachings and doctrines. Mary and Joseph had left Jerusalem for home following the annual feast of the Passover. Thinking Jesus was among the large group of travelers heading back to Nazareth, they did not worry about him until the end of the first day's journey. Traveling back to Jerusalem to look for their misplaced son, they found him comfortably situated in the temple amid the teachers—asking and answering questions, listening, and discussing. When confronted by his parents regarding the situation, he replied with unusual understanding for a boy of his years: *Why were you searching for me? Did you not know that I must be in my Father's house?* (2:49). Early on, Jesus made a practice of worship that became a pattern in his life.

The verses that follow the Passover event divulge more about Jesus' worship habits once he was an adult. Verse 17 begins, *He stood up to read, and the scroll of the prophet Isaiah was given to him.* Luke discloses that Jesus began to teach following this public reading of Hebrew Scripture. Jesus not only attended synagogue worship, he participated fully, even to the point of teaching. It was Jesus' custom to observe the Sabbath by attending and participating in synagogue worship.

Challenging the System

Inasmuch as Jesus upheld the Sabbath and frequented local synagogues, he also challenged the traditional worship system of Judaism, focusing upon abuses. Jesus was not a status quo person. Status quo people might have an assortment of names to call him: rabble-rouser, boat rocker, mover and shaker. New Testament Scriptures are full of incidents where Jesus challenged the system, sought to change the game rules, and shook up Jewish authority figures. (See table 1.)

But Jesus did not challenge everything about his tradition. As we have established, Jesus worshiped frequently within the Jewish tradition. However, where worship practice had become stale, empty, or suffocating, Jesus had the ability to see through the form to the way things really were. His pattern was to examine and challenge the relationship and intent of ritual gone sour, not to throw the proverbial baby out with the bath water. Jesus recognized the status quo as not all bad, nor all good. Conversely, he recognized innovation as neither all bad nor all good. Rather, Jesus seemed able to discern what was at the heart of worship. The core of worship—mercy, doing good, truth and right motives, ethics, love, generosity, inclusiveness, justice, love of God, righteousness, inner purity, freedom and compassion, servitude and humility, faith, and repentance—concerned Jesus far more than worship's outer ceremonial shell.

TABLE 1: JESUS' ACTIONS CHALLENGE THE SYSTEM

Jesus' Actions	*Significance*	*References*
The cleansing of the temple	**Declares temple is a place of worship for all peoples, undermines sacrificial system of the temple, and claims authority as Messiah**	*John 2:13-22* *Mark 11:15-18* *Matt 21:12-13* *Luke 19:45-48*
Interview by Nicodemus	**Challenges entire Jewish system of birth, heritage, corporate identity, rank, and privilege when he declares,** *Very truly, I tell*	*John 3:1-21*

	you, no one can see the kingdom of God without being born from above (3:3)	
Conversation with Samaritan woman at the well	**Challenges Jerusalem as center of worship when he declares,** *But the hour is coming, and is now here, when the true worshipers will worship the Father in spirit and truth, for the Father seeks such as these to worship him* (4:23)	*John 4:5-42*
Heals paralytic & forgives his sins	**By forgiving sins, Jesus undercuts practice of temple sacrifice and atonement; he declares** *I desire mercy, not sacrifice* (Matt 9:13a)	*Mark 2:1-12* *Matt 9:1-8* *Luke 5:17-26*
Defends his disciples for not fasting	**Challenges fasting**	*Mark 2:18-22* *Matt 9:14-17* *Luke 5:33-39*
Heals lame man on Sabbath	**Breaks the Sabbath committing an act of kindness**	*John 5:1-47*
Plucks ears of corn on Sabbath to satisfy a need	**Declares** *the Sabbath was made for humankind, and not humankind for the Sabbath* (Mark 2:27); *I desire mercy and not sacrifice* (Matt 12:7b)	*Mark 2:23-28* *Matt 12:1-8* *Luke 6:1-5*
Heals man with withered hand on Sabbath	**Argues for the spirit of the law over legalism; the Sabbath is about doing good and saving lives**	*Mark 3:1-6* *Matt 12:9-14* *Luke 6:6-11*

Teaches a new standard of righteousness regarding murder, adultery, divorce, oaths, retaliation, and love of enemies	**Stresses ethics over rules and regulations of Jewish system**	*Matt 5:21-48*
Denounces hypocritical motives of Pharisees in almsgiving, prayer, and fasting	**Stresses righteousness over hypocrisy**	*Matt 6:1-18*
Commends anointing by sinful woman	**Argues for love, generosity, and inclusiveness over laws of ritual purity**	*Luke 7:36-50*
Defends disciples for eating with unwashed hands	**Threatens whole system of ritual purity when he stresses heart over ceremony:** *there is nothing outside a person that by going in can defile, but the things that come out are what defile* **(Mark 7:15)**	*Mark 7:1-23* *Matt 15:1-20* *John 7:1*
Heals a man born blind on Sabbath	**Acts in the spirit of the law over the letter of the law; argues that Sabbath is about doing good and saving lives**	*John 9:1-41*
Fails to wash his hands before breakfasting with a Pharisee	**Denounces ritual purity in favor of inner purity, justice, and love of God**	*Luke 11:37-54*
Heals a crippled woman on the Sabbath	**Argues for freedom and compassion over ceremonial law**	*Luke 13:10-21*

Heals a man with the dropsy on the Sabbath	**Argues for humility, justice, and inclusiveness over ceremonial law**	*Luke 14:1-24*
Receives and eats with sinners	**Practices inclusiveness in his eating habits over laws of ritual purity**	*Luke 15:1-32*
Lodges with Zacchaeus, a sinner and publican	**Practices inclusiveness over laws of ritual purity**	*Luke 19:1-28*
Rebukes Scribes and Pharisees over their hypocrisy	**Denounces show over servitude and humility; tithing over justice, mercy, and faith; ceremonial cleansing over cleansing of the heart; outward beauty and cleansing over inner purity, truth, and righteousness**	*Mark 12:38-40* *Matt 23:1-39* *Luke 20:45-47*
Commends poor widow's gift	**Denounces show and superfluity over real sacrifice and generosity**	*Mark 12:41-44* *Luke 21:1-4*
Commends his anointing by Mary of Bethany	**Denounces jealously and criticism over generosity and extravagant love**	*Mark 14:3-9* *Matt 26:6-13* *John 12:2-8*

From the isolated glimpses into Jesus' ministry (as shown in table 1), we see the Master practicing, in J. M. Nielen's phrase, "a contradictory approach combining both freedom and constraint."[33] Although Jesus had grown up within the Jewish system of worship and kept the Sabbath by frequenting local synagogues throughout his ministry, "his proclamation cannot be fitted into the existing order and is associated with radical criticism of traditional worship."[34] A careful and calculated tension between form and freedom is evidenced in the life, teachings, and ministry of the Christ. Critical of temple worship, which practiced exclusiveness, showy spirituality, and legalism over justice, Jesus espoused a system of worship that was grounded in lifestyle.

Evidence of the worship he practiced was shown throughout what we know of his brief life.

Not unlike the prophets before him, Jesus preached about worship *in spirit and truth* (John 4:23). He practiced a lifestyle that emphasized doing good over obeying rules, operating from truth and right motives over hypocrisy, practicing love, generosity, inclusiveness, and righteousness over laws of ritual purity. (See table 2 for a summary of how Jesus' worship in spirit and truth challenged traditional worship practice.) But these concepts were not new. The Twelve prophets, in particular, preached about similar worship reforms. Most radical among Jesus' ideas about worship, perhaps, was his message of faith and repentance for the forgiveness of sins over the practice of blood sacrifice for atonement.

TABLE 2: SPIRIT AND TRUTH OVER TRADITION

Worship in Spirit and Truth	Traditional Worship
Mercy	Sacrifice
Doing Good	Obeying Rules
Truth and Right Motives	Hypocrisy
Heart	Ceremony
Spirit	Legalism
Ethics	Rules
Love, Generosity, Inclusiveness, Justice, Love of God, Truth, Righteousness	Ritual Purity
Inner Purity	Outer Beauty
Freedom and Compassion	Ceremony
Servitude and Humility	Show
Justice, Mercy, and Faith	Tithing
Faith and Repentance for the Forgiveness of Sins	Sacrifice for Atonement

Jesus spent his adult life trying to impress upon the people he met that worship was an expression of the heart rather than strict adherence to prescribed rules and regulations. The Gospels show Jesus trying to persuade people of Palestine that worship's outer display is only as genuine as the heart that motivates it and the life that reenacts it apart from the synagogue.

In all its elements, . . . Christian worship is the action of God, of Jesus, and of the community itself for the community, and therefore the upbuilding of the community. From this centre it can and should spread out into the wider circle of the everyday life of Christians and their individual relationships. Their daily speech and acts and attitudes are ordained to be a wider and transformed worship.

—Karl Barth

Working from within his own tradition, Jesus' actions seem to ask, Where is my tradition liberating? Where is my tradition binding? Where does the status quo need innovation? Where does the status quo lead me to a right relationship with the Holy One? What is at the heart of this practice? What practices are merely cultural manifestations? The Scriptures tell us how Jesus worshiped within the prevailing worship system of his day, got involved, dug deep, and worked at maintaining and improving his tradition as a way people may find relationship with God. How might we use his pattern today?

Practicing Inclusiveness

We have no evidence that the adult Jesus practiced or espoused the ritual purity rites of the Jewish cultic system. However, we do have evidence that he challenged them. While many arguments can be made for his reasons, an abiding concern for inclusiveness seems to undergird Jesus' actions. We find Jesus frequenting the company of sinners, people considered by Jewish religious authorities as unclean or impure, and simple, common folk. Among these flawed characters were his disciples—including four fishermen and a tax collector—the Samaritans and Greeks, women, lepers, paralytics and cripples, people with unclean spirits and demons, people dead or thought dead, harlots, a woman with an unclean issue of blood, those blind and deaf, adulterers, publicans (tax collectors), and the two criminals nailed to crosses beside him at Golgotha. Jesus' inclusiveness enveloped not only the circumspect leaders of his day, but the rejects and discards of respectable Jewish society. He brought them all into his circle of love.

A certain dimension to Jesus' inclusiveness can also be seen not only in the company he kept, but also in his praying. Jesus prayed in Aramaic, the common language of the people. Among other things, by praying in the vernacular, the method and the message of Jesus' praying were open to all.

Furthermore, Mark's account of the condemnation of the temple (11:15-19) cites Jesus quoting from the Hebrew Bible when he claims, *Is it not written, "My house shall be called a house of prayer for all the nations"?* (11:17a).[35] The phrase *for all the nations* (or *for all peoples*) cuts through the exclusiveness of the Jewish worship system. Jesus opens worship to all people.

Jesus: Our Ultimate Example of True and Sincere Worship

Paul Waitman Hoon, in the preface to his scholarly text *The Integrity of Worship*, asserts "God's self-disclosure in Jesus Christ shall determine worship in his Name."[36] Hoon is saying the life and example of Jesus Christ is the "integrating reality for all liturgical reflection, decision, and practice."[37] Jesus' life and witness determines worship with integrity—not the changing moods of culture, not the legalistic rulings of organized religion, not the government or any other ruling system, not even our own experiences nor the spirit of the age. Jesus Christ is the standard and controlling factor. And Jesus lived and practiced a life of worship that grew out of his intimate relationship with a Daddy-like God.[38]

In Jesus' life and ministry we see examples of how the Blessed One desires our worship and our lives to be conducted. To reiterate, God seeks inwardly pure worshipers who practice mercy, goodness, truth, love, generosity, inclusiveness, justice, righteousness, compassion, servitude, humility, and ethical living—seven days a

The integrating reality for Christian worship is the Word, Jesus Christ, who in his work, person, and present Spirit performs these functions and bestows upon worship and upon our thinking about worship the wholeness that alone makes it true. Thus theological integrity is to be understood Christologically.

—PAUL WAITMAN HOON

Let all the study of our heart from henceforth be to have our meditation wholly fixed in the life of Christ. His teachings are of more virtue and of more strength than are the words of all angels and saints; and [anyone] that through grace hath the inner eye of his [or her] soul opened to the soothfast beholding of the Gospels of Christ shall find in them hidden manna. . . . Wherefore if we desire to have the true understanding of his Gospels we must study to conform our life to his life as nigh as we can.

—GERHARD GROOTE (1340–1384)

The mystery celebrated is never exhausted or fully contained in any act of worship. Liturgical rites authentically celebrated point to the vision and the heavenly liturgy of Christ of which all earthly celebrations are but hints and guesses.

—Don E. Saliers

week. Our Sunday worship practice—whatever its form, wherever its place, whenever its time—must illuminate Christ's example, thereby helping us see God and find motivation for lives of faith.

A young high school student once proclaimed, "A demonstration of true and sincere worship can most readily be seen in the ultimate example—Jesus Christ."[39] In *Worship*, Evelyn Underhill makes a similar conclusion: "A constant loving contemplation of [God's] realized perfection and timeless glory, and a constant effort to actualize that glory with the frame of human experience . . . is the substance of this life of worship."[40] Indeed, Jesus, the Christ, is the True Liturgy. With so perfect an example before us, how can we not choose to imitate him?

A passionate longing to glorify [God] upon earth, in all ways and at all costs, is the inspiring cause of every outward action of Christ's life. This spirit of trustful, unlimited, and worshipping love is the real spirit of the Gospel.

—Evelyn Underhill

Questions to Ponder

1. How do you react to the concept that *you* are God's true temple as part of the incarnate body of Christ?

2. What implications do being a part of the body of Christ and God's true temple hold for you? What implications do being the body of Christ and God's true temple hold for the life of your church?

3. In what ways does your church assume responsibility as the body of Christ, God's true temple?

4. In what ways do you attempt to imitate Christ? In what ways does your church attempt to imitate Christ?

5. Does your personal orientation lean more toward maintaining the status quo or toward innovation? List specific traits, actions, and attitudes that support your present position.

6. Is your church oriented more toward maintaining the status quo or toward innovation? How is this so? Make a list.

7. If Jesus were to enter your church to cleanse it of all objects, practices, and attitudes that stand in the way of pure and inclusive worship, what would he get rid of?

8. Divide a piece of paper into two columns: one "cost" and the other "promise." Further divide the paper horizontally: the top half representing "developing an innovative approach" and the bottom half "maintaining the status quo." Working within each quadrant, consider and list the costs and promises of each position. (See diagram 1.)

DIAGRAM 1: COST AND PROMISE

	COST	PROMISE
Developing an innovative approach		
Maintaining the status quo		

Implications for Our Worship

The scriptural models for worship presented in this chapter, like prisms, illuminate for us the multifaceted character of worship. Each model reveals elements central to the experience of authentic worship. At the same time, no single model demonstrates every aspect of worship. From different angles, each model reflects some of the many elements of worship, thereby giving us standards for gauging and evaluating our own worship practice.

NOTES

[1] Ralph P. Martin, *Carmen Christi: Philippians ii.5-11 in Recent Interpretation and in the Setting of Early Christian Worship* (Cambridge: University Press, 1967), 19.

[2] Evelyn Underhill, "The Nature of Worship," *Worship* (New York: Crossroad, 1985), 3-19.

[3] Annie Dillard, *Holy the Firm* (New York: Harper, 1977), 68-69.

[4] R. B. Y. Scott, "Exegesis," *The Interpreter's Bible*, ed. George Arthur Buttrick, vol. 5 (Nashville: Abingdon Press, 1952), 209.

[5] G. G. D. Kilpatrick, "Exposition," *The Interpreter's Bible*, ed. George Arthur Buttrick, vol. 5 (Nashville: Abingdon Press, 1952), 205-206.

[6] Opinion expressed by Raymond Bailey in class lecture, *The Worshipping Church 4020*, at The Southern Baptist Theological Seminary, Louisville KY (Spring 1982).

[7] Kilpatrick, "Exposition," 207, 211.

[8] Page H. Kelley, "Isaiah," *The Broadman Bible Commentary: Proverbs-Isaiah*, ed. Clifton J. Allen, vol. 5 (Nashville: Broadman Press, 1969), 211.

[9] Franklin M. Segler, *Christian Worship: Its Theology and Practice* (Nashville: Broadman Press, 1967), 9.

[10] L. H. Coleman, "Genesis 20:1 to 22:24: The Sacrifice of Isaac," *Bible Book Study for Adults: Genesis (Part I)*, 1/1/82 (October-November-December 1978).

[11] Wilbur C. Lamm was a frequent writer for The Sunday School Board of the Southern Baptist Convention. No source documentation is available.

[12] Segler, *Christian Worship*, 16.

[13] Clyde T. Francisco, "Genesis," *The Broadman Bible Commentary: General Articles, Genesis-Exodus*, ed. Clifton J. Allen, vol. 1 (Nashville: Broadman Press, 1969), 189.

[14] Walter Russell Bowie, "Exposition," *The Interpreter's Bible*, ed. George Arthur Buttrick, vol. 1 (Nashville: Abingdon Press, 1952), 642.

[15] Ibid., 642-43.

[16] Harold W. Tribble, *From Adam to Moses* (Nashville: Convention Press, 1934), 26.

[17] Bowie, "Exposition," 645.

[18] Page H. Kelley, *A Nation in the Making* (Nashville: Convention Press, 1969), 52.

[19] Raymond A. Bowman, "Exegesis," *The Interpreter's Bible*, ed. George Arthur Buttrick, vol. 3 (Nashville: Abingdon Press, 1952), 794.

[20] Underhill, *Worship*, 46-47.

[21] Walter B. Shurden, *The Doctrine of the Priesthood of Believers* (Nashville: Convention Press, 1987), 137, 87.

[22] Segler, *Christian Worship*, 74.

[23] Don W. Stewart, *Matthew 5–7: Design for Discipleship* (Nashville: Convention Press, 1992), 78-79.

[24] William Powell Tuck, "The Lord's Prayer," *Formations* (July/August 1992): 36.

[25] Segler, *Christian Worship*, 31, suggests the Model Prayer may include a logical sequence of attitudes appropriate in worship, but he does not develop this thought any further within the text.

[26] These and other names are used by Evelyn Underhill in her classic text on Christian worship, *Worship* (New York: Crossroad, 1985).

[27] Rich Mullins, "Awesome God," *Songs for Praise & Worship* (Nashville: Word Music, 1992), 40-41.

[28] George A. Buttrick, "Exposition," *The Interpreter's Bible*, ed. George Arthur Buttrick, vol. 7 (Nashville: Abingdon Press, 1952), 312-13.

[29] I must clarify that due to the autonomy of the local church within the historic Southern Baptist Convention, individual congregations are free to include or preclude from worship any element of their choosing. Fortunately, I have worshiped with Southern Baptist congregations who routinely voice confession within their worship service; but by and large, my exposure has been with congregations who omit confession and pardon completely and routinely from their weekly orders of worship. Historical reasons abound to justify this practice, but these are not my concern in this volume.

[30] William L. Dols, "Critical Background," *The Bible Workbench: A Resource for Living Our Story Through God's Story* 4/3 (1997): 55.

[31] Hulitt Gloer, "A Temple of Flesh and Blood" (3 March 1991), 1.

[32] Ibid., 3.

[33] J. M. Nielen, *Liturgy* (cited above, chapter I, n. 2, David E. Green, to fit Hahn's development of the terms "Gebundenheit" and "Freiheit" in Ferdinand Hahn's *The Worship of the Early Church* [Philadelphia: Fortress Press, 1973], 12).

[34] Hahn, *Worship of the Early Church*, 14.

[35] Jesus is quoting from Isaiah 56:7, which reads *for my house shall be called a house of prayer for all peoples.*

[36] Paul Waitman Hoon, *The Integrity of Worship* (Nashville: Abingdon, 1971), 14.

[37] Ibid., 80.

[38] Jesus addressed God as *Abba* [*Daddy* in Aramaic] in his Gethsemane prayer. See Mark 14:36.

[39] John Tarwater, "The Value of Worship," Southern Baptist Brotherhood Commission Breakfast, 1988.

[40] Underhill, *Worship*, 221.

CHAPTER 3

What Is Worship?
CHARACTERISTICS AND DESCRIPTIONS

My whole heart I lay upon the altar of thy praise, an whole burnt-offering of praise I offer to thee. . . . Let the flame of thy love . . . set on fire my whole heart, let nought in me be left to myself, nought wherein I may look to myself, but may I wholly burn towards thee, wholly be on fire toward thee, wholly love thee, as though set on fire by thee.

—Saint Augustine of Hippo

As I set out to define worship, I realize how inadequate words can sometimes be to try to describe something as wondrous as worship. But because words are writers' tools, I will make an attempt to capture the essence of worship in eight ways. First, I will attempt to define worship through an explanation of liturgy. Because *liturgy* is such a misunderstood word among worshipers within the free-church traditions,[1] providing a working definition of liturgy seems to be an essential first step. Following this discussion, I will describe worship as action, as God-centered, and as a priority for God and the church. Finally, I will show that worship is holistic, creative, progressive, and incarnational. By the time you have read and studied this chapter, I hope you will have generously added to my lists your own descriptions and definitions for worship.

I often think of the set pieces of liturgy as certain words which people have successfully addressed to God without their getting killed.

—Annie Dillard

Liturgy

The words *liturgy* and *liturgical* originate from the Greek word *leitourgia* meaning *the work of the people.* While these terms are commonly used within religious circles, they somehow remain vague and strange, even foreign, to many worshipers within the free-church traditions. But this need not be so. As I will attempt to show later in this chapter, *worship* may also be defined as *the work of the church* or *the work of the people.* Considered in this way, the terms *worship* and *liturgy* may be considered synonymously. But let's take a closer look. First, liturgy is a multidimensional concept involving the dualities of action and response, expression and impression.

Action. Horace T. Allen, Jr., Professor of Worship at Boston University School of Theology, provides a simple and succinct definition of liturgy: "Liturgy is the form of faith."[2] The liturgy of worship assumes different forms that vary from culture to culture, community to community, service to service, congregation to congregation, and person to person. Basically, when we worship liturgy is what we do and how we do it—our actions. Liturgy, regarded this way, is the form, the shape, and the acts of our worship—the prayers, the silence, the praise, the sermon, the music, and more. What style we use is not really important. Whether our worship is formal or informal is not the issue. Rather, liturgy is the worship of the people of God—spontaneous and ordered, oral and written, sung and spoken, free and formulated, contemporary and traditional, low and high, creative and routine, new and old.

Response. Liturgy, however, is more than simply the forms we use during the worship hour. Liturgy is also the form faith assumes apart from the sanctuary: Monday's response to Sunday's experience, if you will. Liturgy is how God's people live when they are away from the sanctuary. It is their attitudes and actions at work, at play, at school, and at home in reaction to the transforming power of worship. Pushed to this limit, liturgy is essentially everything we do, because, as Christians, we understand that all we do is done in Christ's name. The stuff of our everyday lives—how we conduct ourselves—is, in fact, the essence of our truest worship. Lutheran Pastor

Frank C. Senn calls this life reaction to worship the "enculturation of the liturgy."³ Likewise, Gerard S. Sloyan, Professor Emeritus of Religion at Temple University, captures something of liturgy's duality when he writes,

> Liturgy is deed, liturgy is act. It is acceptance of a message heard, to be sure, but it is more than that. What constitutes the "more" is an important question. Inspirited song? Yes, of course. Bodily movement? That too. Rite, stylized behavior, bespeaking an encounter with the living God? That is of the essence. It can be the celebration of what are called sacraments in some churches and ordinances in others. It may be the observance of marriage in Christ or the commitment of a dead Christian to the earth, the soul commended to God until it rejoins the body on the last day. Processions and chanted litanies, dancing and music making, going vested in bright costumes—all are liturgical behavior.⁴

Expression. Liturgy is a personal and corporate expression of worship. Senn defines liturgy as "the changing self-expression of a community concerned to renew its life and revitalize its mission. In Roman, reformed and free-church traditions, the liturgy must be an authentic expression of the assembly."⁵ Again, liturgy is what we do to worship the Holy One and how we do it. Liturgy is the form, the shape, and the acts of worship, which vary from culture to culture, community to community, service to service, congregation to congregation, and person to person. Michael Warren, Professor of Theology at St. John's University, writes: "Liturgy is expressive human activity, a symbolic expression of the life of a particular group of people. It does for the life of the group what sharing a meal does for married couples.

It is the fact that the texts and rites of the liturgy do not always express who we think we are that constitutes their potential to transform us. Were we to allow ourselves to grow into them, to let ourselves and our minds be transformed by them, then the liturgy's impact on life might be rather greater than anything we can hope for by jazzing up the music or anointing the prayers with doses of our own personal unction—all of which merely leaves us celebrating who we are in our own eyes.

—MARK SEARLE

Eating together embodies more than personal nourishment; it embodies a way of being together."[6] In sum, communities of faith *form to express* their collective faith in worship. But it is also important to realize that communities of faith are also *formed by worship*. The former speaks to the expressive nature of liturgy, and the latter, to liturgy's impressive nature.

Impression. When I speak of the impressive nature of liturgy, I speak of God's use of liturgy to *transform* or *to effect change* in worshipers. Mark Searle, Associate Professor of Liturgy at the University of Notre Dame, makes this claim concerning the impressive nature of liturgy: "Liturgical language . . . is very like ordinary language, though not in the way we normally think. It is concerned less to express our thoughts and feelings than to impress them, that is, to shape and form them by shaping and forming our attitudes, to conform them to those of Christ, the only liturgist."[7]

This is the God who calls, who initiates, who cajoles, who questions us into conformity with that which we were created to be, who whispers and gently pulls us into relationship with the One who cannot be possessed but who desires our attentiveness. Liturgy, at its best, is the way the gathered community "accosts" and responds to our Maker.

—Rebecca Sue Strader

A thoughtful but unidentified writer once described liturgy's impressive power something like this: At times, liturgy functions like saying "I love you" to those we love when we don't really feel like it. Sometimes in our roles of parents, husbands, and wives we feel as though we are simply "going through the motions," not feeling much love for child or spouse. But, nonetheless, we practice the words and actions of love, almost prayerfully, in efforts to reclaim the feelings we are momentarily unable to feel. The analogy applies to worship. Our liturgy—the words and actions of worship—help to bring us to the points of devotion we sometimes can only awkwardly declare: praise of the Unsearchable God we cannot see and whose presence we sometimes do not feel, confession of the sin we have not yet fully claimed, acceptance of the forgiveness we can never fully deserve, offering ourselves into service we do not yet envision, and so forth. In these moments of disciplined worship, the Parent of Good can use the words and acts of our liturgy to train us to become the people we aspire to be. In this way, liturgy is impressive as it *impresses us* or *presses us* to become kingdom people.

Liturgy is far more than doctrine well dressed. There is truth to be sure, but it is truth in the form of music heard so deeply that we are the music; stories told so well that we become actors in the story; prayers prayed with such integrity that we become prayerful; a meal celebrated so graciously that we are nourished and become bread for others.

—Don E. Saliers

Verbs and Action Words

Worship is a verb. The principal Hebrew term for worship is *shachah* meaning to *bow down* or *prostrate oneself*. The Greek New Testament term *proskuneo* is similar in definition—to *kiss the hand toward one* or again, *to prostrate oneself*.[8] Both terms involve much more than subtle human action. To prostrate oneself means to abase oneself to the point of stretching the body facedown upon the floor. A worshiper really has to get involved to lie prostrate. While prostration is not a position worshipers of this age frequently assume, it is important to understand that worship requires action on the part of the worshiper. Worship is something you do. To worship, we must engage our minds, hearts, wills, and bodies. It is rarely enough to spectate, consume, or passively observe. Worship invites us to willing, whole participation, demanding our response.

Worship is seductive. It draws us in. I like the mental image of losing oneself totally and completely in the act of worship. Enveloped, surrounded, and enthralled by worship, yet not spinning out of control. Engaged in worship with all human faculties—mind, emotion, reason, and senses—turned upon God. Cocooned in the presence and praise of the Holy One.

In an age when, through athletics and diet and the intensity of exercise, we have rediscovered our physical bodies, we have neglected the "body" of our Christianity. Liturgy is the sensuality of the Christian experience, the muscle of our mysticism. And we have treated it with all the regard we would pay to a huge, pastel marshmallow.

—Anthony Ugolnik

Consider the following action words for worship listed below. Each descriptive word or phrase suggests that worship is active, not passive. Worship is dynamic, not static. In order to worship, the worshiper must get actively involved.

dialogue	awe
encounter	praise
offering	the work of the church
giving	gathered
conscious communion	sacrifice
the loving response of the creature to the Creator	obedience
	submission
participation	conversation with God
drama	response to God
an intentional act	witness
service	an expression of faith
celebration of God	adoration

Can you think of additional action words and verbs that describe worship? If so, add them to the list above.

Archbishop William Temple's (1881–1944) poetic definition of worship, published in 1942, has become a classic:

> To worship is to quicken the conscience of the holiness of God,
> To feed the mind with the truth of God,
> To purge the imagination by the beauty of God,
> To open the heart to the love of God,
> To devote the will to the purpose of God.
> All this is gathered up in that emotion which most cleanses us from selfishness because it is the most selfless of all emotions—adoration.[9]

Quicken, feed, purge, open, and devote are action words, verbs, dynamic, not static. The conscience, mind, imagination, heart, and will comprise the very essence of humankind, the whole person. Holiness, truth, beauty, love, and purpose are attributes of God. To know God is to know these.

Worship is not performance; it is participation. And if you are not present to participate or if you are present and choose not to participate, worship is diminished for all of us.

—SAMUEL F. WILLIAMS, JR.

God-Centered

Worship is God-centered. When we worship we must focus upon the Holy One. The American contemporary culture has a real knack for focusing upon *self*. How easy it is to get caught up in self-promotion and self-absorption: *my* needs, *my* success, *my* wants, *my* thoughts, *my* feelings, *my* desires, *my* preferences, *my* property, *my* this, and *my* that. On second thought, perhaps this tendency is not so much American as it is human. Selfishness is a symptom of the human condition. Certainly, since the beginning of time this has been true. An ancient biblical example points this out.

The prophet Amos condemned ancient Israel's selfishness and misplaced focus in worship. Israel's worship had no impact upon life the rest of the week. Amos's audience—comprised of the materially rich but spiritually poor, and the religiously privileged but spiritually irresponsible—heard the prophet preach against hypocritical, self-serving worship, which repeatedly failed to produce justice and righteousness. In the sermonette found in Amos 4:4-5, Amos condemns Israel's worship "because rather than focusing attention upon God, it focused attention upon the people."[10] Israel's worship had become an end in itself. What was being done on the Sabbath had no impact upon life the rest of the week. Through the harsh and prophetic voice of Amos, the Most High conveyed hatred for what was being done in the name of religion. Had the people of Israel been less focused upon themselves and more focused upon the Holy One, perhaps they would have understood that worship focused upon God—and away from self—ultimately produces an outward focus marked with generosity and inclusiveness toward the oppressed, the needy, the hurting, and the lost. But Israel was too self-absorbed.

Come to Bethel—and transgress; to Gilgal—and multiply transgression; bring your sacrifices every morning, your tithes every three days; bring a thank offering of leavened bread, and proclaim freewill offerings, publish them; for so you love to do, O people of Israel! says the Lord God.

—AMOS 4:4-5

Worship is God-focused, not *me*-focused or *self*-focused. For humankind, striking such an unselfish pose in worship requires self-discipline and love of God. Difficult as it may be, worship requires it. Bruce Leafblad, Christian worship writer, has argued that "Worship directed away from God is idolatry."[11] Worship focuses upon the Holy One. It is about opening ourselves completely and honestly to God and abandoning or losing ourselves in praise of God. To focus upon ourselves is vanity; to focus upon God is worship.

God is considered the audience of our worship, so the action in worship is directed toward God—for God's hearing, God's seeing, or God's enjoyment, God's sake, and ultimately God's action. Worship is an invitation for God to act on us.

God-centered worship is dominated by the presence of God where God is the center of attention. Earmarked by awe, reverence, and praise, God-centered worship celebrates God and God alone. Robert Bailey describes this dynamic: "We cannot worship rightly until we recapture, as the principle element in worship, the overwhelming sense of awe and reverence in the presence of God."[12] Franklin M. Segler sums up God-centered worship succinctly with these words: "Worship is an end in itself. . . . We worship God purely for the sake of worshipping God."[13]

Priority

Richard J. Foster, in the opening lines of his discussion regarding disciplined worship in *Celebration of Discipline*, 1978, states that "God is actively seeking worshipers."[14] Foster bases his claim upon the many scriptural references to God's efforts to find fellowship with humankind and the Gospel writer's assertion in John 4:23 that God *seeks* worshipers who will worship in spirit and truth. Given these truths, I believe we may safely and confidently assume that worship is a priority of the Holy.

If every program of the church disappeared, worship would still remain, as it has done, when the church has been driven underground by persecution. It would not disappear because it is the essential expression of our relationship with God.

—Bonnie Jean Lamberth

Worship is also the church's first priority. These days the church is up to a lot of good. In addition to religious, musical, theological, and mission education, church programs and ministries include outreach, community social service, evangelism, daycare, recreation, and fellowship. But of all the things a church gathers or scatters to do, worship is the most central.

Worship is the church's reason to *be*. Worship enables the church to be the church. Worship gives the church the sustenance needed to carry out all its other functions, programs, and ministries. Worship is the church's energizing force. Baptist Pastor Samuel F. Williams, Jr. phrased worship's importance in this way to his Virginia congregation: "The first order in the church's mission is worship. All other aspects of ministry are motivated by worship and without worship the Christian church is diminished. Our worship is a gift to the Holy One. It is primarily the offering of our total selves to God."[15]

Holistic, Involving the Whole Person

One of my favorite ways to think of worship is as *montage*, a mixture of carefully juxtaposed elements forming a whole. The term has its roots in cinematography, where a rapid succession of images produces an association of ideas in moving picture format, or where separate pictures are joined to make one that is new. The term applies equally well to literary, musical, and artistic compositions and to the composition of worship. The worship montage combines worship components, elements, forms, symbols, and history with both individuals and community to form a holistic worship event. Not merely a jumble of isolated parts that do not mesh, worship, instead, is *holistic*, a whole unit comprised of many parts in which whole people are invited to participate, fully and completely.

God calls for worship that involves our whole being. The body, mind, spirit, and emotions should all be laid on the altar of worship. Often we have forgotten that worship should include the body as well as the mind and spirit.

—RICHARD J. FOSTER

The dedicated will must bit by bit take up, transform, and unify the dedicated body and mind, welding them into a single instrument devoted to the purposes of God.

—EVELYN UNDERHILL

Picture in your mind another metaphor for worship, an old-fashioned wagon wheel, balanced and complete, with spokes connected by a central hub. For purposes of this illustration, the wheel—like the montage—represents a single worship event or unit while the hub represents the central biblical theme around which the various parts of the worship service may revolve.[16] The spokes that connect, support, and balance the wheel represent the various parts making up a service of worship: elements, components, symbols, forms, history, individuals, and the worshiping community.

Table 3: Parts Contributing to a Holistic Worship Service

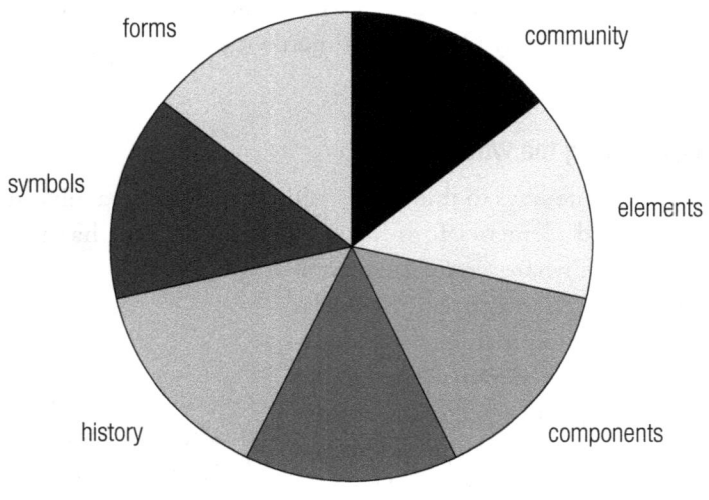

Elements	Components	Whole People	History	Symbols	Forms	Community
preparation	silence	body	traditions	water	*musical:*	those gathered
expectancy	calls to worship	mind	innovations	bread	psalms	local church
attentiveness	doxologies	spirit	creeds	wine	hymns	body of Christ
encounter	praise	reasoning	hymns	cross	spiritual songs	all other saints
revelation	music	senses	writings	dove	anthems	universal church
praise	readings	heart	salvation history	fish	choruses	family of faith
thanksgiving	scripture	soul	scripture	lamb	chants	*great cloud of*
confession	prayers	experience	other saints	palm	instruments	*witnesses*
contrition	assent	personal history		olive tree		*(Heb 12:1)*
pardon	testimonies	emotions		fire	*spoken:*	
cleansing	exhortations	conscience		light	sermons	
calling	sermons	will		wind	testimonies	
offering	baptism	gifts		ashes	exhortations	
sacrifice	communion	calling		rock	drama	
surrender	kiss of peace	commitment		salt	poetry	
commitment	offering	psyche		crismons	creeds	
commissioning		spirituality		architecture		
obedience		social influences		worship space	*written:*	
reliance		education		vestments	scripture	
change		economic status		incense	readings	
blessing					meditations	
					litanies	
					bulletins	
					electronic aides	
					visual:	
					fabric arts	
					dance	
					liturgical colors	
					banners	

My list illustrating the various parts of the worship service is not meant to be exhaustive, but merely an exercise for considering all the pieces that may make up a worship service. (See table 3.) I encourage you to brainstorm, adding to the lists provided. If my metaphors illustrating worship as a holistic unit do not work for you, by all means develop your own.

A worship service that is holistic does not usually happen by chance. Normally, it takes thoughtful and careful planning. In a workshop presented at the 1990 Worship and Music Conference in Montreat, North Carolina, musician Carol Doran and liturgist/hymnist Thomas H. Troeger provided a list of principles and vocabulary for renewing worship. The list includes proportion, congruence, variety, flow, and associations.[17] These principles provide a helpful checklist for worship leaders who desire to plan holistic worship. Each should be considered separately *and* in conjunction with the others when planning worship.

Proportion. Proportion has to do with size, time, or length of the individual pieces of the worship service, like the length of the anthem or sermon, or the amount of time given to praise versus prayer, for instance. If worship planners have one hour to work with in planning a service, careful consideration must be given to the proportion of the various parts of the service if the worship time is to be used wisely and effectively. If a certain number of actions need to be accomplished within the allotted time, no one component should take up a disproportionate amount of time. Proportion not only affects time, but indirectly affects the influence or emphasis of one portion of the service over another and the balance of the entire worship event. Paul Waitman Hoon adds to these aspects of proportion in *The Integrity of Worship*, 1971, when he suggests balance between order and variety, blending of the mysterious and intelligible, balance between verbal, visual, and musical language, and emphasis through time allotment, placement, and execution are also important aspects of proportion.[18]

Congruence. Congruence is how things fit together. Do the parts of the worship service work together in their present configuration? Is a theme being used and do the pieces of the service correspond well to the theme when needed? Does the tone of organ prelude match the overall tone of the service? What types of thoughtful transitions are needed between the parts of the service? Is what is sung and what is said compatible in theme, theology, and intent? Are styles consistent, compatible, or effectively and tastefully blended? These are some of many questions concerning congruence that need to be considered when planning worship.

Variety. Variety deals with form and different ways of doing things. When worship leaders consider variety important, there is at least an attempt to provide something for everyone. Creative worship leaders constantly consider how to vary and offer diversity in form, either in one service or over a period of time in many services. To illustrate, variety in worship may be observed in the following ways: using a combination of hymns, gospel songs, and choruses in one service or over a period of time; sermons presented in ways other than the traditional approach—through monologues, dialogues, brief meditations at different points in the service, or through drama; singing familiar words to new tunes or singing new words to familiar tunes; using different instruments—handbells, organ, piano, orchestral, guitar, or *a capella* singing with no instruments at all; choosing hymns in different meters and keys within one service; planning services around themes that change weekly or monthly; alternating the use of calls to worship that are spoken, sung, or read silently; altering the order of service if the change is logical; enlisting and training different laypeople to lead in worship; or singing the doxology as a call to worship instead of after the collection of tithes and offerings. The list is endless because the possibilities are endless.

Flow. The flow of a service has to do with where the service is going: its direction, movement, and progression. A service that flows is neither overly controlled nor its leadership neglected. Avoiding disruptions and intrusions within a service contributes to good flow. More will be said about flow when the progressive nature of worship is discussed later in this chapter.

Associations. Associations have to do with symbols. When Christians encounter a symbol, they associate with the symbol certain theological meaning. For instance, the cross symbolizes Christ's atoning sacrifice, baptism symbolizes our death, burial, and resurrection into new life with Christ, ashes symbolize grief or penitence, doves symbolize God's Spirit, and so on. Worship leaders concerned about associations will consider the symbols used within a worship service, asking themselves: Have the symbols been interpreted? Have the symbols been interpreted correctly? Have old and familiar symbols been reinterpreted for younger and newer worshipers? Have any symbols been neglected? Will the use of a symbol augment the message and understanding of the sermon? What understanding do the people have of the symbols they routinely see, hear, and reenact? Is more education needed?

Creative and Extravagant

Worship is creative. Worship seeks to be as fresh as a first-time experience. The four Gospels document the creative and extravagant adoration by a woman who breaks a costly alabaster jar of ointment on Jesus' body. (See Matt 26:6-13, Mark 14:3-9, Luke 7:36-50, and John 12:1-8.) Although criticized by the disciples, the woman's extravagance was praised by Jesus: "The woman who came to Jesus did not calculate what her gift of love would cost. Her love was spontaneous, generous, extravagant, overflowing. She acted out of the abundance of her heart. It is why Jesus accepted her gift, her homage."[19] Through her creative and costly gift, she had discovered the meaning of holy waste. Like this woman's gift, worship is creative and extravagant, wastefully full.

Kenneth L. Gibble, bi-vocational pastor and businessman, argues in favor of holy waste in worship. He makes this point in his challenging article, "How Wasteful Can Worship Be?" when he writes, "Holy waste is a good description of the way God creates."[20] Gibble goes on to quote Annie Dillard, author of *Pilgrim at Tinker Creek*, to describe the holy waste of God's creativity: "The creator churns out the intricate texture of . . . the world with a spendthrift genius and an extravagance of care."[21] Inasmuch as God's creativity is abundant and overflowing, so should our worship of the Creator hallmark creative and generous spirits. Such creativity and generosity requires boldness. Richard Foster regards worship as a deliberate and disciplined spiritual adventure calling for boldness, discomfort, and openness. He asserts that worship "is not for the timid or comfortable. It involves an opening of ourselves to the dangerous life of the Spirit."[22]

How may worship be considered dangerous and discomforting? Hearing the biblical message may reproach us, causing uneasy feelings. Conviction of sin is usually very uncomfortable. Confronting sin as a prelude to confession may require boldness and a type of honesty that is unfamiliar. Confession and change may likely produce discomfort. Obedience and commitment require discipline and resolve. Openness—to others, to determining God's will, to the leadership of the Spirit, to service—may challenge and threaten, producing uncomfortable feelings of vulnerability and fear. Worship is dangerous, especially to people who find change disquieting.

If worship does not change us, it has not been worship. To stand before the Holy One of eternity is to change.

—RICHARD J. FOSTER

Describing worship as an *inner adventure,* Wilferd A. Peterson writes that worship "is the personal practice of the presence of God. It is the renewing of our noblest dreams and aspirations that we may rise above defeat, failure and discouragement and have another try at making the most of our lives."[23] Worship is another try, and another, and another, and another. It is forever fresh and new, created and re-created. Worship is the creative work of incarnation, God born within us again and again and again. Like broken vials of precious ointment, we offer our lives to God in worship for re-creation.

Just as God has creative freedom with us in worship—to mold, transform, move, and renew us—we, too, have some creative freedom in worship. Freedom allows worship planners, leaders, and worshipers to discover again and again new and creative ways to worship. This ongoing discovery keeps the worship experience alive and fresh. Worship themes may vary. Liturgy—simply, the ways we worship and the tools we use to worship—may vary. New and freely composed prayers, litanies, and hymns may be created. Old forms and new forms may be used together. The possibilities are virtually endless. Writing to a primarily free-church audience, Robert W. Bailey highlights this freedom and flexibility: ". . . probably the approach to worship that is most consistent with the biblical theology of worship is that which alters each week. . . . The validity in making some alteration in the order of worship weekly is that worshipers learn to come to the sanctuary with a sense of open expectation."[24] Prayer book and confessional churches, familiar with the choices available to worship planners within denominational prayer and worship books, may also vary worship within prescribed forms, making each service fresh and full of expectancy.

Flexibility and creativity in form aids worship practice since worship itself is a creative process. Pastor W. Wayne Price speaks of this in *The Church and the Rites of Passage* when he writes, "One advantage of the free-church tradition is flexibility in worship, thus enabling some creativity in both themes and liturgy."[25] Indeed, the freedom to creatively plan, lead, and worship using both old and new liturgical forms is a highlight of worship within free-church traditions. Yet, anything-goes attitudes or change-for-the-sake-of-change leadership cannot prevail in worship either. With freedom also comes responsibility. Price continues by saying, "The saddest characteristic of the *free-church tradition,* unfortunately, is that everyone tends to do as they please."[26] Just as we cannot make idols of the old and traditional ways, we cannot expect to change simply for the sake of change, nor make an idol out of creativity. Just as we understand that a healthy diet incorporates many different and alternating foods prepared in a variety of ways, we must also understand that worship incorporates changing styles and forms to remain healthy. Worship, by nature, is creative. It involves an ongoing aspect of reformation both in terms of its worship forms and in the lives of worshipers. Worship leaders should want parishioners who approach worship eagerly asking, *What may happen today?* Not worshipers who come expecting *same old, same old.*

The qualifying principle of *balance* may be useful. Finding balance between the tensions of form and freedom is healthy. Unbridled freedom in any form can be dangerous, even in worship. Responsible freedom, exercised with thoughtfulness and discernment, however, can make creative use of old forms. A few examples may be helpful.

First, a musical example. To neglect the use of hymns for an exclusive use of choruses and pop gospel songs would err on the side of freedom. To shun any modern musical forms in worship in defense of an exclusive use of classic and sacred literature would err on the side of form. To strive to find a tasteful and meaningful blend of old and new forms in musical expression would seem to strike a healthy balance in form and freedom.

Secondly, an example concerned with execution of various worship components—calls to worship, confession and pardon, doxologies, lection readings, and the like. To exclude these components and reduce worship to a simple format of praise, offering, and sermon would err on the side of freedom. To include these and other components, using the same language, the same format, the same order, the same style, led by the same voice week after week would err on the side of form. To routinely include these components, but vary their execution—the language, the format, the style, and the presenters—would exemplify a fresh, responsible balance of form and freedom.

Finally, an example involving worship planning. To rearrange a church's worship order week after week after week in order to be creative would err on the side of freedom. To adhere to a rigid order of service—because it has always been done that way—would err on the side of form. To occasionally rearrange and modify an order of service for logical, well-thought-out reasons would represent a balance in form and freedom. In each case, sensitivity and responsibility are prerequisites.

The best creativity and freedom [in worship] happen inside the forms and around them, like good jazz.

—Paul D. Duke

In seeking balance between form and freedom, structure and antistructure, order and spontaneity, I again refer to the work of Doran and Troeger, who suggest simple principles to consider. These are outlined below:

- Avoid polarization between form and freedom.
- Some elements of both form and freedom are needed in worship.
- Maintaining a healthy tension between form and freedom requires intentional planning, not *laisez-faire* leadership.
- Do not make an idol of the old ways.
- No steady diet of one style in worship is healthy.
- Consider appropriate uses, purposes, and effects of change. Try to find *the appropriate moment* when implementing change.
- Freedom and creativity are good during communion, at gathering times, at the coming of a new hymnal, and whenever they can be sensitively woven through the service.
- Form or structure is good at the beginning and end of worship to help people feel secure coming in and going out.
- Consider Jesus' life—an authentic expression of Christian worship—which exemplified both structure and innovation.[27]

Balance is the key. Balance is precisely what Evelyn Underhill argues for when she writes, "[the] Godward life in its wholeness needs and has room for both spontaneity and order, personality and tradition, enthusiasm and mystery, prophecy and sacrifice."[28]

Progressive

The dynamics of revelation and response in worship illustrate, in part, worship's progressive nature. Revelation and response come through God's revelation to humankind and humanity's response, in turn, to the Maker. The progressive nature of worship involves looking backward and forward, but also at the present. Hoon writes about the perspectives of past, present, and future in *The Integrity of Worship*, arguing that this "trifold understanding of movement" is an essential principle of vitality in liturgy.[29]

In worship, we look backward to the genealogy of our faith. We celebrate God's revelation that has been manifested over history—the creation, God's providence, the Redeemer's covenant of redemption, God's redemptive revelation through Jesus Christ in the incarnation, the cross, the resurrection, and the manifestation of power through the coming of the Holy Spirit.[30]

Through this historic glance into the revelation of God's salvation history, we see the Holy One. And as we continue to discern present revelations of the Immortal God, we are compelled to respond in measurable ways. From worship's door, we are set into forward motion. Stepping out on faith, we look ahead to the application of our faith in daily living. This forward movement is part of the progressive nature of worship.

As a result, worship leads us to become progressive people—people transformed by the experience. In worship, we can expect to be motivated to strive to become the people we are meant to be. Just as life and growth are processes, so is worship a progressive process moving us to become kingdom people. Kingdom people do acts of justice, promote peace, practice kindness, act inclusively, and honor God in the service of others.

The progressive aspect of worship is also revealed by how beautifully the components of worship themselves, when thoughtfully arranged, not only add up to make a meaningful whole, but actually lead the worshiper gracefully through a process. Worship does not manipulate worshipers, nor should worship leaders. But worship, when carefully ordered, is logical. A leads to B, B to C, and so forth. The components of a worship service should not be tossed into the hour with little or no regard, but each component should be regarded with respect and examined for where its action may logically lead us. This progressive movement in worship is classically illustrated in the prophet Isaiah's encounter in the temple in the year King Uzziah died. Isaiah 6:1-9, used as a worship model in chapter 2, outlines a fairly obvious worship progression: Isaiah's encounter with the Holy One in the temple produced awe and caused the prophet to praise his Maker. But the encounter also compelled Isaiah to look honestly at his humanity in the light of God's holy reflection. This self-examination produced a humbling awareness, compelling Isaiah to confess his sin and ask for forgiveness. To Isaiah's contrition, God offered cleansing and then called the prophet into service. In turn, God's call prompted Isaiah to respond by offering a life commitment back to the Redeemer. The process continued beyond the worship hour as Isaiah sought to clarify the details of God's call.[31] Clearly, in this passage, one event of Isaiah's worship experience leads to the next in progressive motion. In the words of Richard Foster, "Service flows out of worship."[32] Whatever the consequence of worship—be it service, right living, justice, or something else—the progressive power of worship leads us to something momentous.

Incarnational

Lastly, worship is incarnational. In worship, God calls us to embody the Godly Presence. Such embodiment of the Christ makes Christians. Such embodiment of the Christ makes churches. Such embodiment rightfully bears the image and name of Christ to a watching, waiting world. Christians are the only glimpse of the Redeemer some will ever see. Realizing this, ours is a momentous and humbling responsibility.

Through worship, worshipers experience God anew. Taking God's spirit within themselves, worshipers become new creatures, instruments of God's redeeming love. Worship is a transforming act, gathering and inspiring humanity toward things beautiful, spiritual, and loving. In the incarnational sense, worship is an extremely personal, inward-focused, and earthy event as it works to transform what is carnal to that which is spiritual. For me, the real miracle of the incarnation is that the Christ is reborn again and again in each of us who accept this mantle of responsibility and privilege. Worship is about preparing for and assuming this responsibility. Worship is a place God births people and churches into new life. John 1:14a tells us: *And the Word became flesh and lived among us.* Through the church's worship, the Word continues to become flesh, living in and among us.

What is worship? Worship is the whole-hearted expression of devotion to God in the all-encompassing liturgy of life by both communities and individuals. *O come, let us worship and bow down.*

Our worship gives liturgical shape to the tender yet fierce love of God, which holds all people to be images of the divine, continuing incarnations of the body of Christ.

—REBECCA SUE STRADER

Christians discover Christ's body in the softness of bread and Christ's blood in the sour, sweet tang of the wine. They hear Christ celebrated in song, feel Christ in the embrace of another. The sacramentality of liturgy allows the wholeness of God's being to penetrate the whole of creation.

—ANTHONY UGOLNIK

Community of Christ, who make the Cross your own,
Live out your creed and risk your life for God alone:
The God who wears your face, to whom all worlds belong,
Whose children are of every race and every song.

—SHIRLEY ERENA MURRAY

Worship, in all its grades and kinds, is the response of the creature to the Eternal: nor need we limit this definition to the human sphere. There is a sense in which we may think of the whole life of the Universe, seen and unseen, conscious and unconscious, as an act of worship, glorifying its Origin, Sustainer, and End.

—E<small>VELYN</small> U<small>NDERHILL</small>

Questions to Ponder

1. Can you think of additional verbs and action words that define worship? Make a list.

2. Consider the focus of your church's worship. Is the primary focus upon God, or upon the church family, personalities, the music, the sermon, or something else? If the focus is not upon the Holy One, what skews the focus?

3. Consider the full gamut of your church's programs, ministries, and activities. Make a list. With the help of your study group, prioritize the list from most important to least important, basing your valuations upon your church's current practice and attitudes. What is your church's priority? Why?

4. Can you think of additional metaphors to describe holistic worship? Consider a written composition with thesis, outline, introduction, body, conclusion, words, sentences, paragraphs, and punctuation. Or consider a musical composition replete with form, meter, key, theme, notes, rhythms, harmonies, melodies, and dynamics. Or consider the metaphor of the human body used by the Apostle Paul in Romans 12:4-8 to describe the church. Could this metaphor also be used to describe worship?

5. What additions can you make to the lists describing worship elements, components, whole people, history, symbols, forms, and community?

6. In what ways is worship discomforting to you? What does this mean for you? What might this mean for your congregation?

7. Using the Doran/Troeger principles for renewing worship and a recent order of worship from your church, evaluate your church's worship in terms of proportion, congruence, variety, flow, and associations. (For proportion, it will be helpful to know how long each component of the service lasted.)

8. Considering your church's worship practice, list ways freedom is expressed in worship. List ways form is maintained in worship. Does balance exist between form and freedom? If not, is your church's worship more heavily form or freedom oriented? Why?

9. Using the Sunday bulletin, examine carefully a recent order of worship from your church. Does the order of service suggest a progression of worship events? How? If not, why? What is lacking or what is superfluous?

10. Toward what does your worship move? Service? A deeper commitment? A closer fellowship? Something else?

11. What might it mean for your church to become God incarnate? What might it mean for you?

12. What manifestations of God's incarnation do you see in the life of your church?

NOTES

[1] Free-church traditions historically refer to Protestant denominations such as Baptist, Methodist, Presbyterian, and United Church of Christ, among others. These traditions claim and exercise, to varying degrees, freedom in planning and leading worship, choosing and using liturgy. In contrast, Catholic, Anglican, Episcopal, and Lutheran denominations are not deemed free-church traditions, but rather, prayer book and confessional traditions following set liturgies. However, in recent years, these traditions have transformed to include various innovations in worship.

[2] Horace T. Allen, Jr., "Liturgy as the Form of Faith," *The Landscape of Praise: Readings in Liturgical Renewal*, ed. Blair Gilmer Meeks (Valley Forge: Trinity Press International, 1996), 7.

[3] Frank C. Senn, "The Spirit of the Liturgy, A Wonderland Revisited," in Meeks, *The Landscape of Praise*, 18.

[4] Gerard S. Sloyan, "What Is Liturgical Preaching?" in Meeks, *The Landscape of Praise*, 230.

[5] Senn, "Spirit of the Liturgy," in Meeks, *The Landscape of Praise*, 14.

[6] Michael Warren, "Culture, Counterculture and the Word," in Meeks, *The Landscape of Praise*, 281.

[7] Mark Searle, "The Uses of Liturgical Language," in Meeks, *The Landscape of Praise*, 110.

[8] Franklin M. Segler, *Christian Worship: Its Theology and Practice* (Nashville: Broadman Press, 1967), 5.

[9] William Temple, *The Hope of a New World* (New York: Macmillan, 1942) 30.

[10] Robert G. Baker, *Amos: Doing What Is Right: A Study Guide* (Macon GA: Smyth & Helwys Publishing, Inc., 1995), 79.

[11] Charles Willis, quotation of Bruce Leafblad in "Worship requires top priority," *Facts & Trends* 32/6 (1988): 2.

[12] Robert W. Bailey, "A Theology of Worship," *Search* 13/3 (1983): 17.

[13] Segler, *Christian Worship*, 4.

[14] Richard J. Foster, "The Discipline of Worship," *Celebration of Discipline: The Path to Spiritual Growth* (New York: Harper, 1978), 138.

[15] Samuel F. Williams, "Back to the Basics," *Northminster News* 48/40 (1989): 1.

[16] The thematic approach to worship planning, while an excellent one, is not the only approach to worship planning. See Robert H. Mitchell, *Ministry and Music* (Philadelphia: The Westminster Press, 1978), 95-114, for an excellent discussion of worship planning using four forms: variety, thematic, alternation, and conversational.

[17] Carol Doran and Thomas H. Troeger, "Renewing Worship," opinions expressed in workshop presentation at Worship and Music Conference, Montreat, North Carolina, 24-30 June 1990. My discussion of the principles of proportion, congruence, variety, flow, and associations comes directly from notes taken in this informative workshop. I have simply elaborated upon their ideas in order to clarify and illustrate the principles.

[18] Paul Waitman Hoon, "The Language of Worship," *The Integrity of Worship: Ecumenical and Pastoral Studies in Liturgical Theology* (Nashville: Abingdon, 1971), 279-80.

[19] Kenneth L. Gibble, "How Wasteful Can Worship Be?" *Christianity Today* 25/21 (1981): 17.

[20] Ibid.

[21] Ibid., quoting Annie Dillard, *Pilgrim at Tinker Creek* (New York: HarperPerennial, 1990), 126.

[22] Foster, "The Discipline of Worship," 149.

[23] Wilferd A. Peterson, *The New Book of the Art of Living* (New York: Simon & Schuster, 1963), 12.

[24] Bailey, "A Theology of Worship," 23.

[25] W. Wayne Price, *The Church and the Rites of Passage* (Nashville: Broadman Press, 1989), 55.

[26] Ibid., 64.

[27] Doran and Troeger, conference on "Renewing Worship."

[28] Evelyn Underhill, *Worship* (New York: Crossroad, 1985), 90.

[29] Hoon, *The Integrity*, 283-84.

[30] Franklin M. Segler, *Christian Worship: Its Theology and Practice* (Nashville: Broadman, 1967), 8.

[31] See chapter 2, "Scriptural Models for Worship: Isaiah 6:1-12," for a complete exposition of the passage as it relates to Christian worship.

[32] Foster, "The Discipline of Worship," 140.

CHAPTER 4

Worship Is Not...

Sometimes it is helpful to define something in terms of what it is *not*. For instance, for some it is sufficient to describe fog as *a cloud on the ground*. But for others, additional information is needed, like *fog is not smoke*. In this chapter, worship will be further defined by *what it is not*: preaching, big church, a substitute for Sunday school, extraneous material such as announcements, a variety show, entertainment, a means to an end, evangelism, a security blanket, sermon tasting and music critiquing, nor existentialism.

Preaching, Church Service, Big Church

First change language, behavior will follow. The lesson of this axiom applies to many or all life situations, among them worship practice. The ways we talk about worship affect how we behave in worship. As we consider what worship is not, it seems important, even necessary, to train ourselves to call worship by its proper name—*worship*.

Linguistic authorities advise that language and thought are directly related. In fact, the two are so closely related that language is considered part of the thinking process itself. Language is a syntactic structure that not only aids communication, but also warps and filters meaning and understanding. Language transmits prejudice and attitudes, and according to the experts, every single word we use influences us in one direction or another.[1] We all know the power of words: the wounding pain of a sharp or careless remark, or the caressing touch of kind and gentle words.

Our words reflect our beliefs. If we choose to refer to worship by other names, our labels reveal our beliefs about worship, and in turn, those words affect our behavior in worship. This is why it is important to examine our words—what we call worship. Our choices reflect our understanding of worship, and our worship behavior mirrors the image of that understanding.

How many times have you heard someone ask, "Are you staying for *preaching*?" While growing up in rural Virginia, this was a frequently-used way to refer to worship: *preaching*. Sometimes I still hear the following phrase or others like it: "Are you going to *church* this Sunday?" Or perhaps you have overheard an adult say to a young child transitioning from nursery to worship, "Let's go to *big church*."

If we carefully consider what worship *is* and what worship is *not*, we must also carefully choose what we call our assembly. Worship is made up of a host of components—Scripture, song, prayer, praise, confession, pardon, blessing, and more. Among them is preaching. But preaching—exhortation, sermon, homily, or meditation—is but one integral part among many Christian worship components. To disproportionately emphasize the importance of preaching above all other parts of worship minimizes the other parts, throwing the entire experience off balance.

We make this semantic mistake honestly, for preaching has long been an important factor in Protestant non-sacramental worship. At different times during our Christian heritage—from the early church of the first century, through the Reformation, during the pioneer years of our country, and to the present within the free-church tradition—preaching the gospel has at one time or another been the central hub of worship.[2] To refer to worship as preaching de-emphasizes other equally important aspects of worship such as praise and prayer, confession and pardon, testimony and offering. To refer to worship as preaching assumes that most, if not all, the action of worship is performed by the preacher. This erroneous assumption belies belief in the priesthood of all believers, assigns responsibility for worship to the preacher, and reduces active worship participation to passive attendance. Pastor and author Robert W. Bailey has this to say about the *preaching service*: "The pastor who ceases to call the worship hour the 'preaching service' and stops urging his [or her] members to 'stay for preaching' will be on the right road to teaching his [or her] congregation that worship has leaders not performers."[3]

Words are powerful. Words, like mirrors, reflect our attitudes. Words, like heralds, bear witness to our beliefs. Words, like potters, mold our thinking. Words, like teachers, influence our behavior and the behavior of others. Let us choose them carefully. *O come, let us worship and bow down, let us kneel before the L*ORD*, our Maker!* (Ps 95:6).

A Substitute for Sunday School or Bible Study

If your church is like mine, you have probably witnessed the exodus that often occurs between Sunday school and worship. Have you ever wondered about this phenomenon? In every church, it seems, there are those who regularly attend Bible study but routinely neglect worship participation. Apparently, to some, Sunday school—whether it is called Bible study, Sunday school, Christian education, or church school—functions as a substitute for worship. But education and worship are different. Education and worship have different foci and each fulfills a differing purpose.

A church's educational time usually includes opportunities for fellowship, intercessory prayer, and Bible study within small groups. The small group design facilitates sharing, discussion, and bonding among group members. Caring and ministry are desired by-products of the small group experience. Members learn each other's names. Honesty and intimacy are important facets of the small group experience. Through Christian educational study groups, practical application to biblical principles is taught and learned.

Worship, on the other hand, is the time when the church community gathers for the sole purpose of worshiping God. Worship is the work of the gathered community. Within this appointed time, nothing else claims the community's attention but the Holy One, the one true focus of worship. To regularly expose oneself to the biblical commands and examples regarding worship during the educational hour and then to neglect worship in the next seems ludicrous. But it is done every Sunday. *I was glad when they said to me, "Let us go to the house of the LORD!"* (Ps 122:1).

Extraneous Material Such as Announcements

Like network station breaks and sponsor commercials that interrupt your favorite television programs, announcements break the mood and flow of worship. No matter how well we present them, no matter how well we disguise them, no matter where within worship we place them, no matter what we call them, no matter how well we dress them up, announcements are announcements. And announcements break the mood and flow of worship because announcements are not components of worship.

Perhaps this has happened to you: Three chimes honoring the Trinity rang out as acolytes lit altar candles symbolizing God's light and spirit. As a young boy presented the cross before the solemn assembly, we turned our thoughts to Christ's great sacrifice of love. Skillful organist hands and feet played music for meditation, and the congregation listened: quiet, still, and thoughtful. Then, as the choir sang Engelberg's "When in our music God is glorified," their song of joy called all who gathered to raise unified voices in grateful praise. Together, we stood and sang "All Creatures of Our God and King" as the mighty pipe organ's tones billowed and swelled, modulating higher and higher, undergirding and energizing our song. Following our praise we bore witness to our heart's faith by affirming our belief through a historic liturgy of the church, "The Apostles' Creed." Then came the announcements. What followed was ten minutes of exhilarating news—a lengthy and well-done endorsement of a new Bible study class, reminders about two upcoming Sunday emphases, announcements concerning future guest preachers, a plug for next Sunday's church-wide picnic, an update on the softball team's tournament status, details about the Habitat for Humanity project, introduction to the morning's speaker, et cetera, et cetera, et cetera.

Consider, please, one more scenario: Upon entering the sanctuary, I had been encouraged to focus upon God. The opening voluntaries set the tone for my reflection. The pastor's thoughtful call to worship challenged me to lay aside extraneous concerns and join wholeheartedly in glad praise. I voiced my praise through hymn and litany. I confessed my sin and was assured of pardon. I heard the Scripture proclaimed and my soul was convicted. I voiced my commitment in song with those around me. And just before I was to bring my offering before the Lord—the climax of worship—came the announcements. Carefully disguised as concerns of the church, this two-minute segment strategically placed right before the climax of the service came close to breaking the momentum and flow of worship. Expertly handled, the segment was nevertheless a series of announcements that included welcome to visitors, advertisement of the new orientation class beginning in two weeks, instructions on how to pass the fellowship registration pad along the pews, a reminder of congregational care cards in the pew racks, and a final allusion to the written announcements contained in the bulletin folder. This was undeniably the best announcement period I'd ever witnessed, but the segment still left me with the question, did it need to be placed *here* in the service?

Announcements are important. Churches need ways to share information about programming, fellowship, and ministry opportunities. Welcoming and registering visitors is also important. But a string of announcements within the designated worship time is probably not the answer if worship is given the priority it deserves. Consider the following: Use the bulletin folder or weekly newsletter for announcements of every kind and expect people to read them. People will not read printed announcements if they are not expected to read them or if they know they will hear them announced later. If verbal announcements must be made to the assembly, consider limiting them to congregational concerns and opportunities for ministry, not programming and events. If you must, refer only briefly to printed announcements, urging the congregation to read them. Consider carefully when and how you make any announcements, honestly asking yourself how each announcement relates to worship. Consider positioning brief and essential church concerns either before worship begins—that's before the prelude or any other preparation for worship—or directly before the closing benediction.

Of these two suggestions, the latter better follows worship's progression and flow. Placing church concerns immediately prior to the benediction utilizes the natural break that occurs there and suggests that worship—the work of the church gathered—is complete. This thoughtful placement assumes that once the community of faith worships together, worshipers are then prepared and energized for ministry—the work of the church scattered. Taking a minute or two at the close of worship to alert the congregation to opportunities for service seems a fitting conclusion for worship: Because we have gathered together for succor and strength, because we have worshiped, we are now ready to scatter and minister in God's name. Here are ways we might do this . . . *then come the announcements.*

A Variety Show

There's no doubt about it—we're an entertainment-oriented society. We know what we like and we like what we know. Given this base, it is not difficult to understand why worship of the variety show kind appeals to many people. But worship is not a variety show.

Some worship services resemble variety shows: services where worship components neither fit together nor purposefully progress; services where no discernible focus or central theme emerges; services where announcements, extraneous remarks, and events disrupt worship's mood and flow; and services where entertainment of the congregational audience is the *format du jour*. A muddle of incongruent elements carelessly or thoughtlessly juxtaposed is not what worship is about. While variety is a good thing, in its attempt to provide something for everyone, variety itself is not worship.

To those who enjoy this type of entertainment, variety shows delight and satisfy. *But worship is not a variety show.* Worship's purpose is not to entertain, nor to be fun. Choirs, preachers, and other worship leaders are not performers who seek to entertain or worship for the congregation. The components of worship do not stand alone, but each relates to that which precedes or follows. From beginning to end, worship goes somewhere. Worship is not for spectators, pew critics, or passive audiences. Worship is participatory, engaging, and totally active. Worship is not a variety show, although it does involve rich drama.

Entertainment

The nineteenth-century Danish theologian Søren Kierkegaard provided the Christian community with an excellent, but simple, model for worship: worship as drama. The model compares worship to drama. In worship, we, the congregation, are *actors* before God, the *audience*. Worship leaders—liturgists, ministers of music, pastors, preachers, and others—also function as *prompters*, coordinating, organizing, and assisting the congregation to worship more effectively.[4]

Kierkegaard's model calls for a congregation actively engaged in worship. Worship is not a spectator sport where the congregation sits idle, expecting either to worship vicariously through the worship leaders or to be entertained. The model allows no room for worship by a select few, entertainment of the congregation by the pastor or choir, or lackadaisical involvement in the pew. These all-too-popular, but false, concepts of worship stem from incorrect attitudes about worship participation and misplaced focus: *What do I like, what makes me feel good, what makes me feel comfortable, was the sermon good enough? Was worship fun? Was the choral anthem well executed? Did I like the music selections?* Or o*kay, I'm here—I'll just sit and watch.* Attitudes like these rearrange the model, making the congregation the audience and the worship leaders the actors. Where does the Most High fit into this skewed model? In entertainment-oriented worship, the focus of worship is bent away from God to other concerns.

I hope we do not come to the liturgy as spectators, nor for entertainment or even refreshment, though on occasion it will no doubt provide us amply with both. Rather should liturgy be the simple and powerful effort of people in the midst of life to keep festival in their abundance and to make memorial in their loss, ever striving to make life better and to push its meaning to the furthest reaches of human experience.

—Rachel Reeder

The work of presiders [worship leaders, ministers, liturgists] is to help worshipers enter wholeheartedly and single-mindedly into the new creation that God is fashioning in our midst.

—Yme Woensdregt

The following call to worship reflects the intent of Kierkegaard's model. Instead of drama, here the metaphor is music and dance: *Dance! Children of God! Lose yourself in the choreography of the Spirit. Life is a dance and God is the orchestra. It is good to be alive!*[5]

Kierkegaard's model portrays a congregation of worshipers actively focused upon the Holy One. The model strongly suggests that the work of the church gathered is to offer its acts of worship individually and corporately to God who is present and attentive to all our offerings.

A Means to an End

Worship is not a means to an end. We do not worship to feel good, to experience pleasure, to ease a conscience, to impress a neighbor, to grow a church, to please a parent or spouse. Instead, "worship is an end in itself." Franklin Segler makes this point in his book *Christian Worship*. "When we try to worship for the sake of certain benefits that may be received, the act ceases to be worship; for then it attempts to use the Ancient of Days as a means to something else. We worship God purely for the sake of worshipping God."[6] Worship is an end in itself. Period.

To be spectators,
that's what we like,
isn't it?
No involvement,
no participation,
not too close,
just sit back and watch.
Be a critic.
If it isn't professional enough,
or isn't popular,
it's the performers!
I won't come back.
I want my money's worth—
at church.

—James L. Christensen

[Worship's] purpose is not renewal (although it may), instruction (although it might), or even impetus to mission (although it does). As an end in itself Christian worship does not have a meaning, it is meaning.

—W. Paul Jones

There is no purpose to worship—other than to worship.

—Yme Woensdregt

Evangelism

Evangelism is a coveted by-product of worship, but worship is not evangelism. Nor is evangelism the focus of worship. The jubilant praise of God's people, the perceived sincerity of their confessed sin and the gratitude of their pardon, the convicting testimony of song and sermon, and the climatic offering of life and resource in worship all bear witness to the greatness and goodness of the Godhead. And to the lost soul enveloped within such a worshiping assembly, to the one to whom such powerful witness is borne, evangelism may indeed take place. But the focus of worship remains God, not evangelism. Worship remains the work of God's gathered community. In worship, the community of faith gives offerings of praise, talent, and commitment. Yes, because of the powerful witness of worship, the spectator among the gathered may indeed find salvation. Because of the energizing effect of worship upon God's people, the community of faith finds refreshment that prepares it for its commissioned work outside temple walls: to evangelize the world. *Go therefore and make disciples of all nations, baptizing them in the name of the Father and of the Son and of the Holy Spirit, and teaching them to obey everything that I have commanded you. And remember, I am with you always, to the end of the age* (Matt 28:19-20).

The focus of worship remains God. Conducted by the community of faith, worship not only bears witness to the community's relationship with the Maker, but also enables the community to evangelize.

A Security Blanket

Worship is not a security blanket of comfort, routine, and sameness. Instead, worship is dynamic, active, and challenging, a re-creating force.

Routine and tradition are good things. As a writer, I value routine. Reserving set times for writing increases productivity. Writing regularly perfects skill. Writing—when you might not feel like writing—develops discipline. Routine is good. But routine may also foster rigidity and squash spontaneity if deviation is not allowed.

Tradition is also good. Tradition reflects values, provides windows to the past, and allows us to understand and claim heritage. A knowledge of history grounds and stabilizes us as we live the present and chart the future. But too strict an adherence to past tradition may stifle creativity and growth.

In worship, there is certainly a place for routine and tradition. There is no question that it is right to routinely offer praise, confession, and commitment to the Creator in worship. There is no question that it is important to preserve and practice traditional institutions and liturgies of the church like the Lord's Supper, baptism, confessions, and the Model Prayer. There is great value in a church community celebrating worship in traditional ways meaningful to their collective heritage. But it is equally important to realize that worship, if it is really worship, cannot be the same experience repeated week after week and year after year.

If we use the same order of worship for twenty years, we risk using a lifeless, stale form. If our worship is so predictable that we go through the motions as if by rote, we may reduce our ritual to mere "rut"-ual and predictably leave unchanged, unmoved, effectively disengaged. If we never do anything different, our offerings may no longer be considered our first fruits or the unspotted calf, but something ragged and worn, something dead and devoid of meaning save sentiment. If like Linus, the famed Peanuts comic strip character, who clutches and drags about his dirty and tattered security blanket, we jealously and relentlessly hang on to a particular order of service or way of doing things, we may risk missing out on worship's dynamic and life-motivating force. In our fear of change and the unknown, we may miss a glimpse of the Greatest Unknown. While we may remain secure and unthreatened, wrapped comfortably within the blanket of our hallowed tradition, we may miss the whisper of God's voice and the sometimes disturbing urging of the Holy Spirit. If we expect worship to be comfortable and wrestle with nothing new nor struggle to become God's new creation, we may miss the comforting touch of pardon and the soft kiss of blessing. If we expect the worship experience to be the same week after week, we may lose our saltiness and fail to make a difference in the world. Sadly, if we expect worship to be a security blanket of comfort, routine, and sameness, we may fail to worship at all.

Sermon Tasting and Music Critiquing

During my college years, I was privileged to work in an urban church as organist and music director. They were a cordial people and frequently entertained me in their homes. A frequent occasion for fellowship was over a meal, oftentimes Sunday dinner. However, it was not long before I began to witness a disturbing pattern among these parishioners: Sunday dinner was frequently the forum for extended criticism of the sermon and traditional "roast preacher" was commonly the entree. I soon discovered an unnerving dissatisfaction and deep well of resentment within these otherwise loving people. While they treated me with great kindness, I discovered the church was a hotbed of bickering, fussing, and fighting. Worship produced a churning foment of angry discourse. As I look back and ponder their witness, I realize the worship these good people once held dear had somehow ceased to be worship, and they languished and writhed in pain. Worship had become to them what I call "sermon tasting," a dysfunctional habit of critique and criticism, which left them empty and dissatisfied.

Whatever is imposed on the hearing and the sight of people cannot be worship in spirit and in truth. Liturgy, which must be so defined, is not a presentation submitted for audience critique. It engages people, inviting them to criticize themselves.

—Gerard S. Sloyan

Had I sat in the congregational pew instead of on the organ bench within the choir loft, I might have witnessed yet another perspective over Sunday dinner: music critiquing. I might have heard, *I don't like the anthems that minister of music chooses. The choir sounds terrible. I'm not singing new hymns I don't know. Why can't we sing more of the old hymns? I wish Mrs. Solo Singer wouldn't sing so often! Her voice wobbles and squeaks.*

The sermon may be awful and the music pathetic. The choir may be bad and the music director may lack training. Unfortunately, these situations exist. Ugly forms can inhibit worship. But sermon tasting and music critiquing is not worship. To allow the sermon or the anthem to completely make or ruin worship relegates the congregation's role from active worshipers to critics and spectators. As Kierkegaard's model of worship so graphically suggests, preachers and choristers are not entertainers and the congregation is not an audience. God is the audience of our worship and every person who worships is an actor before the Holy One. Thankfully, God is merciful.

Existentialism

Existentialism, with its emphasis upon the subjective experience, is not worship. It seems we're up to our ears these days in a subjective mess of existentialism when it comes to worship. It is no wonder that this is so when one considers the diverseness of today's congregations and their divergent tastes in worship.

Researchers tell us that the baby boomers (those born between 1946 and 1964) are a "multiple choice generation" who pick and choose—smorgasbord style—between what they like and dislike when choosing a church. These adults hungrily seek self-gratification and self-fulfillment. When it comes to worship, boomers desire a blended traditional style, "combining elements of traditional worship with more contemporary elements found in non-traditional worship programs."[7]

To the post-baby-boomer generation born between 1964 and 1983—the busters—everything is relative. "They don't believe in absolute truths. Anything goes. They live in a society where everybody does what's right in their own minds." As a result, busters are experimental. While they want to make a difference, it is difficult to get them to commit unless the experience has real meaning for them.[8]

The third group of adults alive today are people born before 1946. The technological and medical advances of our era have increased life expectancy to new levels. As a result, the ranks of this older population group continue to swell in numbers. Among this population segment are faithful church attendees who cling to traditional worship forms and find both boomers and busters difficult to understand.

> *... the liturgy is not primarily a "work of art." The point of worship is not the production of aesthetic experience but the encounter and dialogue with a living God.*
>
> —DON E. SALIERS

While each population group deserves careful consideration, we must beware of the inclination to concentrate so much on what makes *me* feel good and what *I* like in worship that we fall prey to the tendency to culturally over-condition and corrupt worship. Paul Waitman Hoon, author of *The Integrity of Worship*, calls this tendency to exalt beauty over holy, imagination and feeling over conscience and will, art over substance, taste over truth, aesthetic over biblical, appreciation and impression over decision, and contemplation over commitment the "corruption of aestheticism."[9] When the emphasis of worship is existential—attempting always to feature and tantalize the subjective experience—it ceases to be worship.

Worship is not preaching or big church, a substitute for Christian education, extraneous material such as announcements, a variety show, entertainment, a means to an end, evangelism, a security blanket, sermon tasting or music critiquing, nor existentialism. Worship is none of these things. Instead, worship is an active encounter with the Living God who remains the sole focus of all worship.

Questions to Ponder

1. What do you call worship? What do you hear worship being called within your congregation?

2. Does your church experience an exodus between Sunday school and worship? What are the possible reasons members of your congregation omit worship participation? What are some possible solutions?

3. How are announcements and welcome handled within your church's time of worship?

4. How long is your usual worship time? How much of this time is routinely given to announcements and welcome?

5. Does your congregation's worship ever resemble a variety show? In what ways?

6. For what reasons do you worship?

7. In the "drama" of worship, what role do you assume?

8. To what degree and in what ways does your congregation participate in worship?

9. What traditions within your church's worship does your church jealously guard? Considering each tradition, how do they contribute to or diminish worship?

10. Is the Lord's Supper observed in the same way every time? Why? Why not?

11. How often does your church's order of worship change? In what ways does it change?

12. How does your congregation react to change within worship? Cite possible reasons for their varied reactions.

13. Following worship, what thoughts and feelings do you frequently find yourself expressing? What testimony do you hear others give?

14. Using your church enrollment, what percentage of your congregation belongs to the buster group? The baby boomers? Those born before 1946?

15. How does the population mix within your congregation affect worship in your setting?

16. How would the various segments of your congregation define their time together in worship?

NOTES

[1] Dwight Bolinger and Donald A. Sears, "Mind and Language," *Aspects of Language*, 3rd ed. (New York: Harcourt, 1981), 134-57.

[2] See Franklin M. Segler's discussion of "The Preaching of the Word" in *Christian Worship: Its Theology and Practice* (Nashville: Broadman Press, 1967), 126-33.

[3] Robert W. Bailey, "A Theology of Worship," *Search* 13/3 (1983): 17-27.

[4] Søren J. Kierkegaard, *Purity of Heart*, trans. Douglas Steere (New York: Harper, 1938), 163ff.

[5] Excerpt from the call to worship from a service of worship at Myers Park Baptist Church, Charlotte, North Carolina, 22 September 1996.

[6] Segler, *Christian Worship*, 4.

[7] Michael Duduit, "Boomers and the Bible," *The Tie* 62/2 (1994): 10.

[8] Terry Lackey, "Reaching Boomers and Busters," *Facts & Trends* 40/4 (1994): 6.

[9] Paul Waitman Hoon, "The Concern for Worship," *The Integrity of Worship: Ecumenical and Pastoral Studies in Liturgical Theology* (Nashville: Abingdon, 1971), 23-78.

CHAPTER 5

Components of Christian Worship

Scriptural models provided in chapter 2 identified various worship elements. Isaiah's temple experience (Isa 6:1-12) reveals eight elements: commendation (praise), confession and contrition, cleansing, calling, commitment, commissioning, and clarification. Abraham's worship encounter over the near sacrifice of Isaac in Genesis 22:1-19 includes encounter, revelation, obedience, separateness, expectancy, preparation, attentiveness, surrender, change, and blessing. In the Model Prayer of Matthew 6:9-13—if we use it as a model for worship—we find elements of praise and adoration, submission, reliance, and confession and pardon. I list these again here in order to differentiate between *elements* of worship and *components* of worship, which for the purposes of discussion within this chapter, I maintain are different.

Components, like building blocks, are the materials that worship planners use to build orders of worship. They are the tools that help worshipers experience and express such elements as awe, praise, submission, or commitment. For example, one way to express or experience praise (an element) is through music (a component). While an element is an act of worship—an expression or experience, a component is a way to accomplish worship acts—a means, a tool, a form, a medium. The terms I use, components and elements, are arbitrarily chosen and could be easily identified by different words. I offer this explanation for the sake of effective communication and understanding.

In this chapter, we will examine numerous components that enable congregations to worship. Among these are gathering, centering, silence, call to worship, doxology or praise, music, readings, prayers of various types, congregational assent, testimonies and exhortations, sermon, baptism and communion, kiss of peace, and offering. Where appropriate, illustrations will be provided to clarify further the form and function of each worship component.

For continuity's sake, let us assume that the samples provided within this chapter are written for a service of worship with the theme "New! You Are a New Creation" from 2 Corinthians 5:17: *So if anyone is in Christ, there is a new creation: everything old has passed away; see, everything has become new!* The setting is spring. The pre-Easter themes of introspection and confession, and the Easter themes—renewal, revival, new life, *newness*—shape the liturgy. Where deemed appropriate, the samples will be connected to this theme, but as it is not necessary, nor even desired, to tie every single component of worship to a theme, some examples will remain general in nature.

Gathering

While worshiping with various congregations and denominations during the course of a calendar year, I became disturbed at the indiscriminate but frequent mix of fellowship and worship within worship services. I worried how I might address the important matter of family and community-building, fellowship and *koinonia*, within a book about worship when it appeared that so few congregations recognized that the gathering rituals of greetings, announcements, church family business, and fellowship are not really components of worship. After reading James F. White's thought-provoking essay "Coming Together in Christ's Name," the answer became clear.[1] White opens his essay with this claim: "Worship is the most important thing the church does, and coming together in Christ's name, the most important thing that happens in worship. It may also be the most overlooked."[2] Before discussing creative ways to apportion the time and space for gathering, White admonishes "us not [to] be disturbed by the noise and shuffle of people arriving. Meeting is important; assembling is part of Christ's work among us. It deserves to be recognized with sufficient time and space."[3]

Church families must be given opportunities for building community, making announcements, rehearsing new music and unfamiliar service materials, and taking care of family business when most of the congregation is present. But churches also need to understand that conducting church business is not worship.

Individuals and communities worship. We worship individually within groups. We worship corporately while seated individually side by side.

Corporate worship at its best is done by communities, not groups of strangers, although strangers may effectively worship together if one considers the holy catholic church a community. But for the moment, let's consider the local church, a family of believers who worship together regularly at a set time and place. The health and depth of their community relationship affects the quality of their corporate worship. The community is built up not only by its worship, but by its many other opportunities of interaction—musical and educational programs, fellowship opportunities, common meals, outreach projects, committee business, and so forth—where names are learned, friendships forged, and time is spent together. Community is formed by being and doing together. When a local community of faith assembles for corporate worship, the individuals comprising the community worship side by side, and the group worships as a whole. The quality of the worship experience affects both the individuals and the gathered community. If worship truly takes place, these people and this community leave better prepared to face and influence the world.

All this is to say that the building up of community—apart from worship and also through the worship event—is a necessary and essential aspect of local church life. The better job a local church does at building a community of healthy relationships, the better chance it has for worship. Worship and community function within a cyclical relationship: worship aids community, and community aids worship. Aside from the circular relation the two share, however, the building of community and the worship of God are two separate acts. Both are important. In fact, both are essential. But each is different and deserves its own place and focus.

What seems to happen far too often is the designated worship time becomes a disorganized mix of fellowship, family business, and worship all rolled into one. The mixture sometimes becomes so scrambled that true worship becomes difficult, if not impossible, because worshipers are asked to focus in so many directions at once. What is called worship is in effect an indiscriminate conglomeration of business and fellowship, periodically interrupting the prayers and praise of God's well-intentioned, but confused people. To one of the family, this blend of fellowship and worship may be so normal and feel so comfortable that the intermingling of family matters within worship is not recognized as a disruption at all, but a part of worship itself. Perhaps it is on some level.

But to the visiting stranger trying to worship within such tangle of fellowship, family business, and worship, the experience falls short of worship's grand potential. As a visitor in many different congregations over the past two years, I often left services asking myself how might a visitor find community and common ground except through the liturgy? But more important, why would it ever make sense repeatedly to break the flow and rhythm of worship with anything that draws our attention away from God, the ultimate focus of our worship?[4]

Consider these examples.

(1) The setting is a small church. The congregation boasts on its street-side sign, "Visitors are expected." Yet, in reality, their welcome to me that crisp morning included only a passing remark about the unusually cold weather as I entered the sanctuary, a brief and rather perfunctory statement from the pastor during the service, and a simple hello from a couple of folks following worship. No handshakes, no introductions, no names.

As I looked around the room from my place on the nearly empty pew, I noted the casual dress of the congregation. A few senior adults donned the usual Sunday attire, one young woman had clad herself in a flimsy summer dress, but many of the adults and most of the children outfitted themselves in an assortment of jeans, slacks, tee shirts, and tennis shoes. Small children remained in the service, wriggling, talking, walking on pews, and lying on the floor. One young boy parked his shoes in the aisle and sat in his sock feet. The casualness in dress was also reflected in worship style.

It dawned on me I was observing a family. My mind created its own scene of a family at home—children sprawled on the floor coloring and poring over the Sunday funnies, Dad lounging on the sofa flicking the remote from game to game, apron-clad Mom giving the last touches to dinner, a teenager setting the table—a family simultaneously together, both relaxed and busy, taking care of family business. This is what I saw in this small and close-knit community of faith who seemed to have gathered for the purpose of building and celebrating family. They called it worship.

For the first half-hour of the designated worship time, this assembly, at best, gave me an outsider's glance into an intimate family scene. I never felt a part of it, only an observer to the family ritual. Amid this family of faith, I remained a stranger. I felt invisible.

Eight minutes of announcements followed the call to worship. During this interlude, I learned the specific way to cook chickens for the church bazaar, was invited to an upcoming midweek dinner, and was told of a newly instigated service project. A five-minute prayer segment followed that included the pastor's listing prayer concerns, soliciting additional prayer requests from congregational members, and voicing a pastoral prayer on their behalf. A hymn was sung and then we returned to our family emphasis with a five-minute children's message. It was not until twenty-seven minutes into the worship hour that the focus began to shift away from family concerns toward God. Finally, thanks to a segment of liturgy from the denominational worship book, I began to acquire a temporary sense of community within the larger family of faith to which this local body and I both belong. As a visitor, as a stranger among these people, my only hope for community that crisp October morning was through the liturgy, not through the business.

While everything I saw and heard within this community was important, I left wondering how much of it was actually worship. Please consider another example.

(2) The setting is a medium-sized congregation. The order of service printed in the bulletin begins with the entry, "Gathering of the Community." During this time, the sanctuary pews filled gradually as people entered the sanctuary. At 10:59, a skillfully played Bach prelude and fugue opened the formal part of the service. Talking continued. A rousing choral anthem followed. Still, some parishioners continued to talk. Despite the murmur of voices surrounding me, the music of organ and anthem began to prepare me for praise. But much to my disappointment, what followed was eighteen minutes of family business: welcome to guests, announcements, a tribute to the organist, and numerous lengthy program promotions. At 11:30 we stood to sing a hymn of praise. I was not in the mood.

I left these two services confused by what I had witnessed. While strongly affirming the need for a time and place to conduct family business and to build community, I questioned its placement within the worship service.

In order to maintain and protect worship's integrity—while simultaneously respecting and nurturing community-building—it seems churches need to seriously and prayerfully consider providing adequate gathering times whenever large populations of the church gather, like on Sundays. Gathering time is an essential prerequisite for worship, perhaps even a component, which begins or ends the service. It deserves a space of its own. Once sufficient gathering time is provided, gathering rituals need not be mixed with worship, interrupting its flow and rhythm. Once worshipers have been afforded adequate gathering time and space, they will be more receptive to entreaties to center or focus themselves for worship.

Examples follow that illustrate how three churches provide gathering time and space separately but in conjunction with worship. As you will see, each situation is slightly different. While one church designates gathering as an event that both precedes and follows worship, another treats gathering as a foyer to worship. The third encourages gathering as an extension of worship and provides a separate space for the event.

(1) The setting is a medium-sized church, a Sunday in early January. As I entered the church foyer, the warmth of its large, roaring fire quickly replaced the chilling effects of the wintry weather outside. The narthex, tastefully decorated with rugs, sofas, and armchairs, resembled a parlor, and the space was filled with a large gathering of people talking happily with one another as they warmed themselves near the blazing hearth. I had arrived early for the 11:00 service, as had these folks. No one seemed rushed to leave the warmth of the room or the fellowship of their friends. Since I was a stranger to those gathering, I ventured ahead into the sanctuary where some worshipers sat quietly in the silent room. As I sat down to prepare myself mentally and emotionally for worship, other worshipers left the narthex gathering and found their places among the pews. Organ music helped prepare me further for worship. Worshipers continued to enter the sanctuary reverently and quietly. Following the service, additional fellowship time was encouraged. At this time, I was greeted by many worshipers. Many lingered in fellowship beyond my visit.

(2) The setting is a Baptist church where I worshiped while a seminary student in the early 1980s. Like most, if not all, Baptist churches (and perhaps other denominations also) in the greater Louisville area, this church gathered for worship at 10:45. The gathering ritual included greetings, announcements, family time, and addressing various church family concerns. Once this was done, worshipers refocused and began worship with the opening notes of the organ voluntary. In essence, the church gathered from 10:45 until 11:00, and then worshiped for the hour following.

(3) The setting is a large congregation, noted for its eclectic and ecumenical theological stance. This church takes worship seriously. Opportunities for

silence, meditation, lighting of altar candles, and music for organ or piano precede the call to worship, which begins the collective part of the worship service promptly at 11:00. The rhythm and flow of worship is zealously respected, and few, if any, gathering acts are conducted within the worship hour itself. Following the service, though, the congregation is routinely invited and encouraged to reassemble in the fellowship hall for the coffee-fellowship hour where emphasis is turned away from worship to community-building and family.

The differences between the former and latter examples reveal how gathering and worship are conducted. Each congregation, by its actions, seems to acknowledge and emphasize the family aspect of churchgoing. But the latter three churches seem better to understand that time, attention, and space need to be given to gathering and worship, but to each separately. The latter congregations guard worship time jealously, while providing their respective families of faith ample Sunday morning opportunities for fellowship. In each case, the quality of worship was remarkably better, and as a visitor among them, I was able to feel immediately at home in the worship of God.

Consider building gathering time into your Sunday morning schedule, either directly before or after the worship service. If gathering and community fellowship times seem to be indiscriminately mixed into the worship service, ask yourself why. What contributes to this? Consider seriously the placement of the kiss of peace, especially if your church's interpretation is primarily an extended greeting or a moment of fellowship. In this form, the kiss of peace may be functioning as an interruption to the rhythm of worship. (A discussion of this ancient rite comes later in this chapter.) If gathering is taking place under the roar of loud organ music, consider putting an end to the competition by providing a designated gathering time. If the gathering time you choose precedes worship, allow the organ prelude to signal the end of gathering and the beginning of centering for worship.

Whether you consider gathering an act of worship or as a preliminary to worship, consider designating time and space for this important aspect of church life. Do all you can to preserve, protect, and develop family and community within the life of your congregation by providing gathering time and space. Then, likewise, do all you can to preserve, protect, and develop worship as a separate action with a separate focus and direction. Because of their tandem relationship, gathering and worship will each enhance the other.

Questions to Ponder

1. What opportunities are given your congregation for gathering and community-building on Sunday mornings? Are these adequate? If so, how? If not, how?

2. How does gathering take place on Sunday morning within the life of your congregation? Is gathering intermingled with worship or given a special time and place? Why? Why not?

3. How may a visitor in your worship find community or common ground?

Centering

Part of the gathering ritual for a local Methodist church with which I am familiar, includes something called "centering." What occurs during this brief time sandwiched between the greeting of guests and the organ voluntary is a shift in focus. The pastor invites those gathered to turn their attention from fellowship to worship as he provides them with a simple statement interpreting the theme of worship for the day. His words function as a call to worship entreating worshipers to focus their thoughts on worship. As the organ voluntary begins, the room falls quietly into contemplation. Each time I have visited this congregation, the procedure was the same, and each time I was given the opportunity to center myself for worship. (A discussion of calls to worship comes later in this chapter.)

The dedicated will must bit by bit take up, transform, and unify the dedicated body and mind, welding them into a single instrument devoted to the purposes of God.

—Evelyn Underhill

In other settings, the organ prelude provides the centering time, which is drawn into sharper focus by a call to worship following the music. Still other settings print written theme interpretations, pithy quotations, or contemplative excerpts on spiritual topics in the worship folder for worshipers to read silently and ponder in preparation for worship.

In a day and age when we are bombarded by information, sales pitches, traffic jams, crying children, midnight sirens, blaring TVs and radios, roaring planes overhead, and ringing phones, a moment or two—perhaps even five or six—of centering time provides a welcomed interruption to the life noise that constantly besieges us. Worship is serious enough to contemplate. How wonderful it is to be given a chance to focus on worship—to quiet oneself after dashing from the parking lot, to change gears after teaching a Sunday school lesson, or to distance oneself from the ever-pressing cares of the world—before attempting to worship the Holy One in spirit and in truth. *Whew, I need that.* What about you?

Questions to Ponder

1. What opportunities for centering are provided for worshipers in your setting?

2. How might an opportunity for centering affect for your church's worship?

Silence

The LORD is in the holy temple; let all the earth keep silence! (paraphrase of Hab 2:20). We seem to want to fill every living moment outside worship with sound—TVs, radios, stereos, mindless chatter, cars and computers that talk back to us, loud bistro-styled restaurants, whirring fans and air conditioners, beeping watch alarms and pagers, even conversations with ourselves when we are alone. The cacophony can be deafening.

Our propensity for constant sound carries over into our worship. We want walking music, processional music, praying music, ushering music, interlude music, mood music. We want words and music to fill every moment. When unplanned and pregnant pauses interrupt the action, we fill the awkward spaces with our squirming, our fidgeting, and our murmuring and whispering. Why is our culture so intent upon filling every moment with sound?

Habakkuk reminds us that God hears and sees our noisy living. *But God is present in the world; let all the earth keep silence before God's presence.* Certainly, Hababbuk's message to the captive Hebrew nation was concerned

[God told Elijah,] "Go out and stand on the mountain before the LORD, for the LORD is about to pass by." Now there was a great wind, so strong that it was splitting mountains and breaking rocks in pieces before the LORD, but the LORD was not in the wind; and after the wind an earthquake, but the LORD was not in the earthquake; and after the earthquake a fire, but the LORD was not in the fire; and after the fire a sound of sheer silence. When Elijah heard it, he wrapped his face in his mantle and went out and stood at the entrance of the cave. Then there came a voice to him that said, "What are you doing here, Elijah?"

—1 KINGS 19:11-13

with more than mere noise. The prophet reminds his ancient audience, and his modern one as well, that the Holy One is present in the world. The Holy One witnesses the din of noisy lives filled with acts of violence, oppression, exploitation, idolatry, and all manner of wrongdoing. The Holy Other observes our noisy minds cluttered with questions, worries, untamed thoughts, and mental lists of things we must do. Likewise, the Holy One attends the clatter of our noisy hearts, crowding out contemplation, reverence, and communion with God.

Silence is a necessary component of worship. We can never disengage ourselves from the pandemonium of life without a little silence. Without silence, how may we ever gain perspective and discern the meaning of life?

The story found in 2 Chronicles 5:11-14 shares a glimpse of the festivities and worship surrounding the consecration of Solomon's temple. Pastor Samuel F. Williams, Jr., shared with his Richmond, Virginia, congregation that sometimes silence is the only possible meaningful response:

> On the day the temple of Solomon was dedicated, 120 trumpeters, along with assorted harpists and singers, players of lyres and cymbals, "made themselves heard in unison in praise and thanksgiving to the LORD." They raised their song, writes the Chronicler, "in praise to the LORD." And when they had finished, no one said a word.
>
> There was not a single "Amen"; there was no applause. In fact, there was only one, silent response.[5]

Dr. Wayne E. Oates, Professor of Psychiatry, writes, "There is a silent self in all of us—yearning to be nurtured."[6] Oates explains that "Nurturing silence, . . . is the growth of the power of discernment as to what will be the focus of your attention, care, and commitment."[7] In worship, our ultimate focus is upon the Holy One. The final, culminating act of our adoration is the offering of ourselves to God. These actions require concentration and focused thought, determination and discipline. Providing moments of silence before the worship service and periodically within worship gives worshipers opportunities for proper focus upon God and self. Worship, when you think seriously about it, demands silence.

Pay attention to silence. It has a voice of its own.

—K. BRADFORD BROWN

Questions to Ponder

1. What opportunities for silence are provided for worshipers in your setting? How much time is given to this component of worship?

2. Within your study group, experiment with two-minute segments of silence. Have one member clock the time and make observations as the group concentrates upon meditation or private prayer. Observe how long it takes for coughing, fidgeting, and shuffling to cease. Observe how long it takes the group to become comfortable. Ask all members to discuss how they felt during the timed segment and how each used his/her time.

3. What does a worship leader do about a small child (or children) who doesn't quite understand the importance of periods of silence in worship and whose noise ruins the experience for all? How is worship formative for children and adults alike?

Call to Worship

In the words of seminary professor G. Temp Sparkman, author of *Writing Your Own Worship Materials*, the "call to worship is literally an invitation to participate in worship. Along with the prelude or opening voluntary, it has a tone-setting function."[8] In this practical guide, Sparkman illustrates many types of calls to worship and provides worship leaders with this list:

- A call establishing a motif or theme
- A call away from the world to worship
- A call for celebration
- A call from nature
- A special happening or calendar event
- An expression of how the Holy One greets us in worship
- A call from the news or a current event
- A call defining worship
- A call quoting or paraphrasing Scripture

A call to worship may be spoken or sung. It may be composed by people within your own congregation or borrowed from the great hymnic literature of the church. A call may be prose or poetry and may take the form of a solo, a choral anthem, or a responsive reading between leader and congregation. Calls to worship come in many forms. But whatever the form, a call to worship is a brief and succinct invitation to worship set in the tone and language in keeping with a particular service of worship. The call to worship is an important component of worship because it helps the congregation focus upon what is about to happen.

Sample Call to Worship
A scriptural call to worship to be read antiphonally by leader and people:

Leader: O God of Morning and night, Earth, sky and sea, Creature, bird and humankind,

People: You called our world into being. You call us even now.

Leader: O God of mercy and hope, who called to Hagar and Ishmael in their time of trouble,

People: You call us now, Deep unto deep, Spirit touching spirit, stirring our souls.

Leader: O God of burning bush and angelic flame, who called Moses for freedom's purpose,

People: You call us now to be a new people of inclusion, reconciliation, and peace.

Leader: O God of Israelite slave and covenant peoples,

People: You call us now from the masters and gods that enslave us to new relationship with you.

Leader: O God, the First, who has called generations from the beginning,

People: You call us now. Like Deborah, like Gideon, like Samuel, like Isaiah, you call us according to your purpose.

Leader: O Creator and Living God, who formed and made us, redeemed us, and called us by name,

People: You call us now to become your children.

Leader: O Living Stone, who called us a chosen race, a royal priesthood, a holy nation, your own people,

People: You call us now, from darkness into light, to proclaim your mighty acts to friend, neighbor, and stranger.

Leader: O God of Spirit, who makes all things new, and who called us by new names.

People: You call us now to walk in newness of life, to serve in newness of spirit. Like new bottles and new garments, you re-create us as a people of new spirits and new hearts, ready to sing new songs.

Leader: O Great God of Creation, who makes all things new,

All: You call us even now. Mold and make us—this hour—into your new creation.

Questions to Ponder

1. Is a call to worship routinely used in your church's worship? Considering the types of calls to worship suggested by Sparkman, what type or types of calls to worship are used in your setting?

2. What different forms (i.e., spoken, sung, danced, written, etc.) do the calls to worship take in your church's worship?

Doxology or Praise

A doxology is a liturgical expression of praise. Dialectically, it is both an element and a component of Christian worship. In the comprehensive sense, the whole of worship is doxology, as is belief and the application of faith to life situations. Geoffrey Wainwright makes this clear in his systematic theology of worship, *Doxology: The Praise of God in Worship, Doctrine and Life.*[9] The way we spend our time and live out our lives on a day-to-day basis is, indeed, *our truest worship*. More specifically, doxology also encompasses acts of praise in worship. But first, some background may be in order.

Many, perhaps all, Christian hymnals include one to several settings of Thomas Ken's Trinitarian doxology often set to variations of Louis Bourgeois's Genevan Psalter arrangement. In recent years, there has been resurgence among hymnists in setting Ken's doxological phrases to various hymn tunes. This innovation may seem creative to us, but in reality, the practice is not new. Historians tell us the practice of appending Trinitarian doxologies to the ends of existing hymns was common among Reformers of the nineteenth century. But even before that, doxological use in psalmody and hymnody traces easily to the early church and pre-Reformation traditions.[10]

In addition to setting the familiar lines of Ken's doxology to new tunes, new versions of this well-known doxology have been penned in recent years. Framed here in the non-gendered words of Neil Weatherhogg, 1988, this Trinitarian doxology remains a recognizable favorite among Protestant peoples:

> Praise God, from whom all blessings flow;
> Praise Christ, all people here below;
> Praise Holy Spirit evermore;
> Praise Triune God, whom we adore.
> Amen.[11]

According to hymnologists Harry Eskew and Hugh T. McElrath, Ken's famous "doxology has undoubtedly been sung more than any other four lines in the English language."[12]

But the term *doxology* means so much more than Ken's familiar Trinitarian formula or the church's respective "Greater" and "Lesser" Doxologies, *Gloria in excelsis* and *Gloria Patri*. While all liturgical action within worship may be deemed doxological, we will momentarily focus upon specific acts of praise within Christian worship.

As stated in an earlier chapter, praise is an *element* of worship. Scriptural models describe incidences of praise within the worship experiences of biblical personalities. Elementally, doxology may assume varied executions: spoken, sung, communicated through interpretive movement, or silently voiced by contrite hearts. Likewise, praise may occupy various positions: prostration, seated, kneeling, dancing, standing, with raised hands, even lying on one's back facing the starry heavens. More specifically, the doxological element may find shape in various worship components: the music of hymns, anthems, and chants; readings of all kinds; calls to worship; recitation of creeds and affirmations of faith, and so on.

In the greater sense, doxology or praise is an element that encompasses all that we are and all that we do—both individually and collectively, in worship and through the liturgy of life. Doxology, in the lesser sense, is a component of worship when it functions as one of the many building blocks comprising Christian worship services.

Question to Ponder

When considering the rhythm of worship, praise is often a peak experience. Discuss the ways your congregation expresses praise in worship.

Music

Music is a medium. In worship, this medium takes two forms: music *with* words and *without*.

Music with Words. Music with words may be expressed in three main ways: congregationally, chorally, and vocally. Congregationally, music finds shape in hymns, gospel songs, choruses, and chants. Music compositions take form chorally through anthems, cantatas, oratorios, introits, and responses, and vocally through solo or ensemble literature. In any of these forms, church music with words is music that bears the biblical message. God's salvation story proclaimed in worship through sermons, testimonies, exhortations, prayers, confessions, pardons, calls to worship, amens, litanies, Scripture, benedictions, and other worship components may not only be spoken, but also sung.

The anthropological point that is of significance for theology is that singing clearly demonstrates worship—and therefore the divine kingdom and human salvation—to be an affair of the whole person, mind, heart, voice, body.

—GEOFFREY WAINWRIGHT

When scheduling music with lyrics within a worship service, consider first the message of the text because the textual message is the best indicator of function. Next consider the tune. Are the words and music of this piece well married? Does the music enhance or detract from the message? Since music serves an important tone-setting function, ask yourself if this particular piece matches the tone of the service you are planning. Once these three aspects—text, tune, and tone—have been thoughtfully considered, determine the best placement of the piece.

Placement and treatment of a musical selection can either maximize or diminish its effectiveness. A few specific examples may be helpful. If the choral anthem is a rousing composition with a message of general praise, it might be used most effectively near the beginning of the service with other components of praise. But if the anthem is a prayer, placing it before or after confession and pardon or pastoral prayer may increase its effectiveness. If the anthem is a blessing or benediction, schedule it as such, allowing it to function as the composer intended. Pastor and hymn writer Tom Jackson views the anthem as an extension of the sermon and frequently places it following the sermon when considering it this way.

Take care to avoid *routine* placement of any musical selection. To routinely place a choral anthem before the sermon makes no sense if the message and function of the anthem is seriously considered. To sing a benediction and then discount its effect by speaking a second one makes no sense if the function of the musical selection is taken seriously. To read Scripture when Scripture may also be sung makes no sense, if the singing of Scripture is considered a valid mode of communication within worship. Instead of routine placement or treatment, allow the text, tune,

Music proclaims the Word by supporting the text.

—Frank C. Senn

and tone of the music to dictate its position and use within worship. Thoughtful placement of musical components within worship is a necessary step to using music effectively in worship.

Music without Words. Not all church music combines score with text. Music without words, another important component of worship, takes shape through keyboard and instrumental genres: organ, piano, orchestral instruments, rhythm and electronic instruments, recorded orchestral accompaniments, and special effect instruments. Apart from its accompaniment function supporting singer and text, music without words serves a primarily meditative function.

This meditative or tone-setting function must be carefully considered when choosing music without words. A loud and rousing organ prelude to worship would not set the proper tone for a service planned around a contemplative theme. Nor would a somber or dark voluntary work within an upbeat service of praise and thanksgiving. Once the tone of the worship event has been determined, choose musical selections that match and compliment this tone. This is a good argument for including the musicians in long-range worship planning efforts.

Whether through the musical-verbal combination of music with words or meditatively through instrumental genres of music, music in worship remains an essential and effective building block. Like speech, like silence, like symbol, music is a medium through which worship may be expressed.

Questions to Ponder

1. List and discuss the many ways music *with words* is used in worship in your church.

2. List and discuss the many ways music *without words* is used in worship in your church.

In their superb book, Performing Literature, *Beverly Whitaker Long and Mary Frances Hopkins make the point that written texts are "arrested performances," Speaking those texts aloud, therefore, is not so much something we do to them as it is something they require of us.*

—Charles L. Bartow

Readings

Scripture readings, responsive readings, dramatic readings, and liturgical readings such as calls to worship, confessions, prayers, and affirmations of faith in written form fall into this category. Chief among them is the public reading of Scripture.

A well-read Scripture passage can come alive for those who listen. Conversely, nothing can kill a Scripture reading faster than a poor reader—unskilled, ill-prepared, or expressionless—limping or racing through a passage. Equally detrimental to the public reading of Scripture is an animated or overly dramatic reader. But Scriptures read correctly and beautifully by skilled voices grip the attention of the hearers. Through such a presentation, not only is the Scripture message remembered, but it is also honored and given its rightful place of respect. In Geoffrey Wainwright's words, "The continued reading of the scriptures in church keeps the vocabulary, grammar and syntax of the biblical revelation before the people."[13] Effectively read, the story draws us in.

Just as a choir or soloist must practice before presenting a musical offering, so must a reader prepare. A well-rehearsed reader will have studied the passage for meaning and nuance and read the passage aloud many times before any public reading. Names and words difficult to pronounce will have

We may take the task of reading the Scriptures and attending to the reading of Scriptures in worship lightly, failing to discern what God is up to with us in that effort. A faithful, that is, a full-of-faith rendering of the Scriptural word in terms of both denotation and connotation demands more of us than a casual glance through the text before we skip up to lectern or pulpit. It demands prayerful, cerebral, imaginative preparation.

—Charles L. Bartow

been tackled and conquered prior to any public pronouncement. The meaning of the passage will have been determined early in the process so that the reader may select and practice the proper tone for the presentation. A good reader will be cognizant of occasional eye contact with the congregation, ample voice projection, and confident composure. All these add to the effectiveness of any public presentation, spoken or otherwise.

Consider enlisting and developing a group of dramatic readers within your congregation. Certain talented people within your church body acquainted with the dynamics of public speaking, singing, or drama may come to mind. These people could be instrumental in selecting and training others to lead in worship by reading Scripture or leading antiphonal congregational readings. The group might meet monthly or new readers might be coached individually by experienced readers.

If the group meets monthly, consider a studio format. Selected readers would come to the meeting prepared to give public readings. Following each reading, the group would constructively critique the presentation, considering inflections, volume, pauses, speed, and pacing. The ensuing discussion should open the way for learning about effective public reading. Insightful suggestions regarding the reading of a particular Scripture may also surface during discussion. Of course, not every reader will be willing to subject himself or herself to this type of critique, but certain readers will rise to the challenge. Be certain to encourage and reward these pioneers for their contribution to the learning experience. Whether you critique or not, all readers involved in the group should

Sadly, when [the Bible is] read in public, the minimum attention is paid to whether the verses for public hearing come from a prison cell or a charismatic procession, and dull monotone is too often the preferred register for "reading the Bible." The imagination and sensitivity we would show a child when reading her a poem, an adventure story, or a letter from her grandmother, we fail to offer a congregation when opening the lively oracles of God.

—JOHN L. BELL

Far from being an exercise in self-indulgence, or even self-expression, speaking words with color is an exercise in self-immersion. What is required of us is that we immerse ourselves in the explicit logical content and implicit emotional content of whatever is being read.

—CHARLES L. BARTOW

periodically read aloud before the studio group in preparation for reading aloud before the congregation, a much larger group. Only select readers, chosen in advance, should be subjected to group critique.

Consider enlisting and developing a group of liturgists from among those in your congregation gifted as writers and poets. Organize an ongoing Bible study group for these people. During the first hour of your group meeting, lead the group in a thorough study of a select Scripture passage. Following the study time, encourage group members to compose new liturgy, using the Scripture passage studied as a base. Exercises might include paraphrasing Scripture or composing calls to worship, invocations, offertory prayers and sentences, litanies, and responsive readings for inclusion in the worship service. Provide some instruction or guidance for writing liturgy. Practice composing liturgy as a group. Then allow group members to choose how they will complete their assignment most comfortably, creatively, and productively—individually, in groups, as a homework assignment, or some other arrangement of their own choosing. Give each composer an opportunity to share his/her completed work or work in progress with the group at the next meeting.

When selecting readers—and those who write liturgy—for corporate worship, first consider carefully giftedness. Next develop talent, but always expect preparation. Just as an actor rehearses lines and as a musician practices a score, so must a reader prepare to read for the most effective public reading of Scripture or liturgy. In the process, Scripture is honored.

Questions to Ponder

1. Read aloud Psalm 51 and Psalm 66. How are these psalms different? How do these differences affect the ways each should be read aloud?

2. Consider the many gifts of your congregation's members. Who among you is a gifted reader or public speaker? Who among you is a gifted writer or poet?

3. In your setting, how might gifted people be enlisted or volunteer for worship leadership?

4. What opportunities for ongoing worship leadership training exist in your church?

There are generally three kinds of prayers used in public worship: (1) fixed or liturgical prayers in which all of the prayers are read in public worship; (2) spontaneous or extemporaneous prayers, which are prayed without planning; and (3) prayers given extemporaneously after preparation. In this third method of praying there is both discipline and freedom, both planning and spontaneity. Many of the Free Churches believe this is the best plan for vital worship.

—Franklin M. Segler

Prayers

Within worship, many different types of prayers may occur, each with a different purpose. In this section a variety of worship prayers will be examined and illustrated. The list is not exhaustive. Among the prayers included are invocation, silent prayer, litany, bidding prayer, offertory prayer, and benediction.

Invocation. Simply put, an invocation is an acknowledgment of God's presence. Certainly, the Infinite God is already present whether we issue an invitation or not, but through the invocation, a congregation explicitly recognizes God's abiding presence in their midst. Through this opening prayer of praise and adoration, a congregation calls upon God to help them worship in spirit and in truth. The purpose of the invocation, then, is to lead the congregation to become conscious of God's presence among them and to help them open their hearts to receive God's blessings in worship.[14]

Usually a short and succinct prayer, an invocation's form or language will depend upon the theme or tone of the ensuing worship service. To plan and coordinate the invocation with other components of the worship service adds vitality to the total worship experience.

Sample Invocation

A thematic invocation based upon Scripture:
O Creator God, Author and Finisher of all creation, Alpha and Omega, create in us this hour new hearts, new minds, new souls afire—transformed, renewed, re-created—so when we leave this place we may serve in newness of spirit and walk in newness of life with new songs on our lips, as new and different people. Amen.

Confession. Confession is at once an element of worship and a viable component. Sometimes confession may find expression in readings, hymns, or, more obviously, in prayers of varying types. Litanies, bidding prayers, pastoral prayers or collects, or the silent strains of closeted hearts may be confessional in nature. I include this discussion of confession as a component within the subsection of prayers because whatever form confession takes—litany, hymn, responsive reading—confession remains, simply and unequivocally, a prayer.

A number of things happen in confession. In confession, humanity recognizes its sinful state and unburdens its soul before the Maker. To this release, petition for forgiveness and cleansing is understood, if not audibly voiced. Such entreaty cannot be understood as anything but prayer. The Model Prayer as a model for worship holds that confession, forgiveness, and pardon are viable and important aspects of every prayer and every act of worship. In confession, worshipers open themselves up to God. In this honesty, worshipers may confess not only that which separates them from viable relationships with God and others, but worshipers may also confess their trust, their joy, and their hope in God. Confession, in this larger sense, involves laying our whole selves on God's altar, asking God's forgiveness for our shortcomings, praying God's transforming help for change, and accepting God's blessing for what we do well.

Four examples of prayers of confession are provided, each in a different format. The first illustration is a confession composed by a group of Swedish women. The poem confesses a lack of faith and calls for God's restoring help. The second confession is a Scripture-based litany adapted from a portion of the Liturgy of Confession of the Moravian Church; the third is a simple prayer following the theme "New! You Are a New Creation"; the fourth example is a hymn of confession penned by poet and liturgist Thomas H. Troeger. The latter three prayers could be used together *in one grouping in the order provided* or used singly in separate services of worship.

Example 1
God,
I confess before you,
    that I have had no faith in my own possibilities.
That in thought, word and deed I have shown contempt for myself and for
    my ability.
I have not loved myself as much as others,

neither my body nor my looks,
nor my talent nor my own way of being.
I have let others direct my life.
I have let myself be scorned and mistreated.
I have trusted the judgment of others more than my own,
and allowed people to be indifferent and malicious to me without objecting.

I confess
that I have not developed to the extent of all my capacities,
that I have been too lazy to fight for a just cause,
that I have wounded myself in order to avoid controversies.

I confess
that I have not dared to show how brave I am,
have not dared to be as brave as I really can be.

God, our Father and Creator,
Jesus, our Brother and Redeemer,
Spirit, our Mother and Comforter,
forgive my self-contempt,
raise me up,
give me faith in myself and love of myself.[15]

Example 2
Litany of Confession
A litany based upon Scripture to be read responsively by leader and people[16]

Leader: Thou high and lofty One, Who inhabits eternity, Whose Name is holy, Who dwells in the high and holy place, but with those also who are of contrite and humble spirits, give us grace to bring Thee the sacrifice of a broken and contrite heart, which Thou, O God, does not despise.

People: Hear us, gracious Lord and God.

Leader: Lord God, merciful and gracious, long suffering, and abundant in goodness and truth, keeping mercy for thousands, forgiving iniquity and transgression and sin, and Who will by no means forgive the unrepentant;

incline Thine ear and hear; for we do not offer our supplications before Thee relaying on our own goodness, but on Thy great compassion.

People: Hear us, gracious Lord and God.

Leader: Create in us a clean heart, O God; and renew a right spirit within us. Restore unto us the joy of Thy salvation; and uphold us with Thy free spirit. Have mercy upon us, according to Thy loving-kindness; according to the multitude of Thy tender mercies, blot out our transgressions, through Jesus Christ, our Savior.

People: Lord, have mercy upon us. Amen.

Example 3
Prayer of Confession
To be read aloud by the congregation in unison:

Creator God and Divine Redeemer, we come again to your throne, cloaked in the sin of our humanity, yet exposed, naked and poor, before the light of your great knowledge and truth. You approach us again and again through friend, family, and creation, but we fail to acknowledge you. You have sent your Word to guide us, but repeatedly we fail to follow. You speak to our hearts with the stirrings of your Spirit, but we fail to listen. We are tired and worn, weighed down by worldly cares, harsh words, erred judgments, lost opportunities, botched relationships, and empty worship. Renew our spirits and lift us to new heights. Take hold of us, Lord, and mold us into new vessels filled with your Spirit. Clothe us in the beauty of your righteousness and set our feet on right paths. Recreate in us humble and obedient spirits, Lord. In the name of the Creator, the Son, and the Spirit ever among us. Amen.

Example 4
Hymn of Confession

As a chalice cast of gold, Burnished, bright and brimmed with wine,
Make me, Lord, as fit to hold Grace and truth and love divine.
Let my praise and worship start
With the cleansing of my heart.

Save me from the soothing sin Of the empty cultic deed
And the pious, babbling din Of the claimed but unlived creed.
Let my actions, Lord, express
What my tongue and lips profess.

When I bend upon my knees, Clasp my hands or bow my head,
Let my spoken, public pleases Be directly, simply said,
Free of tangled words that mask
What my soul would plainly ask.

When I dance or chant your praise, When I sing a psalm or hymn,
When I preach your loving ways, Let my heart add its Amen.
Let each cherished, outward rite
Thus reflect your inward light.[17]

Silent Prayer. Time allowed for silent prayer can become a cherished opportunity within the worship service. Sometimes coupled with the congregational prayer of confession or the pastoral prayer, these precious moments of silence can be used by worshipers to commune silently with God specific and personal concerns or to sit quietly and listen for God's still, small voice.

Frequently, our discomfort with silence causes worship leaders to cut this time short, often too short for a worshiper to collect his or her thoughts, much less to begin to pray. Many times I have been encouraged to pray silently by a worship leader, and just as I began to formulate my thoughts and began to pray, the worship leader broke the silence. This scenario, experienced time and time again, suggests that worship leaders may be more anxious about silence than the worshipers themselves.

Fifteen to thirty seconds of silence is not long enough. The first fifteen to thirty seconds is nothing more than preparation time before the praying begins. It takes this long for most of us to relax, center, and focus. With coughs silenced, squirming ceased, and tensions relaxed, real silence ensues, and within its soft and enveloping arms we, like Elijah, may find God.

I recommend two minutes. At first, this may seem like an eternity. If you are leading worship, time it. Your tendency will be to break in sooner, filling the space with words and movement. But two minutes will give worshipers time to relax, prepare, and meditate. Two minutes will allow people to approach the throne of grace with personal and heartfelt concerns and

Never mind that some worshipers are not yet disciplined enough to make use of silence. Those who can should be given the gift, and the others, in time, can learn.

—Paul D. Duke

petitions. Two minutes will allow worshipers to offer prayer and praise using their own words, emotions, and spirits.

Provide silence—quiet, simple, godly silence. Soft organ music in the background is not desired as this will serve as a distraction to many and is easily manipulative. Provide silence in which people can be still and commune privately with God. God, through psalmist's pen, admonishes us: *Be still, and know that I am God!* (Ps 46:10a).

Litany. A litany is a responsive prayer. In response to brief petitions made by the minister or worship leader, the congregation responds with frequent and fixed responses.[18] A litany may be compared to a gospel song: the petitions voiced by the worship leader compare to the stanzas, and the repeated responses by the congregation function as the refrain.

Litanies, like prayers, may serve many purposes: confession, petition, praise, dedication, intercession, commitment, benediction, and so on. The following litany, based upon Psalm 51, is a prayer of confession. The poetic structure of psalms lends itself easily to antiphonal readings and litanies such as this. Hal H. Hopson arranged this responsorial psalm for congregational use. While the composer intended for the responsorial psalm to be sung by cantor and congregation, it may also be effectively spoken. If spoken, omit the opening refrain (shown in italics) and allow the worship leader to begin the reading.

Psalm 51
A responsorial psalm of confession in litany form that can be spoken or sung:

Create in me a clean heart, O God.
Have mercy on me, O God, in your loving-kindness; in your compassion blot out my offenses.
Wash me through and through from my wickedness, and cleanse me from my faults.
Create in me a clean heart, O God.

For I know my sinful ways, they are ever before me.
Against you, you alone have I sinned and done what is wrong in your sight.
> *Create in me a clean heart, O God.*

Purify me, I shall be clean, like waters of spring, I shall be whiter than snow.
Create in me a clean heart, O God, and renew a right spirit within me.
> *Create in me a clean heart, O God.*

Do not banish me from your presence, and take not your Holy Spirit from me.
> *Create in me a clean heart, O God.*[19]

A second responsorial psalm composed by Hal H. Hopson paraphrases Psalm 104 into a litany of praise. Again, if the litany is spoken rather than sung, skip the opening refrain (shown in italics) and allow the worship leader to begin with the verses.

Psalm 104

A Litany of Praise:

> *O Lord, send down your Spirit, and make us new again.*

Lord, how great you are! How beautiful the world you made.
The moon and stars on high, the flowers and the hills,
O God, you made them all, They still are in your hand.

> *O Lord, send down your Spirit, and make us new again.*

Lord, you formed the seas—the waters wide from land to land.
All creatures in the seas, All creatures on the earth,
O God, you made them all, They still are in your hand.

> *O Lord, send down your Spirit, and make us new again.*

Lord, we bless your name, your glory shout forevermore.
You free us by your hand, You guide us by your love,
I'll sing my whole life long, And you will be my song.

> *O Lord, send down your Spirit, and make us new again.*[20]

Bidding Prayer. Professor James F. White offers an excellent explanation of the bidding prayer in his book *New Forms of Worship*. White states that a bidding prayer is "where the minister asks the congregation to pray for a series of concerns, leaving moments of silence after each bid so the people can formulate their own prayers on the same topic. Sometimes the minister sums up these silent prayers after each silence with a collect and then bids us pray for the next concern."[21]

Theoretically, congregational responses to a leader's bidding prayer might also be voiced aloud. For instance, in the context of a midweek prayer service, members of the congregation might be encouraged to offer aloud brief sentence prayers in response to the leader's biddings. For greatest effectiveness, however, this latter version of the bidding prayer may require worship leaders to teach people how to pray aloud.

A few years ago, M. Mahan Siler Jr., led the congregation he served in prayer using the phrases of the Model Prayer. Phrase by phrase, Siler guided the congregation through the Model Prayer. His brief biddings included, first, a phrase from the Prayer, followed by an interpretive statement or question to inspire private meditation and silent prayer. Following each bidding, adequate periods of silence gave worshipers time to offer individually composed prayers before Siler moved on to the next phrase. Allowing the Model Prayer to guide in this way, the congregation filled in the blanks silently between the pastor's biddings. Lasting less than five minutes, this bidding prayer served as the main prayer of the service. This simple formula uniquely and effectively blended the Model Prayer, a pastoral prayer, and the silent prayers of the people into one.

Offertory Prayer. An offertory prayer is a simple prayer of dedication offered either before or after the collection of tithes and offerings. Any number of offerings may be dedicated through this brief prayer: time, talent, personality, service, will, spiritual gifts, money, and other resources. In a sense, this prayer summarizes a congregation's attitude regarding offering. Three sample offertory prayers follow that could fit any service along any theme.

Example 1

Great Wisdom and Faithful Parent, we acknowledge your goodness and generosity to us your children. Help us to become better stewards of our resources, our talents, and ourselves. Use us in your service. Accept now and use these gifts we bring. In the name of God the Creator, Jesus the Model, and the Holy Spirit the Comforter. Amen.

Example 2

Giver of Life, we acknowledge that all good gifts come from you. Accept our humble gifts and help us accept the challenge of faithful service, presenting ourselves as offerings, and thereby fulfilling our individual callings to be your ministers. Amen.

Example 3
Majestic God, we know that only through devotion is any great thing done. Our offering of money is but one expression of our commitment to you. We lay this offering before you both out of the obligation of stewardship and from the joy of being your children. Accept what we bring, in the name of the Model Steward, Jesus Christ, our Advocate. Amen.

Benediction. When my husband Mack and I were married, our friend Paul D. Duke concluded the ceremony with a benediction. Clasping each of us by the hand and looking deep into our faces, Paul offered us this blessing: *Now hear this good word: The L*ORD *bless you and keep you; the* LORD *make his face to shine upon you, and be gracious to you; the* LORD *lift up his countenance upon you, and give you peace* (Num 6:24-26). The Aaronic blessing, given from God to Moses to Aaron and his sons, and subsequently to the people of Israel, is perhaps my favorite of all priestly benedictions. It is one of many found within the Scriptures.

May God bless you and keep you;

May God's own face shine upon you and be gracious to you;

May God's own countenance be lifted upon you, and give you peace.

—NUMBERS 6:24-26; NON-GENDERED VERSION BY PAUL D. DUKE

Now unto the One who is able to keep you from falling, and to present you faultless before the presence of Glory with exceeding joy, To the only wise God our Saviour, be glory and majesty, dominion and power, both now and ever. Amen.

—JUDE 1:24-25; VERSION WITH NON-GENDERED LANGUAGE

Another favorite comes from my childhood. If I close my eyes and listen intently, I can still see my pastor father's outstretched hand and hear his pronouncement: *Now unto him that is able to keep you from falling, and to present you faultless before the presence of his glory with exceeding joy, To the only wise God our Saviour, be glory and majesty, dominion and power, both now and ever. Amen* (Jude 1:24-25, KJV).

Many benedictions are found within Scripture. Many of these priestly blessings close the writings of the Apostle Paul. Consider these scriptural benedictions: Deuteronomy 31:8, 2 Corinthians 13:13, Hebrews 13:20-21, 1 Peter 5:10-11, and Revelation 22:21.

Having read each of these scriptural benedictions, one should find it apparent that a benediction is a *blessing directed to people.* Sometimes benedictions may also include a charge, sometimes stated, other times implied. Frequently the charge is connected in some way to what has taken place in worship. The charge, like the blessing, is also directed to the people. One Baptist church frequently refers to the benediction as "The Blessing," whereas another typically names the benediction "Charge." The person who offers the benediction acts as priest extending God's blessing or charge to the recipient. With this functional definition closely in mind, it is easy to see that a benediction is a different sort of prayer. Unlike most prayers, which are directed *to God,* a benediction is directed *from God* to people.

In many churches, ministers conclude the worship hour with a closing prayer. More often than not, however, this closing prayer—offered to God before a congregation of bowed heads and closed eyes—is called a benediction. But if we carefully consider the scriptural examples, a closing prayer is one thing, and a benediction another. How we receive the benediction—with eye contact or with bowed heads and closed eyes—may change its impact.

First, however, let's consider the many acceptable postures for prayer. Most of us close our eyes and bow our heads when we pray, a posture often learned from childhood. Jesus, standing before Lazarus's tomb, *lifted up his eyes* in prayer to God (John 11:41-42, KJV), but in Gethsesame, Jesus *threw himself on the ground and prayed* (Matt 26:39). King Hezekiah *turned his face to the wall and prayed to the* LORD (2 Kgs 20:2). Peter, at Dorcas's deathbed, *knelt down and prayed* (Acts 9:40). David, the psalmist, prayed through song, poetry, and dance. Paul, in his letter to the Thessalonians, admonished this first-century church (and us) to *pray without ceasing.* If we are to take Paul's admonishment seriously, we may assume a constant *attitude* of prayer, which may cause us to momentarily and spontaneously to pray during work, while driving the car, when waiting in the doctor's office, at any time, in any place. Obviously then, there are many postures we may assume in prayer. But our posture in receiving a blessing may affect its effectiveness.

In keeping with its historical use and purpose, I strongly suggest that a benediction—wonderfully good words of blessing from God to God's people—should be offered and received with heads up and eyes open. When we look deep into faces of those we bless in God's name, the good words of comfort, hope, and peace we share will penetrate not only eyes, but hearts and souls as well.

In this stressed and troubled world, people need a word of blessing. This is exactly what the benediction provides—*a good word, a word of blessing*. Good words of blessing may be delivered by word or song, spoken or sung. They may be scriptural, Scripture-based, or newly composed. By whatever delivery or composure, there can be no better way than with full eye contact between priest and recipient. When I give a good word of hope to another I want to look into that person's eyes. St. Jerome (c. 342–420) once wrote: "The face is the mirror of the mind, and eyes without speaking confess the secrets of the heart."[22] When another blesses me with words of encouragement and direction I am touched not only by the warmth and sincerity of their voice, but also by their eyes.

In keeping with our *newness* theme, I offer to you the following benediction, a paraphrase of the benediction offered by the imprisoned Apostle Paul to the church at Ephesus (Eph 3:20-21): *Now to God who is able to do immeasurably more than all we can ask or imagine, according to the power that is at work within us, to God be glory in the church and in Christ Jesus throughout all generations, for ever and ever! Amen.*

Questions to Ponder

1. Using orders of service from recent worship services in your setting, identify and discuss the different types of prayers used in your church's worship.

2. Is a time of confession and pardon routinely included within your church's worship? Why? Why not?

3. Within your study group, experiment with two-minute segments of silence. Have one member clock the time and make observations as the group concentrates upon meditation or private prayer. Observe how long it takes for coughing, fidgeting, and shuffling to cease. Observe how long it takes the group to become comfortable. Ask all members to discuss how they felt during the timed segment and how each used his/her time.

4. As a group exercise, form pairs in your group. Have each couple face each other and offer to each to the other the following blessing: *You are God's beloved (daughter/son) in whom God is well-pleased.* After each has had his or her turn and a few moments to react to the blessing, encourage group members to share with the group how this personal blessing impacted them. How did you feel? How did you respond? Were you surprised at your reaction? Was giving/receiving the blessing a positive experience?

Congregational Assent

In this section, two forms of congregational assent will be discussed, one ancient and one modern: the congregational amen and applause.

Congregational Amen. *And all the assembly said, "Amen" and praised the* LORD (Neh 5:13). This ascription of assent is referenced numerous times within Old Testament writings. While the amen is used as a general form of assent for both individuals and assemblies, the frequent Old Testament reference illustrates the amen as a form of congregational accord in conjunction with praise to God. (See also Deut 27:15-26, 1 Chr 16:36, Neh 8:6, and Ps 106:48.) Years later, the Apostle Paul, in his letter to the church at Corinth, referred to the early church practice of congregational amens in 1 Corinthians 14:16.

Consider the biblical examples of congregational amens. Deuteronomy 27:15-26 records a fragmentary account of an ancient Hebrew liturgical ceremony of blessings and curses. Although these verses present no blessings, but only a series of twelve curses, "Each is followed by the rubric, *And all the people shall answer and say* (v. 15; in the remaining verses it is simply *shall say*), and the word to be uttered by all, *Amen*. . . . The people's response to each of the curses as read, *Amen,* is, as generally known, an adjective used adverbially to express strong assent, 'assuredly, truly.'"[23] Here the Levites, in call and response form, issue a number of directives in the form of calls to covenant to which the people respond alternately, *amen.*

In 1 Chronicles 16, we find King David—thankful that the ark of the covenant is at home at last in Jerusalem—making offerings and appointing ministers to invoke, thank, and praise the Lord on behalf of the people. Within the service of dedication, David offers a psalm of thanksgiving to which all the people answer, *Amen!* The account tells us that their assent was followed by additional acts of praise: *". . . Blessed be the* LORD, *the God of Israel, from everlasting to everlasting." Then all the people said "Amen!" and praised the* LORD (1 Chr 16:36). Through their voiced assent, the Jerusalem congregation made David's psalm their own expression of thanksgiving. Afterward, they continued to participate in worship through other acts of praise.

In Nehemiah 5 we find Governor Nehemiah dealing with an economic problem plaguing the Jewish community. After Nehemiah's exhortation, which offers a solution to the problem, the assembly commits to do as Nehemiah instructs them. Voicing their resolve through a joint amen, this renewed people continue their worship by offering praise to God (Neh 5:13).

Nehemiah 8 chronicles yet another example of the congregational amen. Here the priest Ezra, standing before the people gathered in the city square, reads from the *book of the Law of Moses*. When Ezra opens the book, the people stand and listen attentively. *Then Ezra blessed the* LORD, *the great God, and all the people answered, "Amen, Amen," lifting up their hands. Then they bowed their heads and worshiped the* LORD *with their faces to the ground* (Neh 8:6). There was nothing passive about this Scripture reading. The chronicler pictures a people actively engaged in worship: rising to their feet; listening with opened ears, hearts, and minds; and responding with hearty amens, lifted hands, and bodies bowed low. Participation and respect figuratively jump from this passage.

Finally, a brief look at Psalm 106 reveals Israel at prayer. In Psalm 106, the Israelite community confesses its sins and requests deliverance from its exilic state. The biblical account ends the prayer with a doxology to which the following phrase is appended: *And let all the people say, "Amen"* (Ps 106:48b). Here prayers of confession and petition are offered on behalf of the Israel congregation, and the people prayerfully respond, *Amen.*

In each of these biblical examples, the congregational amen serves both a participatory and responsorial purpose: an answer to a call to covenant, an expression of thanksgiving and prelude to praise, a voiced resolution in response to exhortation, an expression of respect for Scripture, and a joint response to prayer offered on the congregation's behalf.

Used sparingly, the congregational amen is an effective response to action within the worship event. Its very use implies action on the part of the congregation. The congregation who voices a collective amen following the public prayer of a leader communicates that it has prayed corporately and silently as the worship leader has prayed individually and aloud. Defined *so be it* or *so it is* from the Hebrew,[24] the responsive amen voiced by the congregation first calls for active listening and prayerful attention, then heartfelt or mindful assent or intention.

Applause? Among modern congregations, the outbreak of applause occurs with increasing frequency in services of worship. Opinion is divided on whether applause within worship is an appropriate expression. What is most troublesome about applause is its direct link to the entertainment world. We are an entertainment-possessed culture. Applause, a cultural form of spontaneous approval, praise, and acclaim, may subtly place the congregation in the role of audience and worship leaders in the roles of performers. This rearranged configuration relegates the congregation from active participants to passive onlookers who occasionally voice approval with their hands. Worship leaders become performers. If the congregation likes what a leader does, he or she is rewarded with the gift of applause. Quite often the worship leader is heard to exclaim, "Let's all thank the musicians with a round of applause!" Church music in particular suffers from the applause expression that reduces solos and anthems to entertaining show pieces rather than the testimonies and offerings they are intended to be.

To the person who defends congregational applause as a new form of the congregational amen, I must encourage him or her to consider seriously the plausibility of the claim by asking the following questions. When does applause most frequently occur—following a solo or anthem, or following a prayer, Scripture reading, sermon, or call to worship?

My exposure to congregational applause leads me to believe applause is more a form of approval for a job well done, an expression of honor for someone, or a way of expressing likes and dislikes than it is form of congregational participatory assent, at least within the more traditional worship settings. More often than not, applause in worship occurs following musical offerings, worship events led by children or youth, or special speakers.

In all my years of worship participation, I've never heard a congregation respond to a prayer or Scripture reading with applause. If regarded as a modern-day amen, applause could also be an appropriate response to sermon, Scripture, or prayer. But more often than not, applause is reserved for the favored musical performance or performer. This major inconsistency leads me to question the validity and appropriateness of applause in worship, whether contemporary or traditional in form. There may be a couple of exceptions, however.

One exception may be found within traditionally black communities of faith. Repeated worship experiences with a Baptist church in Roanoke, Virginia, helped me reevaluate my thinking about applause in worship. Within this worship setting, vocal and physical demonstrations were the norm: clapping, standing, swaying, jumping, shouting, and raising hands, in addition to such vocal expressions as *uh-huh, Yes sir, All right, Yes—oh yeah, Preach on, What's that?* Vocal and physical expression within this worship tradition is rich, liberated, and free. Within this context, clapping is not merely an expression of gratitude or pleasure reserved for a great soloist, superior choral anthem, children's group, or favored speaker. Instead, applause reverberates as an enthusiastic and participatory expression of encouragement and assent to preacher and sermon, to new converts rising from baptismal pools, and to decisive members walking the aisle during invitation time. In the highly participatory, body-involved style of the black church, clapping is a natural expression of assent, gladness, and thanksgiving.

Nothing that was done during the weeks I worshiped with this expressive congregation—including the applause—seemed remotely linked to entertainment. And, remarkably, as I worshiped with this lovely congregation, I soon joined in the simplicity and fervor of its poetic worship. I found myself wanting more liberal expressions of freedom within my own tradition of worship.

A second exception may be within the developing contemporary tradition of worship, although inconsistencies still exist within this new form. As I worshiped recently with an evangelical Presbyterian congregation who uses exclusively contemporary forms in worship, applause seemed more appropriate in worship within this totally contemporary context. The opening call to worship, a rousing contemporary pop gospel song by a well-trained singer, elicited some rhythmic clapping during the upbeat number and drew hearty applause at its end. Added to the jubilant applause were also whistles and hooting noises from some enthusiastic congregational members. Elsewhere within the service, however, other charismatic responses were noted: raised hands, shouts of hallelujah, applause, hmms of assent during prayers, a few amens, other whistles and hoots, and verbalizations of "um-um," and "preach it, brother" during the sermon. Obviously, a freedom and consistency for vocal expression in many forms exists within this worshiping community. And this is good. In this setting—combined with other physical and vocal expressions—applause seems more appropriate, although the inherent link to entertainment is ever present.

Perhaps if congregations clapped for new Christians rising from the waters of baptism or for those who walk the aisle in acts of decision, clapping elsewhere within worship would seem more congruent, more participatory, possibly more reverent. Perhaps if worshipers encouraged the preacher with periodic clapping during sermons, clapping elsewhere within worship would seem more appropriate. But this is seldom the case. More frequently we reserve our applause to entertainment-oriented events—sports events, musical concerts, theater, and laud for public figures and heroes—not responses to exhortations, prayers, and spiritual commitments. Our inconsistency when it comes to applause, at least within many traditions of free worship, convicts us of our inappropriate use.

While expressions of gratitude to a singer, choir, or speaker are not necessarily bad or wrong, it is essential to remember that people who sing or speak in worship offer their songs and their words to God, not to congregations. Our approval or disapproval is, therefore, inappropriate. What counts is God's response. Our applause in these instances signals our displaced focus from God to performer. Applause in this context cannot be an act of worship. What are our alternatives?

Questions to Ponder

1. Within the context of your church's worship, is an amen sung at the close of every hymn? Why? Why not? How is this practice different from the responsorial assent of the biblical amen?

2. Considering your church's worship practice, suggest times and ways the congregational amen might be effectively used.

3. Worshipers within the black church tradition actively involve themselves in worship through verbal expressions and physical movements. How might all congregations get more involved with the sermon?

4. How might all congregations learn liberation and freedom in worship? Many congregations seem uncomfortable with silence and noise in worship and somewhat uncomfortable with their bodies. How might we educate to effect change?

5. Is applause a frequent, sporadic, or nonexistent occurrence within your church's worship? When does applause most frequently occur? What events seem to trigger the applause response?

Testimonies and Exhortations

Within my Baptist background, testimonies and exhortations in worship are the exception rather than the norm. In my experience, testimonies are most frequently reserved to revival or renewal services. These evangelistic-oriented services are usually longer in length and less formal than a full-orbed service of worship on Sunday morning. The longer length allows for testimonies that, if unrehearsed, can often be quite long.

Exhortations, a frequent observance among Pentecostal and charismatic gatherings, are virtually nonexistent in most free churches, unless you consider the annual stewardship emphases in churches where members—in a type of combination testimony-exhortation style—encourage fellow members to give generously and cheerfully in support of next year's budget. Exhortations, by definition, include encouragement, strong urging, advice, or spiritual admonishments.

Churches might do well to encourage and develop the artful presentation of testimonies and exhortations in worship as another means to involve congregational members in worship leadership. Like other effective public presentations, preparation and rehearsal are critical to testimonies and exhortations alike. To be effective, these presentations need to be brief, succinct, and well executed.

Questions to Ponder

Are testimonies or exhortations used within your church's worship? In what ways are these effective components of Christian worship? In what ways are they ineffective?

Sermon

I really do not consider myself a preacher, but through the years I've listened to many sermons and preached a few times myself. Experience continues to teach me there are many more mediocre preachers and average sermons than great ones. A good sermon is a wonderful thing, but a poor sermon, well, is torture. Because I have not been instructed in the skills of homiletics, I will limit my comments to perspectives one might reasonably acquire as a faithful listener of sermons. To the preachers who will read this text, I hope my suggestions will be viewed as a simple but viable form of feedback from the pew.

A sermon may be identified variously as the homily, exhortation, commentary upon Scripture, a message or meditation, or even preaching. James F. White, in *New Forms of Worship* (1971), writes: "Preaching in worship is shaped by its context as counterpart to the reading of Scripture lessons."[25] Perhaps this is why the best preaching is tied closely to scriptural themes.

Thematic Relation. A well-planned and coordinated worship service will always express some scriptural theme. For effective planning, it is essential for all involved in planning and leading worship to be sensitive to that theme. For this to happen, some planning scheme must be developed by those who plan worship. Various options are available and these have been discussed in other sections of this book. But in the final analysis, someone must be responsible for the coordinating process of worship planning. To have no plan is not acceptable. The best possible plan organizes worship—sermon, music, and all other components—around a focal Scripture passage.

Some worship leaders routinely use the common lectionary as a selection guide when choosing Scripture and planning worship. The common lectionary is an exceptional tool for long-range planning. Some ministers of music rely on pastors to provide Scripture selections and sermon topics in order to coordinate music with the word. But this must be done months in advance. Whatever the strategy, someone must choose the Scripture well in advance of a given Sunday so that all involved in the planning process can be responsible planners and effective leaders. When the sermon, music, and other worship components reflect the message of a central Scripture passage, beautiful things may happen in worship. To the astute worshiper, the absence of this type of planning is as obvious as its usage.

Balance and Length. A sermon is one component among many in worship. To disproportionately emphasize the importance of preaching above all other parts of worship not only minimizes the other parts, but throws the entire experience off balance. Balance is the key.

Of all the sermons I have heard, many have been too long—too long to fit proportionately into the service with the other worship components, too long to fit into its allocated time slot without running over time, too long to hold the congregation's fleeting attention, too long because insufficient preparation caused the preacher to be wordy and repetitious, and too long to remember the main points after leaving the service. Mostly, just too long. "Studies show that the typical senior executive can concentrate on a project for only *six minutes* at a stretch because of distractions."[26] What is more, the Northwestern School of Speech reports that "the attention span of an audience is approximately *nine* seconds. If you don't *do* or *say* something that catches and reaches their attention *every nine seconds,* it's daydream time for the folks out front."[27] These figures say a lot about contemporary audiences. How may these facts help us understand congregations and their receptivity to preaching?

As a listener and one who thoroughly appreciates a good sermon, I can say that fifteen to eighteen minutes is long enough unless the preacher is absolutely splendid and captivating. Fifteen to eighteen minutes allows a preacher to say something substantive, but does not allow the speaker to ramble aimlessly, be overly wordy, or become repetitious. In fact, limiting a sermon to this brief time frame encourages the preacher to prepare. It seems more than reasonable that a preacher would want to be well organized, well prepared, clear, concise, and as polished as his/her skills allow. These attributes of good preaching give listeners an honest chance to pay attention, hear, understand, and remember.

Varied Style, New Forms. When my father was in seminary, the typical sermon formula was *three points and a poem*. Apparently, the homiletic professors in his day found this skeletal frame for sermon-building effective. Perhaps it was. Perhaps it still is. But I dare say nothing works well all the time without variation. As a listener of sermons, I suggest that preachers vary their style and the format of their sermons from time to time. Variety is an excellent tool for adding freshness and vitality, which can capture the attention of even the dullest, sleepiest minds.

Many different types of sermons exist. The various options will not be discussed here. That is topic enough for another book and further study. My advice is simple. If yours is the responsibility of preaching on a regular basis, take advantage of every opportunity available to you for continuing education, study, practice, and the perfecting of your skills so that you may continually increase your effectiveness as a proclaimer of God's holy word.

Outlines and Note-taking. Some preachers publish sermon outlines in the order of worship. This practice helps worshipers more easily grasp the main points of the sermon and remember them long after the delivery is complete. Since I frequently take notes while listening to sermons, having a published outline makes my task even easier. In fact, having a published outline probably encourages note-taking, and note-taking—at least for me—promotes active listening. Publishing an outline is an option some preachers may wish to consider if note-taking, active listening, and retention are desired outcomes. This technique would not work for all people or for all sermons.

Sermon Talk-back. Some preachers invite sermon talk-back from their parishioners. Dialogue about the sermon with the preacher may take different forms: through formal congregational talk-back meetings following worship, through small discussion groups, or through individual and informal conversations with interested listeners. Still other preachers engage interested segments of the congregation in sermon preview sessions where key ideas are shared and discussed in advance of Sunday's delivery. Done in this manner, sermon preview sessions function as another facet of preparation for the preacher. For preachers who wish to engage congregational members in deeper and broader ways beyond the usual one-way monologue of the sermon, these innovations may prove interesting, challenging, and extremely beneficial to spiritual growth. Talk-backs are probably not for everybody, however, and probably should be conducted in a separate space from the sanctuary where intimacy and conversation can be nurtured more effectively.

I leave you with this concluding thought about sermons proposed by James F. White: "The sermon has probably had to change more often than any other part of worship. We still sing eighteenth-century hymns and recite sixteenth-century prayers, but such a time lag in preaching would be unthinkable. Change in preaching may well be a sign of its enduring vitality."[28]

Questions to Ponder

1. What proportion of worship time is given to the sermon in your setting? How does this time allotment balance with the time given to other components of worship?

2. Do the sermons you hear/deliver parallel with the Scripture, music, and other worship components? Why? Why not?

3. By what system is Scripture chosen for the worship services in your church? Who makes the choices? Are all with worship leadership responsibility involved in long- and short-term worship planning? Why? Why not?

4. In your setting, by what means do worshipers provide feedback to the sermon? Consider all avenues: formal and informal, organized and unorganized, public and private, positive and negative.

Kiss of Peace

Within Christian liturgy, "the kiss of peace is the ritual hinge between social ethics and common praise."[29] Geoffrey Wainwright, in his systematic theology, *Doxology*, makes this assertion and goes on to argue that the kiss of peace (or the *pax* or passing of the peace) is most likely based upon Jesus' injunction found in Matthew 5:23-24: *So when you are offering your gift at the altar, if you remember that your brother or sister has something against you, leave your gift there before the altar and go; first be reconciled to your brother or sister, and then come and offer your gift.* The social implication of worship is clear: collective worship cannot take place until members mend their broken relationships. Whole and healthy communities worship, but broken communities divided by conflict cannot worship.

Through the ages, the use and placement of the kiss of peace within worship has varied: before or after communion, before the offering and consecration of gifts, in conjunction with infant baptism, after intercessions as a seal of prayer, and possibly as the opening or customary ending to worship within the early church as suggested in the Pauline epistles.[30] Sometimes it is not used at all.

Frequently among congregations within free-church traditions, contemporary practice of the peace has become an extension of the welcome, a friendly greeting to guests and other worshipers, an opportunity within worship to fellowship with members and make introductions to guests. Usually placed near the beginning of worship, and sometimes at the end, this simple expression through handshake, hug, or words of spiritual blessing emphasizes good will and right relationships, the hallmarks of a healthy community who are about to worship together or who have just worshiped together.

Sometimes worship leaders provide helpful suggestions of what to say during the kiss of peace: *The peace of God be with you* to which the response *And also with you* may be made; or simply *Peace* or *Shalom* signifying a blessing of God's peace. At other times, the peace, left solely to the discretion of the congregation, runs the risk of becoming a rowdy interval of loud talking, backslapping, laughing, and involved conversations with friends as people wander about the sanctuary. Executed in this manner, the kiss of peace appears to be nothing more than a free-for-all, where nearly anything goes. Unfortunately, for some congregations, this is exactly what happens.

But if a deeper understanding of worship is what your congregation desires, the kiss of peace—as any other liturgical act—deserves periodic, if not weekly, interpretation. Explanations need not be lengthy nor pedantic, but may take the form of a simple introductory remark like, *Do this because* . . . or perhaps, *When you do this, say* . . . .

If the kiss of peace is maintained as merely an extension of the greeting to members and visitors gathered for worship, it may, in this form, be a trite gesture lacking the richness of the ancient rite. For instance, when it is used in this way, members of a congregation may be lulled into thinking that visitors have been duly greeted and no more interaction is required between them. As a frequent visitor within the worship services of many churches and denominations the past two years, I can attest that many members awkwardly handle the peace. At best, a handshake between member and guest is exchanged, but more often than not, members fail to introduce themselves by name, fail to speak to guests again following the service, and offer no blessing in God's name. Given in this way, the peace becomes a perfunctory expression of forced friendliness, insincere and clumsy. Such a lazy practice seems to relieve member-hosts of any further hospitality following the worship hour and allows them to leave follow-up to designated greeters and ministerial staff.

However the peace is expressed within a congregation, there needs to be an understanding of what the practice actually means, why a congregation does it, and how to do it well. Otherwise, a congregation left to its own devices may simply shake hands and force a smile before waiting for the next directive from the worship leader.

Given its varied historical practice, the peace may be practiced differently on different occasions, so long as worshipers understand what is expected of them. If used as an extension of the welcome or greeting, a position very early or very late in the service seems valid. If more directly linked to the mandate of Matthew 5:23-24, placement before the offering or directly before or after communion seems better. What is important here is that worship leaders and congregations know what they do and why in worship. Ritual without understanding is empty and ceases to be worship.

Questions to Ponder

How and when does your congregation practice the kiss of peace? What interpretation is given to this ancient rite? How often is interpretation provided?

Offering

The time for offering and commitment is deemed by many—and certainly this author—the climax of worship. Offering symbolizes a people's commitment to God. In a real sense, what a church does with its time of offering and commitment summarizes what a church believes and what has transpired within the worship experience preceding it. For Evelyn Underhill, sacrifice is the sum of worship.[31] Because I view offering and commitment as

Placing the offering after the sermon and the response hymn will no doubt be startling to traditionalists. The explanation is that the offering is also "response" to God's Word, not just a perfunctory act to support the church budget or to show one's loyalty to the "program." We give our money to God in token of giving ourselves in a complete dedication. Contributing to the offering following the sermon is one way of saying "Amen" to God's will, as expressed in [the] Word, read and preached.

—DONALD P. HUSTAD

a combination event and the apex of worship, I recommend the offering and its related parts—the collecting and presenting of tithes and offerings, the invitation to commitment and the dedication of life—to be near the end of the worship service.

Considering the scriptural models from an earlier chapter, you will recall that Isaiah's commitment came late in his worship experience. Because Isaiah encountered and worshiped God, Isaiah was then able make a committed response to God's call. Likewise, Abraham's renewed commitment to the Lord came late in his encounter on Mount Moriah. What happened between Abraham and God that morning changed Abraham forever, and with new understanding, Abraham was able to renew his commitment to the God he worshiped.

By examining the significance of sacrifice through the historical lenses of the great prophets and psalmists, "the spirit of penitence and self-oblation, and the mystery of communion, which are dramatized in the ritual sacrifices still remain . . . the very essence of worship."[32] As we give our offerings we must not forget that much more is involved than mere tithes and monetary offerings. The prophet Micah sums up this thought beautifully in poetic Hebrew verse: *With what shall I come before the Lord, and bow myself before God on high? Shall I come before him with burnt offerings, with calves a year old? Will the Lord be pleased with thousands of rams, with ten thousands of rivers of oil? Shall I give my firstborn for my transgression, the fruit of my body for the sin of my soul? He has told you, O mortal, what is good; and what does the Lord require of you but to do justice, and to love kindness, and to walk humbly with your God?* (Mic 6:6-8)

More than an envelope stuffed with dollar bills goes into the offering plate in worship. The essence of *ourselves* is the real gift the God of love requires. Nothing less is fully acceptable. No personal check or handful of coins can ever be sufficient without life commitment. The life of the giver is the essence of the offering. *Life commitment* is the basis for the generous giving of time, money, personality, spiritual gifts, and other resources.

Consider the emphasis your church gives to offering and commitment. How are the offering and other times of dedication handled by your congregation? Are these times sacred? Consider the contrasts of these two real-life situations.

(1) The setting is Sunday morning within the worship hour of a small-town congregation. The church routinely worships in a semiformal style with reverent and tasteful presentations and historically good music. The

offering—concerned primarily with the collection of tithes and offerings—is routinely scheduled midway through the order of service, following praise and pastoral prayer. A call to give is issued by the minister and an organ or choral music selection is presented during the collection. As the collected gifts are placed upon the offering table at the front of the sanctuary, the congregation dedicates the offering through the singing of a hymn stanza or doxology.

Attitudes as they are among the finance committee members of this particular congregation put an entirely different spin on the worship gesture just described. For years, members of the church's finance committee have whisked the money away from the ushers out the back door of the sanctuary and counted, bagged, and deposited the morning collection during the worship hour. As a result, select members leave worship for responsibilities in the counting room or for trips to the bank. When repeatedly petitioned by their new pastor to alter their routine in order to allow the congregation to present their offerings symbolically to God upon the altar, the best response this practical group could remedy was this:

As the congregation rises to its feet to dedicate its gifts, ushers walk to the front of the sanctuary bearing two empty plates. A clever committee member came up with the idea of turning two extra plates upside down on top of the empty ones—like lids—so no one would know the plates were empty. One insightful member of the committee routinely leaves a penny in one of the plates so no one can accuse the ushers of bringing empty plates to God's altar.

The willfulness of this committee's furtive act may almost seem comical at first glance. After all, we must be practical about counting a congregation's money. People are busy these days and counting receipts during worship saves valuable time, one might argue. It's *just* a symbol, so what does it matter that there's no money in the plates? But frankly, weekly exposure to this blatantly hypocritical act gnaws and rubs against a person's sense of integrity in worship. What must the Holy One think of this empty gesture? What does it reveal about this church's attitude toward worship?

Please consider a contrasting example.

(2) The setting is an urban Baptist church made up primarily of upper middle class parishioners. The church routinely worships in a formal style where every aspect, to the tinniest detail, is thoughtfully planned and professionally presented. A strong and healthy sense of worship prevails among this

reverent and serious congregation. The offering is routinely located late in the service: following praise, following confession and pardon, following Scripture and sermon, following concerns of the church and pastoral prayer. During the collection of gifts, an offertory anthem is presented. Then the choir sits down.

Gradually, with crescendoing strains from organ pipes, the presentation of offerings begins. As the escorted offering plates pass by the aisles to quire, the organ billows and swells in ever-crescendoing and broadening sound, momentum builds, worshipers rise to their feet turning faces and bodies to the centrally-located altar, and lungs and voices sing loud doxologies of praise and glad alleluias. The offering, delivered to the altar by acolyte hands, is ceremonially presented to God. Momentarily, a prayer of dedication stills the house before a final hymn and priestly benediction.

What a stirring culmination to worship. It is difficult, perhaps impossible, not to get caught up in the drama and ceremony of this symbolic presentation.

Two divergent attitudes are expressed by these congregations. Each enactment reflects attitudes concerning worship and commitment. The attitudes reveal what is important and not important to each congregation.

The strongest statement I am likely to make in writing this book is that *worship is the most important thing a church does.* Worship is the work of the church gathered. Worship enables a congregation to function effectively once it is scattered. If worship is our most important task, both individually and corporately, how can we give anything less than our best effort?

Questions to Ponder

1. Where is the giving of the offering placed in your usual order of service? What reasoning determines this placement?

2. Examine your usual mode of gathering and dedicating the offering. What do your actions symbolize? What rich symbolism is lost in your church's current practice?

3. Is your emphasis upon offering adequate? In what ways is the emphasis adequate? In what ways is the emphasis inadequate? What changes might be made?

4. Is anything more than the giving of money emphasized in your current offering practice? How is the emphasis made in your setting?

NOTES

[1] James F. White, "Coming Together in Christ's Name," *The Landscape of Praise: Readings in Liturgical Renewal* (Valley Forge: Trinity Press International, 1996), 152-56.

[2] Ibid., 152.

[3] Ibid., 153.

[4] Please refer to the exposition of Isaiah 6:1-12 in chapter 2, "Scriptural Models for Worship," for a discussion the rhythm and flow of worship. See also chapter 3, "What is Worship? Characteristics and Descriptions," for a discussion of worship's progressive character.

[5] Samuel F. Williams, Jr., "Piece of Mind," *Northminster News* 52/16 (1993): 1.

[6] Wayne E. Oates, *Nurturing Silence in a Noisy Heart* (Garden City: Doubleday, 1979), quote from text on book jacket.

[7] Ibid., 9.

[8] G. Temp Sparkman, *Writing Your Own Worship Materials* (Valley Forge: Judson Press, 1980), 17.

[9] See Geoffrey Wainwright, *Doxology: The Praise of God in Worship, Doctrine and Life* (New York: Oxford UP, 1980).

[10] Harry Eskew and Hugh T. McElrath, *Sing with Understanding* (Nashville: Broadman Press, 1980), 60-61, 73-74.

[11] Neil Weatherhogg, "Praise God, from Whom All Blessings Flow," *The Presbyterian Hymnal: Hymns, Psalms, and Spiritual Songs* (Louisville: Westminster/John Knox Press, 1990), number 591.

[12] Eskew and McElrath, *Sing with Understanding*, 117.

[13] Wainwright, *Doxology*, 19.

[14] Franklin M. Segler, *Christian Worship: Its Theology and Practice* (Nashville: Broadman Press, 1967), 114.

[15] A confession composed by Swedish women, quoted by Elisabeth Moltmann-Wendel in *I Am My Body: A Theology of Embodiment* (New York: Continuum, 1995), 54-55.

[16] This litany is adapted from the liturgy of Moravian Church. See *Hymnal and Liturgies of the Moravian Church* (n.p.: Provincial Synods of the Moravian Church in America, 1969), 10.

[17] Thomas H. Troeger, "As a Chalice Cast of God," *New Hymns for the Lectionary: To Glorify the Maker's Name* (New York: Oxford University Press, 1986), 6-7. The hymn is set to the tune INWARD LIGHT by Carol Doran, who co-authored the text with Thomas H. Troeger.

[18] Segler, *Christian Worship*, 16.

[19] Hal H. Hopson, *10 Psalms* (Carol Stream IL: Hope Publishing Company, 1986), 10.

[20] Ibid., 12-13.

[21] James F. White, *New Forms of Worship* (Nashville: Abingdon, 1971), 212.

[22] St. Jerome (c. 342–420), *Letter 54*, referenced in John Bartlett, *Familiar Quotations*, ed. Emily Morison Beck, 15th ed. (Boston: Little, 1980), 128.

[23] G. Ernest Wright, "Exegesis," *The Interpreter's Bible*, ed. George Arthur Buttrick, vol. 2 (Nashville: Abingdon Press, 1952), 490, 492.

[24] Robert Young, *Analytical Concordance to the Bible* (Grand Rapids: Wm. B. Eerdmans Publishing Company, 1970), 32.

[25] White, *New Forms,* 175.

[26] Ron Hoff, *"I Can See You Naked": A Fearless Guide to Making Great Presentations* (New York: Andrews and McMeel, 1988), 138.

[27] Ibid., 138.

[28] White, *New Forms,* 173.

[29] Wainwright, *Doxology,* 143.

[30] This idea regarding the opening and closing of worship within the early church is expressed and developed by editors Cheslyn Jones, Geoffrey Wainwright, and Edward Yarnold in *The Study of Liturgy* (New York: Oxford UP, 1978), 356-57.

[31] Evelyn Underhill, *Worship* (New York: Crossroad, 1985), 48.

[32] Ibid., 53.

CHAPTER 6

Inclusive Language, Inclusive Worship

Enlarge the site of your tent, and let the curtains of your habitations be stretched out; do not hold back; lengthen your cords and strengthen your stakes.
—Isaiah 54:2

The salvation epoch found in the second section of Isaiah, chapter 54, seeks to console Israel, exiled and discouraged. In the first strophe (Isa 54: 1-3) of the poem, the ancient poet encourages Israel not to hold back: *Enlarge the site of your tent, stretch out the curtains of your dwelling, lengthen your cords, strengthen your stakes.* The poem encourages a barren and depressed Israel—estranged from God, laid waste by the Babylonians, driven into exile, divided and displaced—to take heart, hope for reconciliation, expect restoration, and wait to receive limitless bounty and blessing. Lyrically and metaphorically, the poet speaks of God as husband, exiled Israel as God's barren and estranged wife, and Zion—reconciled and restored Israel—as a wife with many children, pregnant, filled with possibility.[1]

Many applications of truth may be found within the wisdom of this Hebraic literature. Yet when I consider how the worshiping church might understand the profundity of this passage, I return again and again to the idea of inclusion. Centuries later, Jesus Christ, our True Liturgy, practiced a life of inclusiveness, setting for us a perfect example of love that is both wide and broad.[2] We see a prophetic hint of this inclusive love ruminating within the Isaiah 54 passage.

Following a discussion of the power of language, two areas related to language and inclusive worship are also discussed: naming God and receiving others. I encourage you to open yourself to the possibilities each presents.

The Power of Language

Language is powerful. With language we may heal or hurt, include or exclude, clarify or obfuscate. In your experience, what other powers might language hold?

Language comes in many forms. Its most obvious form through words probably comes to mind first—the written, read, spoken, and sung forms of communication. Words are an essential part of worship, giving us many ways to pray and praise, confess and sing, receive the word of God, bless and be blessed. Words give us ways to speak of God and of others.

The unspoken languages of silence, gestures, and body language also communicate, often with great distinction and intensity. For instance, sometimes what is not said is far more powerful than what is spoken. And of course, we all know a full vocabulary of nonverbal gestures practiced daily by our culture. Consider how quickly certain gestures come to mind. Sometimes a person's body language—a stiff neck and set jaw, folded arms, a wink, downcast eyes and fallen chest, a springy step, a smile, a frown, fidgeting limbs—reveals more than its sender consciously knows or wants known. As with any other language system, positive or negative images may be expressed through body language, gesture, and silence.

There are many ways to communicate and many language systems in which to do it. These systems are not strangers to worship. Worship employs a myriad of languages that speak on various levels: audibly, verbally, visually, psychologically, sensually, subconsciously, consciously, intellectually, emotionally, and nonverbally. Not only are we shaped by our worship, but we are also molded by the language of our worship. Carol Lakey Hess states it this way: ". . . in relation to the shaping function of our worship, we can say that everything we say (and do not say) and do (and do not do) during that time of communal gathering forms us as the people of God."[3]

Hess goes on to explain that "There are roughly three ways that our corporate worship shapes us: explicitly, implicitly, and silently. We are shaped *explicitly* by those things that we confess and present publicly: the theology we proclaim, the topics we study, the language we use, the ideas we convey, the images we present, the hymns we sing, and much more as well."[4]

We are also shaped *implicitly* by the manner in which we speak and function. Hess provides this example: "When we speak of 'mankind' rather than 'humanity' we are implying that the male element of humanity is the standard."[5] Moreover, when we speak exclusively of God as *father* we imply God is male or that there are no other metaphors for naming the Holy One. When our ministers or worship leaders are predominantly white males, we imply that Caucasian men represent the standard in worship leadership and ministry. When we refer to fellow Christians as *brothers* we imply that our *sisters* in Christ are nonexistent, subordinate, or unimportant members of God's family. When we cling to antiquated rules of grammar that purport to represent both sexes through the generic use of masculine pronouns such as *he, his, him,* and *himself* or nouns like *man, men,* or *mankind,* we make women "linguistically invisible"[6] through implication.

Finally, Hess states we are also shaped by what is *silent,* giving this example: "When we use only male images of God, we emphasize only certain aspects of the divine character."[7] Furthermore, when we fail to speak out against injustices our silence betrays our lack of compassion. When we fail to practice inclusiveness, mercy, and justice our silence mocks Jesus' example.

Yes, language is powerful. Language is particularly powerful in worship.

Questions to Ponder

1. Consider the many ways words are used in worship. Make a list by brainstorming with your study group.

2. Consider the explicit language of your worship. What is being communicated? How is God being portrayed? Who is being represented? Who is being excluded?

3. Consider the implicit language of your worship. What is being communicated? How is God being portrayed? Who is being represented? Who is being excluded?

4. Who are the linguistically invisible people for your church?

5. Consider the silence of your worship. What is being communicated? Who is being represented? Who is being excluded?

6. Who are your worship leaders? Consider how each is similar to the other leaders in terms of race, sex, and age. What did you discover? What might their similarity (or dissimilarity) be saying?

God Language: Alternatives for Naming the Holy One

One of the ways we use language in worship is through our attempts to name God. Most of the ancient images and names for God, which come to us from Scripture, are set in patriarchal language. Understanding that canonized Scripture was written by—so far as we know—a small population of males who lived within a patriarchal society that regarded women and children as chattel, it is not so surprising that biblical language is primarily—

God of many Names
gathered into One,
in your glory come and meet us,
Moving, endlessly Becoming.
God of Hovering Wings,
Womb and Birth of time,
joyfully we sing your praises,
Breath of life in every people.
Hush, hush, hallelujah, hallelujah!
Shout, shout, hallelujah, hallelujah!
Sing, sing, hallelujah, hallelujah!
Sing, God is love, God is love!

—Brian Wren, 1986

but not exclusively—patriarchal. The ancient writers spoke and wrote using the language and metaphors known and understood by them in their attempts to describe the indescribable I Am. Knowing this historical context and taking into account our own, it seems right to consider the ways we may broaden our vocabulary about the Holy One while remaining true to the integrity of the biblical revelation about God's character.

An important first step is to realize language is not reality, only a representation or description of reality. Furthermore, God is beyond our naming. In Brian Wren's phrase, "God is beyond all imaging . . . ."[8] So basic is this concept to the message of the

We must admit, however, that all of our words are inadequate to fathom the reality of God. We are engaged in attempting to express that which is beyond our ability to express.

—Harold M. Daniels

Scriptures that it is one of the Ten Commandments: *You shall not make for yourself an idol, whether in the form of anything that is in heaven above, or that is on the earth beneath, or that is in the water under the earth.* The commandment of Exodus 20:4 disallows idol-making in any form, even with words. Without realizing it, our words—our names for God, our ways of thinking and doing—can become graven images. God is beyond our naming and beyond all imaging.

. . . images of God in language must not become idols. However hallowed by tradition, however enriching and suggestive, however profoundly they move us, our metaphors and names for God are not themselves God.

—Brian Wren

Wren, one of the renowned hymn poets of this century, offers the following advice: "If we draw on a variety of God-images and let them balance, enrich, and clash with one another, we shall be following the instincts of biblical faith and the methods of many biblical voices. Allowing God-images to *clash* is important, because it reminds us that we are approaching that which is beyond all images."9

My best language will be like a finger pointing at the moon, and I shall be foolish indeed if I confuse the moon with my finger.

—Brian Wren

Alternatives for Naming God

Beyond Male or Female. Through the prophet Hosea, God makes this identifying revelation: *I am God and no mortal, the Holy One in your midst . . .* (Hos 11:9b). The Holy One is beyond all human imaging. God is neither male nor female. Knowing and understanding this, there remains no sound argument for using exclusively masculine language to name or reference God.

The image of God as father refers to the good *relationship* between a parent and child. Couched in comfortable language, which mirrors a human relationship those of us with good fathers may easily understand, the personal image of God as father is not so bad. However, to those with irresponsible, drunken, or abusive earthly fathers, the exclusive use (or perhaps even the limited use) of this imagery is extremely problematic. Yes, God is like a loving father, but God is more than this. God is also like the best mother—life-giving, devoted, nurturing, fiercely protective, and tender. God is like the very best parent this world of love-starved orphans has ever imagined. But God is more than this.

The image of God as father is probably the most pronounced of all biblical names, yet the Bible and our vocabulary are full of other characteristically masculine images that portray, in lopsided fashion, the Holy One as powerful and mighty, exerting dominance and control.[10] God

But surely, it may be objected, Christ Himself taught us to regard God as a Father. Are we to reject His own analogy? Of course not, so long as we remember that it is an analogy. When Christ taught His disciples to regard God as their Father in Heaven He did not mean that their idea of God must necessarily be based upon their ideas of their own fathers. For all we know there may have been many of His hearers whose fathers were unjust, tyrannical, stupid, conceited, feckless, or indulgent. It is the relationship that Christ is stressing.

—J. B. Phillips

imaged as Lord, King, Almighty, Warrior, Conqueror, Protector, and Master imply for us relationships of slavery, servitude, and subjection, not love. The predominant use of these royal and warrior images over others assigns to God the attributes of a brutish male despot who would not be tolerated in any modern, free society. While the concept of God's omnipotence may be sound, God is infinitely more than this.

Since the pages of the Bible, and subsequently the words of our hymns and liturgies, are filled with masculine images of God, where do we find words for God that counter these one-sided images? We start with the Bible.

Non-Patriarchal Biblical Images.
Virginia Ramey Mollenkott, in her book *The Divine Feminine: The Biblical Imagery of God as Female,* provides a valuable resource for those interested in searching the Scriptures for feminine images of the Holy One. I commend the book to your reading. Table 4 illustrates only a small sampling of the many feminine images of God within Scripture.[11]

God is beyond all imaging, but God's holy and impassioned otherness strikes sparks from the anvil of our imagination and experience, and those sparks register linguistically as similes and metaphors. It therefore seems true to biblical faith to use strong and vivid God-images, in considerable variety. Then we can let each image have full impact on our imagination before moving on to another, which may connect or clash with it.

—Brian Wren

TABLE 4: SAMPLE OF FEMININE IMAGES FOUND WITHIN SCRIPTURE

Category	Example	Reference
God as a Woman Giving Birth or Mother	**you forgot the God who gave you birth**	*Deuteronomy 32:18*
	now I will cry out like a woman in labor	*Isaiah 42:14*
	borne by me from your birth, carried from the womb	*Isaiah 46:3-4*
	we are God's offspring	*Acts 17:26-29*
	what is born of the Spirit is spirit	*John 3:6*
	everyone who loves is born of God	*1 John 4:7*
God as a Nursing Mother	**O taste and see that the Lord is good**	*Psalm 34:8*
	I bent down to them and fed them	*Hosea 11:4*
God as a Midwife	**Yet it was you who took me from the womb**	*Psalm 22:9-10*
	shall I open the womb and not deliver?	*Isaiah 66:9*
God as a Mother Bear	**I will fall upon them like a bear robbed of her cubs**	*Hosea 13:8*

God as a Female Homemaker	as the eyes of a maid to the hand of her mistress, so our eyes look to the Lord our God	Psalm 123:2
	parable of the woman who lost one of ten silver coins	Luke 15:8-10
God as a Mother Eagle	**I bore you on eagles' wings**	Exodus 19:4
	As an eagle stirs up its nest and hovers over its young; as it spreads its wings, takes them up, and bears them aloft on its pinions, the LORD alone guided him	Deuteronomy 32:11-12
	hide me in the shadow of your wings	Psalm 17:8
God as a Mother Hen	**in the shadow of your wings I will take refuge**	Psalm 57:1
	How often have I desired to gather your children together as a hen gathers her brood under her wings	Matthew 23:37 Luke 13:34

The Bible contains many other feminine images for God. I challenge you to research these, and then with new eyes and new understanding reread the many biblical passages containing feminine word-pictures for the Holy One. As you read and study, remember that God is *both* male and female and *neither* male nor female. Like all other words and images describing God, these images are merely metaphors and our feeble attempts to know and describe the Indescribable I Am.

Personal and Non-personal Metaphors. In *What Language Shall I Borrow?* Brian Wren makes this claim: "Nonpersonal metaphors are needed to protect us from cozy God-images tailored to our own perceptions, and to

With the advantage of the whole Hebrew and Christian Scriptures to guide our thinking, we are enabled to understand that recognizing Yahweh's female component is not a reversion to paganism, but rather a deepening toward a fuller and healthier orthodoxy.

—Virginia Ramey Mollenkott

encounter God's strangeness and otherness. Without nonpersonal metaphors, our image of God becomes domesticated; without personal metaphors, God is unknowable and alien. Both are needed, in harmony and dissonance."[12] Personal metaphors refer to God in human terms while nonpersonal metaphors speak of God in natural or ethereal ways.

When naming God I suspect we err most often through an overuse of personal metaphors for the Holy One. At this point of over-familiarity and anthropomorphism in our worship, we miss God: God is too familiar to us and our weak praise and adoration reflect this. We think we know God and we assign God familiar human traits because humanity is all we do know. But we don't know God. We don't understand God. Somewhere in all our defining and naming, we have forgotten that God is simply and mysteriously the Great I Am.

According to the Bible, our God is both male and female, and neither male nor female. The language of prayer, liturgy, sermon, and hymnody had best reflect that fact.

—Virginia Ramey Mollenkott

What follows in table 5 is a partial list, a beginning. Gleaned from the poetry and prose of Brian Wren and the writings of Evelyn Underhill,[13] these scripturally anchored metaphors represent both personal (P) and non-personal (NP) alternatives for naming God. I have added a few of my own to the list. Likewise, I encourage you to brainstorm, thinking of additional scripturally sound metaphors for God. Add generously to the list. Experiment with new metaphors, stretching your imagination. Balance your use of personal and non-personal metaphors. God has many names.

Table 5: Metaphors for God

Personal Names for God

Lover	Parent	Midwife of Changes
Potter	Sister	Weaver of Stories
Builder	Brother	Womb of Being
Mother	Spinner	Carpenter
Father	Daredevil Gambler	Parent of Good

Non-personal Names for God

Sun	Moving	Light
Thunder	Endlessly Becoming	Unsearchable
Mighty Torrent	Web of Love	Formless
Justice	Loom of Love	High
Wisdom	Holy	Immortal
Rock	Majesty	Infinite
Spring	Energy	Presence
Shield	Holy One	Star
Fortress	Home	Eternal
Devouring Fire	Suffering God	Transcendence
Creator	Mercy	Wholly Other
Unnamed	Sustainer	Uncreated
Name Unnamed	Holiness Eternal	Infinite God
Being-Becoming	Fire of Truth	Reality
Love	Great	Divine Essence
Life	The One	The Holy
Hope	Provider of All	The Unseen
Beautiful Movement	Beginning & End	Self-existent Eternal
Maker	Alpha & Omega	Absolute God
Maker of Rainbows	First & Last	
Birth of Time	I Am	

Personal Names for Son

Beloved	Counselor	Bridegroom
Friend	Prophet	Prince of Peace
Priest	Servant	
Advocate	Victim	

Non-personal Names for Son

Redeemer	Lamb	Joy
Life-giving Loser	Love	Feast
Word-in-Flesh	Immanuel	Heart
Word-made-Flesh	God with Us	Rock
Savior	Light	Spring
Incarnate	Life	Sun
God in Jesus	Word	Desire of Nations
Messiah	Name	Wonderful
The Christ	Truth	
Anointed One	Crucified	

Personal Names for Spirit

Mutual Friend	Go-Between	Advocate
Matchmaker	Friend	Counselor
Love's Companion	Guide	Breath
Love-Mediator	Guest	Companion

Non-personal Names for Spirit

Wind	Well	Song of Love
Sustainer	Well of Peace	Giver
Comforter	Deep	Paraclete
Nurturer	Fire	God's Voice
Nudging Discomforter	Flame	Fount of our Being
Hovering Wings	Blazing Light	Increate Spirit of God
Breath of Life	Wild Eagle-dove	Divine Presence
Storm of Love	Dove	

Naming the Trinity. Brian Wren offers his readers a set of Trinitarian metaphors for naming the centers of God's personhood: God as Lover, Son as Beloved, and the Holy Spirit as Mutual Friend. Each metaphor works in symbiotic relation with the others. Wren bases his selections upon seventh-century John of Damascus's term *perichoresis* [Greek for *dance around*], a word that aptly describes how the three centers of the Trinity relate to one another. "Perichoresis means that the three Persons continually exchange energy, being, and power, so that each partakes of the other. It suggests a beautiful intertwining, unending dance, whose movement flows to and fro between the dancers. . . . Trinitarian metaphors should strive for that sense of dynamic, intertwining movement."[14] Can you think of others?

I urge you not to hold back. Pray for sensitivity, imagination, and boldness. Experiment and struggle with new metaphors for God. Choose language for God and for people that is both intentional and inclusive. Consider the unspoken language of your actions. *Enlarge the site of your tent, stretch out the curtains of your dwelling, lengthen your cords, strengthen your stakes.*

Just as God has many names, all of them metaphor, our congregation's experiences of God are manifold.

—Rebecca Sue Strader

Language patterns do not finally change until we use new patterns enough for them to sound natural and normal. That takes effort, and it takes a conviction that such changes are worth the effort.

—Phyllis Koehnline

Questions to Ponder

1. In a brainstorming session with your study group, quickly list the names by which your group currently names God. Designate one person to record the names suggested by your group.

2. Working with your list of names for God, indicate beside each name whether that name is masculine/patriarchal (M), feminine (F), personal (P), or non-personal (NP). What does this exercise reveal about your word choices?

The important thing is for language to open up space which does not limit us but which moves us, make[s] us experience, have a breath of other things: "You set my feet in a broad room" (Ps 31:9).

—Elisabeth Moltmann-Wendel

3. How might you expand your list of names for God? Let the Scriptures guide you as you use your imagination to verbalize what you know of God's nature and character.

Receiving Others

Look about you the next time you worship. If your church is like most, the other members of your church are probably a lot like you. Like most worshiping congregations, your church is probably fairly homogeneous, homogenized, and similar. Noting this, Jesus' referral to his followers as *flocks* takes on new meaning as people with similar interests, tastes, educational levels, race, and socioeconomic bases tend to flock together. There is nothing fundamentally wrong with this. There can be great comfort in sameness. Belonging to a group feels good, and a sense of identity may be derived from it. But consider if you will that while we tend to congregate with others like ourselves, we also tend to exclude people who are different from ourselves and to disregard ideas foreign to us. If such a stance becomes our rule—to associate only with those who live where we do, who have comparable education and jobs, who wear the right kind of clothes, who think like we do, who are members of certain clubs—we risk endangerment by insidious threats of closed minds, narrowness, and exclusivity.

One day, should we take serious stock of ourselves, we may come to realize we have become a closed people, and our churches cliques. Then should we compare our tightly held positions and our resistance to change to the life and teachings of Jesus, we would be quick to note the great chasm between our frailty and his perfect, yet threatening, example.

Sometimes the zeal with which we guard and defend our standards—our sense of right and wrong, our purity of principle, our godly ideals, our interpretation of Scripture, our morality judgments—outweighs our expressions of love, mercy, forgiveness, acceptance, and yes, inclusiveness. Unwittingly— and sometimes decidedly—we exclude people who need and desire expressions of God's love, but who may feel, for one reason or another, unworthy and unclean. But did not God in a vision to Peter clarify this issue long ago that *What God has made clean, you must not call profane* (Acts 11:1-18)? And did not an impassioned Paul write to the church at Ephesus about how Christ tore down dividing walls between estranged groups of people?[15]

Whether intentional or unintentional, sometimes our language choices erect barriers that keep certain people out. If our language for God and others is insensitive, archaic, and exclusive, we risk confusing, wounding, and ultimately diminishing the community of faith. Remembering the axiom expressed in chapter 4—*first change language, behavior will follow*—we need to think seriously about our language choices and how these play out in worship. The ripple effect of ill-chosen words can be far-reaching. Although sometimes our actions belie our words, more often language reveals our true mind-set. If we ever hope to change our behavior in worship—we must first understand the power of our language choices and make the necessary changes.

Our faith is a faith that welcomes the stranger and continually opens its boundaries to those marginalized in this life (the poor, the differently abled, the mentally retarded); it is a faith that is concerned about the "other" who is not present in its worship (the homeless, the prisoners, the "enemies"). In fact care for the stranger is what shapes us as a people of God, and what shakes us as a people of God.

—Carol Lakey Hess

In what ways does your church welcome, include, and involve the following groups in the kingdom: the divorced, the widowed, homosexuals, minority groups, ethnic and racial groups, people with tattoos and pierced bodies, disabled people, blended families, single-parent families, people with AIDS, unmarried couples, women ministers, the poor, interracial couples and families, unmarried parents and their children, the infirm, the handicapped, the doubters, the agnostics? Can you identify other people or groups who, at one time or another, feel cut off from the kingdom and disenfranchised by God's people? Who might feel excluded by your church? What might you do to change this?

Questions to Ponder

Although the language framing the following questions is directed toward a study group or congregation, I urge you first to consider many of the questions personally in a time of private devotion. Having done this, reuse the questions in a group setting to examine and discuss the identity, attributes, and practices of your church.

1. Do you consider your church to be a friendly congregation?

2. How does your congregation express friendliness and warmth to strangers worshiping among you? What do you do personally?

3. What measures does your church take to encourage others to visit your church in worship?

4. How do you follow up with visitors after the worship service?

5. Does your church really want visitors and new members?

6. What is your church's demographic makeup? Of your membership, consider the following: ages, race, socioeconomic levels, educational levels, occupations of members (blue collar, white collar, professional, etc.), theological stance (fundamental, conservative, moderate, liberal, etc.), ratio of sexes. What do these studies reveal about your church? How are your members alike? How are they different?

7. Consider the community surrounding your church. How is the community like your church community? How is it different?

8. How might you involve the surrounding community in worship?

9. Is there a prejudice in your church against certain kinds of people?

10. Who do we believe the God of Love excludes?

11. If a person with AIDS wanted to join, become involved, and worship regularly within your church family, how would he/she be received? Would limitations be imposed upon this person's involvement? What might these be?

12. Reconstruct question 11 several times, substituting other people or groups for *a person with AIDS*.

13. Whom would you be dismayed to see sitting beside you in worship?

14. Have you ever felt excluded in any way? How did it feel?

15. Imagine being one of the people from question 12. If you were this person, where would you choose to go to church? What would you look for?

16. Considering the power of language to include or exclude, what does your church's God language suggest?

17. Considering the power of language to include or exclude, what does your church's worship language suggest? Start by searching the hymn texts routinely sung by your congregation. Is the language found in your hymns primarily inclusive or exclusive? Consider other worship language used by your congregation.

18. Considering the power of language to include or exclude, what does your church's people language suggest?

19. Considering the power of language to include or exclude, what does your church's "unspoken language" suggest?

20. To whom does the church belong?

In closing, I would like to share a prayer of thanksgiving and intercession offered by Reverend William L. Dols, Jr.[16] His prayer, eloquently written and delivered, captures for me the essence of inclusive worship and inclusive living:

Lord God of power and might, we intercede—stand up for and speak out on behalf of—those this day throughout the world who are the victims of misspent power and ill-used might. We pray for the poor, discounted and forgotten, near and far away, who are exploited and used by those who have more money or enough votes or bigger armies or influential friends in high places or a better education or know the proper thing to say and how to say it and, most of all, have cultivated deafness to cries for help and blindness to sores and suffering.

We pray for those who are violated because of what they believe or say or refuse to agree or give allegiance to. Mindful this weekend of Waco and Oklahoma City, we intercede for those who feel disenfranchised and left out and whose despair, at ever finding a way in, leads to violence. We intercede for those people—even in our city—who do not know they have power enough or have not yet touched it or found a way to be heard. Jesus reminds us that no one can take God's power from us. Help them like him to use their power to turn the world upside down and begin it all over again in justice and peace.

We intercede for those with status and rank who confuse your gift of power with their prowess and rights and privilege. We pray for people in high places who no longer ask "why" but only how to do more for themselves and less for the rest. We pray for the grace and courage it takes to summon up your power within us and to say NO to their and our greed and YES to you.

As well as for one another we pray for this planet. We give thanks and pray for this fragile earth our island home. We intercede for rivers being robbed of life, of land raped and skies invaded. Invested with the power to preserve and nurture, we choose instead, again and again, to use and exploit and exhaust. We speak up for animals and plants and trees and water and air who are speechless and have only our voices with which to cry out.

We thank you, Lord God, for another day in which to decide again what to do with the power we are. Remind us that our days are not endless—that time and life and resources and even patience run out. You promised Noah by placing your bow in the sky that you will never again destroy us for our misuse of your power. Instead you watch and wait and weep. Thank you, Lord God, most of all, for another opportunity to choose. Amen.

NOTES

[1] These ideas are developed by James Muilenburg, "Exegesis," and Henry Sloane Coffin, "Exposition," *The Interpreter's Bible*, ed. George Arthur Buttrick, vol. 5 (Nashville: Abingdon Press, 1952), 632-34, 632-35, respectively.

[2] The aspect of inclusiveness as a model for Christian worship is dealt with in chapter 2: "Scriptural Models for Worship: Worship Personified: Jesus Christ."

[3] Carol Lakey Hess, "The Shaping and Shaking of Congregational Life," *Reformed Liturgy & Music* 25/2 (1991): 67.

[4] Ibid., 66, italics added.

[5] Ibid.

[6] Brian Wren, quoting Susan Thistethwaite in *What Language Shall I Borrow? God-Talk in Worship: A Male Response to Feminist Theology* (New York: Crossroad: 1995), 61.

[7] Hess, "Shaping and Shaking," 66.

[8] Wren, *What Language Shall I Borrow?* 132.

[9] Ibid.

[10] For a comprehensive discussion on "Dethroning Patriarchal Idols," see Wren, *What Language Shall I Borrow?* 123f.

[11] References are taken from Virginia Ramey Mollenkott's *The Divine Feminine: The Biblical Imagery of God as Female* (New York: Crossroad, 1994).

[12] Wren, *What Language Shall I Borrow?* 206.

[13] This list of personal and non-personal metaphors for naming God was gleaned from the poetry and prose of Brian Wren in *What Language Shall I Borrow?* and the writings of Evelyn Underhill in *Worship* (New York: Crossroad, 1985). It should not be considered exhaustive. Judgments regarding each metaphor's personal or non-personal designation were made by the author.

[14] Wren, *What Language Shall I Borrow?* 202.

[15] Ephesians 2:11-22 references Paul's letter to the church at Ephesus where he specifically addresses Christ's removal of barriers between two historically divided groups: *the uncircumcision* (Gentiles) and *the circumcision* (Jews).

[16] William L. Dols, Jr., "Prayer of Thanksgiving and Intercession," delivered in worship at Myers Park Baptist Church, Charlotte NC, 20 April 1997.

CHAPTER 7

A Matter of Style

The newspaper headline read, "Congregations loosen up the liturgy,"[1] while another reported "All creatures great and small—and slimy—are blessed" in a worship service designed especially for family pets.[2] One California church caters to surfers. The pastor addresses his bathing suit-clad congregation in speech punctuated with surfer analogies while standing "at a podium designed to look like a surfboard sawed in half."[3] As surfers pray, their fiberglass boards rest along undecorated chapel walls, replacing traditional and historic artistic motifs of stained glass with waxed symbols of modern culture. A prominent North Carolina church mailed out worship surveys to its membership soliciting worshiper preferences about the services. William Easum has written a book about the church in the twenty-first century called *Dancing with Dinosaurs* in which he extends the dinosaur metaphor to plateaued and declining churches. One church historian writes, "Today, evangelical churches across the country are torn between the tug of tradition and the pull of style."[4] No wonder.

Cultural Influences

According to Michael Warren, Professor of Theology at St. John's University, "Liturgy embodies the life of a group of people. The dominant culture finds its way into this life just as sand on a windy day at the beach gets into everything, including your sandwich."[5] It cannot be avoided. As we accept the inevitability of cultural influence upon worship, the best questions we can ask ourselves may include: To what extent should we allow culture to invade worship? Whose culture invades our worship? What if no culture invaded worship? Can we disallow it? To what standards shall we hold firm in order to maintain worship's integrity?

With each generation of God's people throughout history, worship changes. As we move into the future, we carry with us worship's vast history. What we do today in worship is influenced not only by modern culture, but by a vast body of tradition preceding our current practice. Much of what we know, understand, and do in worship has been passed on to us by generations gone before. A sense of that history is helpful to an understanding of worship's evolutionary nature.

Worship has evolved through the centuries—from the patriarchs who stood apart from Canaanite worship; to the communal and congregational Mosaic period shaped by the exodus event; to the syncretistic period of the judges where ancient nomadic culture prevailed; to the monastic period of David with movement toward a cultic center, festival celebrations, and the worship of Yahweh; to temple worship of prescribed offerings and sacrifices; to the prophet era that varied with every ruling monarch and his influence; to the synagogue that enabled Judaism to survive through oppression in a non-Jewish world; to worship in New Testament times.[6]

What we know about New Testament worship is limited to infrequent biblical descriptions and allusions, a few instructions concerned primarily with abuses, and a number of fragments and quotations of liturgical material. Ferdinand Hahn, in his scholarly survey *The Worship of the Early Church*, reminds us that "It is a well-known fact that the earliest evidences from which we can derive a complete picture of the structure and sequence of Christian worship date from the middle of the second century."[7] We simply do not have a complete picture nor a detailed account of worship in the early church, only glimpses and extant texts from which we may draw indirect conclusions.

So what about worship in the New Testament? What evidence does its pages reveal? From the Lukan account of the story of the early church in Acts, we may dissect the components of baptism, healing, teaching, and evangelizing done in Jesus' name, the celebration and practice of the presence of the Holy Comforter, and reliance upon prophetic utterance. The Acts 2:42-47 account reveals that the early Christian church devoted themselves to apostolic teaching—recalling miracles, remembering Christ's passion, and testimonies of still-living eyewitnesses—as well as fellowship, collections for the common good, meals, and prayers.

The Pauline epistles of 1 Corinthians, Colossians, and Ephesians, as well as the sub-apostolic treatise of Hebrews, give us additional glimpses into first-century worship. Paul wrote specifically to refute certain abuses of freedom in worship practice in 1 Corinthians and Colossians. His instructions regarding worship are sprinkled throughout his writings and the collections of his followers. Colossians and Ephesians contain quotations from worship materials and hymns. Both letters are couched in worship language and are liturgical in tone. The writer of Hebrews, in didactic mode, opines about the early church's new understanding and practice of worthy and superior worship through Jesus Christ. Ephesians, Titus, 1 Timothy, Hebrews, Colossians, Philippians, and the Gospel of John each contain hymn fragments of various forms. First Peter quotes confessions and hymns and includes a baptismal sermon to new converts. Psalm-like passages are found in the apocalyptic literature of the Revelation to John. All these pieces of evidence seem to suggest that the authors and compilers of the writings that later formed the New Testament used worship materials to compose their manuscripts.[8] Yet despite these many references to early church practice, no church bulletin has ever been found showing us exactly how things were done or in what order. We may only peer at the early church's worship through the pages of the New Testament like children bent before keyholes hoping for a glimpse of what remains largely blocked from sight and understanding. Hahn summarizes our fragmentary view by saying:

> We cannot simply reach back to the worship of the primitive church. The New Testament evidence cannot be made normative in the sense that the various elements and forms must all be recovered and imitated. They must, however, provide a model for renovation and restructuring in the face of all adherence to a later, historically developed form of worship, in the face of all traditionalism and legalism in liturgical matters. The proper form of worship is always proper only to its own age, because only thus can the missionary function of worship and its function in equipping the faithful for service in the world be taken seriously. In this process the crucial principles of the New Testament understanding of worship must be vindicated anew theologically and given appropriate expression.[9]

No orders of worship are set out in the New Testament. On this point we are clear. Following the movement of the Spirit, the worship of the primitive church was full of spontaneity and freedom. No controls were set in New Testament times, except for certain Pauline instructions checking abuses of freedom and his admonitions that everything be done in order and for the good of the community. In the second century, however, Justin Martyr (c. AD 150) provides a partial, but not rigid, order of service: lections, sermon, common prayers, kiss of peace, presentation of bread and cup, praise and prayer of thanksgiving, congregational amens, and administration of the bread and cup by the deacons. Yet, no formal structure for worship was set until the fourth century.[10] In Hahn's phrase, "All in all, we must think in terms of a great range of variations, especially in the earliest period; only gradually did practice tend toward uniformity."[11]

Our worship is—and rightfully so—a response to God that reflects our particular places and situations in this world. However, if that is all that it is, it will be much more parochial and narrow than a response to the gospel ever should be. It will fall into becoming a mere reflection of the culture around us rather than the alternative and transformative means of grace it is meant to be.

—Carol Lakey Hess

To this day, the evolution of worship practice continues—developing, altering, mutating, augmenting, subtracting, adding—as we experiment with worship forms, orders, and styles. In the words of Lutheran pastor Frank C. Senn, "Christian liturgy retains traces of the various cultures through which it has passed and to which it has been adapted. We chant a Hebrew 'Amen,' sing Greek canticles, pray the rhythms of Latin rhetoric, assemble in Gothic buildings, listen to German chorales preludes and extend an American handshake at the greeting of peace."[12]

In the early 1800s, English poet Percy Bysshe Shelley (1792–1822) penned the lines, "Naught may endure but Mutability."[13] The insight of his poetic mind—that the only thing in life that lasts is change—applies well to the mutational and evolutionary nature of worship.

One Essential Style

A given tradition or congregation will have an essential style of worship set in a familiar structure. This style will naturally vary between congregations, denominations, and cultures. People will always identify with others most like themselves, and where churchgoing is concerned, they will join where they feel a part of things and at one with others gathered. If this were not so, there would be only one denomination, one church, one doctrine, one polity, and one changeless style of worship the world wide.

Within Protestant American culture, four basic worship styles exist: liturgical, traditional, contemporary, and blended. Hallmarks of liturgical worship include adherence to the Church Year and use of liturgical colors, multiple lectionary Scripture selections, classic and sacred anthem literature, congregation hymns and chants, the inclusion of confession and pardon, and a balanced emphasis between word and table, among other distinctions. Traditional worship includes a strong sense of dignity and reverence, sacred anthem literature, congregational hymn and gospel song singing often led by a song leader, a primary emphasis upon word, and often a single reading of Scripture related directly to the sermon. Contemporary worship is typified by a relaxed, almost casual, approach to worship, exemplified in the dress, language, and demeanor of leaders and worshipers alike. Music accompaniment is most often provided by a band and led by an ensemble of singers. Anthems are replaced with tunes by pop artists while choruses take the place of hymns. Hymnbooks are displaced by overhead projectors and pews by moveable chairs. Orders of service are often abbreviated to include only praise, offering, prayer, and sermon.[14] Blended forms will be discussed at length later in the chapter.

Some churches worship exclusively within one style, while others homogenize one or more of the four, thereby creating for themselves a distinctive style all their own. Some congregations experiment with one or more

While there may not be a single fixed order of worship in the Reformed tradition, it is nevertheless the case that most communities of faith have a given order for their worship. There is a weekly structure that is familiar to us. There is a rhythm by which the community has come to understand and celebrate its faith, and praise God week by week. There is a pattern in which the gathered community feels at home, a weekly pulse which helps the congregation be reoriented toward God again and again, which heals the brokenness of the particular community, which guides the church as it seeks to be transformed by the renewing grace of God in worship. In that sense, the liturgy is a given, a constant, in which the congregation may live.

—YME WOENSDREGT

styles, while others decide that a consistently blended form of worship represents for them an approach that is at once ecumenical, inclusive, and broad.

Within each of these basic styles—liturgical, traditional, contemporary, and blended—there are variations of formality and informality. Each congregation settles at some level of formality that either their leadership or their people find comfortable. One might assume that the liturgical and traditional worship styles tend to be more formal and the contemporary style typically less so, but this is not necessarily the case. Some liturgical services, for example, are quite informal. The degree of formality or informality in worship adopted by a given church varies among congregations.

In the end, however, most churches settle into one essential style—formal liturgical, informal contemporary, informal traditional, informal liturgical, or some unique combination. The chosen style will, in time, serve as an identifying mark for the congregation. Tradition and people in leadership roles may lock some congregations into an almost unchangeable style, while other congregations may routinely feel free to experience differences in worship. The end is the same, however. Most churches settle into one essential style uniquely their own.

Always pushing against a church's essential style is the influence of culture. To what degree contemporary cultural affects or is allowed to affect worship is of major concern to worship leaders and worshipers alike.

Fast Food or Thanksgiving Dinner?

Ours is a culture of fast food. The overweight status of most Americans attests to our dietary habits. We are a self-centered and impatient culture who wants *what* we want *when* we want it. We are a people of now. Electronically armed with keypads, computer mice, remote controls, and microwave ovens, we are free to choose, click, and instantaneously change the world around us with the touch of a finger. Bombarded by choices at every turn, we have much to do and little time to do it. We have thrown good manners and civility out the window. Anything goes. The world is a cafeteria of options just waiting for us to grab and devour. We are a-consumer-oriented society. It is no surprise, then, that we approach worship as consumers, wanting *what* we want, *how* we want it, *when* we want it, *NOW!*

One purpose of this book is for those who are serious about worship to pull aside, slow down, and think long and hard about this fascinating and complex subject. Any serious study of worship must look in all directions—

past, present, and future—asking: What are our roots? What essential style do we espouse in worship? What does this practice mean? Why do we do what we do in worship? Where do we go from here?

For a moment, consider confession, an ancient component of worship. In order to confess, we must first know ourselves. To know ourselves, we must look deep into our souls and examine the essence of who we are. Looking into our past enables us to know ourselves more completely and to interpret present feelings, motives, and actions. If I may stretch the analogy, worship is a lot like confession. If we are to worship with integrity, we must first know the truths of past traditions, the evolution of practice, which brings us to the present, and interpret contemporary expressions using standards of biblical truth, time, and history. To do less is at best superfluous and narrows our understanding to only present realities and personal whims.

While it is inevitable that prevalent culture will affect current worship practice, we must seriously ask if we are ready and willing to throw away everything traditional and historic for the sake of contemporary styling. To do so seems biblically unsound, selfishly unwise, narrow, and unhealthy.

We come together to remember; that is our reason to hope and our mission as church. If we as a church lose our memory, we will also have lost our identity. One of the major functions of ritual is to keep memory alive by communicating the values and meanings that bind a group together.

—Margaret Mary Kelleher

Worship has changed through the centuries. Culture has altered it and will continue to do so. But worshipers must guard against losing all sense of what has come before in order to ensure integrity in what we pass along to the next generation. Robert Webber, professor of theology at Wheaton College in Illinois and a prolific writer on the subject of Christian worship, speaks in favor of blending traditional and contemporary forms in worship: "The traditional has depth; the contemporary has relevance. I think that in many of our churches we don't have depth or relevance. . . . A lot of contemporary worship is just rah-rah, ... It's valentines to Jesus. It's a novelty, and I don't think it's going to last."[15]

Just as a habitual fast-food diet of pizza, burgers, soft drinks, and fries is an undeniably unhealthy approach to nutrition, worship experiences that cater exclusively to the limited and worldly tastes of contemporary culture are equally unhealthy and should be a subject of utmost concern. Worship is more like a feast—a Thanksgiving dinner—with gathered friends and family than a quick trip to the burger stand or local pizza parlor. Worship is a big deal. Its diet is large and varied—rich with tradition, tempered and tried over the passage of time, alive in the presence of the Spirit, fresh with the first blush of contemporary expression. Worship is deep and wide, tall and broad.

Concerning Hymns and Choruses

Whenever worship styles are discussed, someone usually asks, what about hymns and choruses? Churches intent upon offering contemporary worship experiences, to a large extent it seems, are discontinuing the use of hymns in favor of praise choruses. To many church musicians and liturgists, this is an alarming practice. Hymnologist Harry Eskew, in a 1996 interview by Terri Lackey, made this remark: "Discounting the significance of singing hymns at church would be like dismissing the importance of learning history at school."[16] Lackey's interview with Eskew uncovered this abiding concern: "A fear among many hymnologists and worship traditionalists is that church music ministers are turning away from hymns and using more choruses. . . . Often churches make little or no use of hymnals, thus neglecting the tradition and educational benefit of hymns. . .

The scantest touch of grace can heal
A wound that's bled for years
If first we dare to reach and feel
Beyond our pain and tears.
Observe a hand stretched out to brush
The hem of Jesus' gown.
That bleeding woman trusts one touch
Will make her body sound.
She cannot see the savior's face,
But lunges for his robe:
At once a surge of healing grace
Where stubborn blood has flowed.
Like her, O Christ, we reach for you.
One touch is all we need.
We stretch for grace to make us new
And heal our wounds that bleed.

—THOMAS H. TROEGER, 1985

. A concern among many hymnologists is that churches that change their worship style do not abandon the rich heritage of hymns." Furthermore, Eskew continues: ". . . most churches that sing choruses, typically use them for only a short time, discard them, and find new ones. Hymns, however, have long-term effects on churches and individuals."[17]

Eskew and hymnologist Hugh T. McElrath, in their textbook *Sing with Understanding: An Introduction to Christian Hymnology*, make these points concerning the theology of hymns:

1. Someone has said that hymns are the poor person's poetry and the ordinary person's theology. Being the most popular kind of verse in living use, hymns do indeed express what common folk have believed through the ages and what can be affirmed today as true and reliable.

2. The recitation of creeds and confessions of faith makes up an important part of the public worship of many Christians; but in those worshiping groups where this is not the normal practice, the hymn stands as an alternate means of objectifying belief corporately. Replete with the lyric expression of universal doctrine which has been distilled from the church's twenty centuries of experience, the hymnal is truly a book of "grass-roots theology."

3. The hymnal is also a ready means of presenting and teaching Christian doctrine, even though as an instructional tool it is often overlooked. The basic beliefs of most Christians have been formulated more by the hymns they sing than by the preaching they hear or the Bible study they pursue.

4. Besides nurturing the faith, hymns figure prominently in spreading it. Christians from the first century on have proclaimed their beliefs in song, thereby helping spread the tenets of the faith.

5. Because hymns were born out of the conscious human need of their authors to express their faith and devotion, they also minister to the spiritual needs of those who know and sing them.

6. The hymn may thus be considered a ready tool for the major functions of today's church in *worship,* in *education,* in *evangelism,* and in *ministry.*[18]

When we compare hymns and choruses, the theological content of hymns may be compared to a bushel basket, whereas the theological content of choruses may be likened to a thimble. To throw out basketfuls of theology in hymns for thimble-sized portions in choruses borders on the ridiculous, but more and more churches are doing it. Each justifies the waste with good arguments for catering to the likes and dislikes of moderns in order to keep them involved, making worship enjoyable, doing whatever is necessary to

For the fruit of all creation, Thanks be to God.
For [God's] gifts to ev'ry nation, Thanks be to God.
For the plowing, sowing, reaping, Silent growth wile we are sleeping.
Future needs in earth's safekeeping, Thanks be to God.

In the just reward of labor, God's will is done.
In the help we give our neighbor, God's will is done.
In our world-wide task of caring for The hungry and despairing,
In the harvests we are sharing, God's will is done.

For the harvests of the Spirit, Thanks be to God.
For the good we all inherit, Thanks be to God.
For the wonders that astound us, For the truths that still confound us,
Most of all, that love has found us, Thanks be to God.

—Fred Pratt Green, 1970

Wash, O God, our sons and daughters, where your cleansing waters flow.
Number them among your people; bless as Christ blessed long ago.
Weave them garments bright and sparkling; compass them with love and light.
Fill, anoint them; send your Spirit, holy dove and heart's delight.

We who bring them long for nurture; by your milk may we be fed.
Let us join your feast, partaking cup of blessing, living bread.
God, renew us, guide our foot-steps; free from sin and all its snares,
One with Christ in living, dying, by your Spirit, children, heirs.

O how deep your holy wisdom! Unimagined, all your ways!
To your name be glory, honor! With our lives we worship, praise!
We your people stand before you, water-washed and Spirit born.
By your grace, our lives we offer. Recreate us; God, transform!

—Ruth Duck, 1987

grow large churches, and being sensitive to seekers "who may not understand traditional church methodologies, worship services, and language."[19] Yet, it seems wiser to use *both* hymns and choruses than simply choruses alone. The Apostle Paul may have been recommending similar compromise in Colossians 3:16: *Let the word of Christ dwell in you richly; teach and admonish one another in all wisdom; and with gratitude in your hearts sing psalms* [metrical psalms, Scripture], *hymns, and spiritual songs* [gospel songs, choruses] *to God.*

By and large, many of us have learned our theology—rightly or wrongly, correctly or incorrectly—from what we have sung at church. It is fair to say we believe what we sing, and fairer still, we risk becoming what we sing. Knowing this is true, we had better be careful of what we sing. Arguments favoring the exclusive use of choruses to the exclusion of hymns fail to take into account the long-range consequences of such a practice. The exclusive use of contemporary choruses in worship will only serve to stunt the theological growth of churches using them in this manner. In the next thirty years, we will have grown a generation that does not know the richness or theological depth of our hymnic heritage.

Moreover, the exclusive or predominant use of praise choruses over hymns also ignores the wealth of new hymnic literature available through hymnals and hymnal supplements. Contemporary hymnists such as Brian

When Christ was lifted from the earth
His arms stretched out above
Thro' ev'ry culture, ev'ry birth,
To draw an answering love.

Still east and west His love extends
And always, near or far,
He calls and claims us as His friends
And loves us as we are.

Where generation, class or race
Divides us to our shame,
He sees not labels but a face,
A person and a name.

Thus freely loved, tho' fully known,
May I in Christ be free
To welcome and accept His own
As Christ accepted me.
—Brian Wren, 1980

Healthy congregational song requires a balanced diet: We are what we sing.
—Thomas H. Troeger

Wren (b. 1936), Thomas H. Troeger (b. 1945), Ruth C. Duck (b. 1947), and Fred Pratt Green (b. 1903)—to name four among many—are currently producing exceptional hymnody with theological depth, broad ecumenicity, and cultural relevance. If you are not acquainted with these masterful poets, make a point to read and sing some of their fine literature before deciding hymns are a thing of the past. Also, many new hymnals are including works by hymn writers from other cultures and languages, pointing to the universal church.

Our First Fruits

To concentrate simply upon hymns and choruses is to say too little about church music, because the genre includes so much more. Church music comes in many forms and styles and serves many functions. It has been said, "Music transforms the words of worship. It brings us to the boundaries of our finiteness and gives us a glimpse of the expanses of eternity. It deepens prayer and praise, leading us to God in ways that words alone cannot."[20]

Of particular importance to this discussion is the fact that so often when worship style is the topic of discussion in modern forums, church music is the most critical and distinguishing factor. A real-life example illuminates this point. The church, a large congregation of 2,800 members situated in western North Carolina, offers two styles of worship each Sunday morning: two contemporary services (8:30 & 11:00) and one traditional service (9:45). In reality, both styles are similarly liturgical. The greatest difference between the styles of the two services is the music.

Set in the sanctuary, the traditional-liturgical service followed the prayer book tradition of the denomination, and the organ undergirded most, but not all, the singing. Hymns old and new, versical psalmody, and a Taizé chorus offered a blended approach to congregational singing. Worshipers dressed in an assortment of styles with Sunday-best well represented. The choir sang an anthem by a contemporary composer accompanied on electric piano. A Bach prelude and fugue on organ opened the service. A virtuosic toccata played by accomplished hands and feet ushered worshipers from the sanctuary back into the world.

The contemporary-liturgical service, housed in a large, multipurpose room set with temporary altar and attractive banners, began with gathering music by eight singers accompanied by a live band. Two sets of drums, two electric pianos, and a tambourine set the tone of worship—upbeat, lively, in toe-tapping style. Microphoned singers, consistently drowned out by the loud and repetitive accompaniment, led all the music for gathering and congregational singing throughout the service, including the Eucharist. Congregational singing included an assortment of choruses and Scripture songs, all introduced with a crashing cymbal and drum cadence and accompanied loudly by the band. Worshipers of all ages, but predominantly young adults and elementary-aged children, dressed very casually. The basic order of service was repeated from the traditional-liturgical service with certain modifications: no vestments (robes), less Scripture (the Old Testament and epistle readings were omitted), no pulpit (the preacher paced the floor), an offering gathered in baskets (instead of plates), and the language of the creeds, responses, and prayers translated into more casual wording. These many alterations made the service more informal and relaxed, friendlier, I suppose. Once the service ended, I left the worship center to the enthusiastic strains of the band. Nearing the door, I realized how similar the "postlude" sounded to the dance band I'd heard the night before.

The question for each congregation will be WHY we choose to incorporate any particular genre of music. We can "sing a new song" because we are trying to appeal to the culture—or because God is in our midst in new ways that include or will include the people of God in the current culture as well as cultures of the past.

—KARMEN VAN DYKE

Of all the modifications between the two styles of worship I witnessed in this setting, the changes to the music were the most pronounced.

Tragically, somewhere in the transition from liturgical to contemporary, or traditional to contemporary, a rich heritage of church music is being carelessly tossed aside. Somewhere in the transition, the essential elements of awe and reverence in worship appear to be lost. Somewhere textual and musical depth is being traded for less challenging forms—the trendy, the light, and

When people are trained to appreciate the art of music for its own sake, they also want the best music for sacred purposes because they know the sublime sense that grips them when they hear good compositions well rendered. Such music enables people, in fact, to transcend the limits of time, space, and groups by transporting them to the eternal dimension into which liturgy invites and initiates us.

—FRANK C. SENN

the casual. Thirty years from now we will be left with an orphaned generation that will know only the popular idioms of its brief lifetime. They will not know, nor will they appreciate or understand, the legacy once theirs in church music and worship. What is popular today will not be popular tomorrow. Moreover, most of what is popular today will be discarded tomorrow. Orphaned, with no musical heritage, no rich theology of hymns, and no appreciation for anything but the entertaining sounds and vibrations of radio, television, and dance bands, how will this generation lead the church of tomorrow? Where will they lead it? Will they lead it at all?

Harold M. Daniels says it well when he writes, "Trivial music dwarfs our image of God, and cheapens worship. Only the best we are capable of can help us expand our vision of the Holy One. Use of musical styles, popular in a secular culture, but associated with values alien to the faith, are unsuitable for adapting for worship, since the style, or form itself, will always communicate those alien values."[21] The exclusive use of contemporary music and instruments within worship cheapens our worship, making the holiness and majesty of God nearly indistinguishable.

In chapter 3, characteristics and descriptions of worship were discussed. An examination of liturgy began the chapter. An important function of liturgy is to impress—to influence and shape—worshipers into kingdom people. This distinctive and tremendously important aspect of liturgy is all but lost when we allow culture to contour liturgy without constraint. To be certain, culture will always influence liturgy—the music, the language, and the metaphors of our faith—but worship leaders and worshipers alike must exercise cultural responsibility and constraint in what is allowed into worship. In Frank C. Senn's words, "Churches which rely on a particular style of popular (or even ethnic) music are condemned to a sectarianism of age, lifestyle, and cultural particularity, if not of doctrine."[22] While the integrity of church music lies

For on my holy mountain, the mountain height of Israel, says the Lord God, there all the house of Israel, all of them, shall serve me in the land; there I will accept them, and there I will require your contributions and the choicest of your gifts, with all your sacred things. As a pleasing odor I will accept you, when I bring you out from the peoples, and gather you out of the countries where you have been scattered; and I will manifest my holiness among you in the sight of the nations.

—EZEKIEL 20:40-41

First, consider for whom we sing. It is God who receives our praises. Just as we would not invite special guests and give them second best, neither can we offer less than our richest gifts to our Lord.

—Bonnie Jean Lamberth

most critically in harm's way, the same may be applied to the many forms of liturgy.

The worship of God demands our first fruits, our best offerings, the choicest of our gifts. Whether those offerings be music, proclamation, stewardship of gifts, prayers, praise, or confession, they must be our best. Admittedly, all of life is sacred. None of life is profane, not even rock and roll music. But worship seeks to draw us away from the blaring sounds and persuasions of the world toward a newness of life the world cannot match. If we allow contemporary culture to dictate our holy times and override all that is sacred, we may later find we have lost our saltiness and any ability to influence society. Sadly, worship may become little more than a mirror image of the world. How can we defend this position?

The Theology of Worship

What we do in worship—and how we do it—says a lot about what we believe concerning the Holy One and worship. The shape of our liturgy—its components, its elements, its style, its degree of formality or informality, its degree of inclusivity or exclusivity—all speak to our beliefs about worship and our beliefs about God. Worship proclaims to a watching world the answers to questions like the following. To whom do we sing? To whom do we pray? To whom do we offer our gifts? Whom do we worship? What message do we proclaim? How does worship change us?

Chapter 4 discussed what worship is *not*. Among the topics discussed was that worship is not evangelism. Yet the existence of mega-churches, seeker services marketing techniques that target and cater to the unchurched, and the increase in contemporary praise services over more traditional forms, make a strong statement to the contrary. What seems to be happening is this: In their zeal to bring the unchurched into the fold, in their zeal to grow large churches, in their zeal to make the numbers soar, in their zeal to be modern, popular, and attractive, churches are doing back flips and somersaults to pack

Worship that is shaped by a consumerist mentality becomes dependent on exit polls to see if its people will continue to want its product. In a "feel-good" culture, people want less emphasis on sin and sacrifice and more on blessing and abundance. Failure to deliver what people want will mean they shop elsewhere. Such a competitive marketplace tends to silence the prophetic nature of authentic worship that confronts culture with an alternative vision of life.

—David B. Batchelder

the pews. To those engaged in this frenzied activity—with minds set on doing anything to get people in—worship has become the greatest show on earth.

In the process, worship is being marketed as entertainment and being used as a tool for evangelism. And while evangelism is an important part of the church's mission, it is essential to understand that worship is not evangelism. Worship is not a tool. Worship is an end unto itself for the adoration of God and God alone. Using worship for evangelical purposes, in Frank C. Senn's phrase, is to practice "liturgical evangelism."23 Liturgical evangelism not only reduces worship to something other than worship, but reduces evangelism to something other than evangelism—simply "a means of growing the church."24 Some of what is being called contemporary worship today is little more than a clever bait-and-switch marketing strategy to get people in the front door and grow the modern church numerically.

Evangelism is often one of many positive and beautiful by-products of authentic worship. In and through worship, the collective testimony of God's people works as a beacon of light. Permeating every aspect

Worship as an encounter with God and as a public statement of the faith community's identity and meaning has served the purpose of evangelization down through the centuries. It has done this not by consciously turning worship into an evangelism tool, but by letting it have its impact on seekers and visitors. The historic liturgy has both challenged and transformed local cultures, so that seekers and visitors have experienced in the worship of the church an alien reality hospitably presented.

—Frank C. Senn

of their lives, God's radiance fills worshipers, producing a beauty unmatched by anything the world has to offer. In worship, the gospel is proclaimed and celebrated by the community of faith as in no other way. The world's glitter pales at the brilliance of such testimony.

A House Divided

A recent trend in worship engages a smorgasbord approach by offering two separate, distinctively different worship opportunities to the same congregation—one traditional or liturgical and another contemporary. Such a marketing strategy inadvertently encourages division over community, personal preference and choice over compromise and dialogue, and appeal, packaging, and enjoyment (all aspects of modern entertainment) over worship. Furthermore, this cafeteria approach to worship carries serious implications for worship as it seductively lulls would-be worshipers into a passive, consumer, cater-to-me posture. Worshipers cannot be passive. We must be actors—all of us—before God, not the audience.

Division of the church into two parts—the traditional/liturgical group versus the contemporary crowd—also extends serious implications for community. Worship, by and large, is a community event defined as the collective prayers and praise of God's united people. To find a meaningful collective expression of worship through a common liturgy takes work, hard work. The process involves compromise so the liturgy ultimately includes something every person can make his or her offering.

Culture will constantly affect liturgy, washing it with relevance. Liturgy will constantly flex and change, incorporating and shaping old and new forms, history and modern influences, tradition and creativity. But to divide worship into two separate parts is to give up. One worship style for us and one for them seriously wounds community. If worship is the most important thing the church does, and I believe it is, we must do it together. Otherwise, we end up with a church divided against itself—two groups honoring and idoling exclusive forms, unwilling, perhaps unable, to change. Such a closed attitude, impervious to change, cannot produce worshipers. Change is a consequence of worship.

Augment, modify, mix, experiment, vary, and blend. These are worshiping words. Dividing and separating flies in the face of authentic worship as it caters to closed attitudes, exclusivity, and forms that entertain. A weakness of any style—be it liturgical, traditional, contemporary, or blended—lies in its tendency toward exclusivity and tightness of form.

Christian theology, home to many paradoxes, makes both of the following claims: worship and culture are inescapably in conversation; worship and culture are inescapably in conflict.

—Dennis J. Hughes

Blended Worship

As stated, a given tradition will assume an essential style of worship set in a familiar structure. Nevertheless, any worshiper can and should be able to worship with integrity within a variety of styles at one time or another. Some churches, intentional about their worship, experiment with various worship styles, avoid exclusivity of any kind, and expose worshipers to a variety of forms. Such a healthy give-and-take atmosphere encourages worship as it nurtures openness and broadness in attitude. Such a congregation experiences the tender tension between form and freedom and places itself in an open, fertile place where great spiritual growth may occur. It is precisely in this matrix of uncertainty and discomfort that kingdom people and kingdom churches are birthed. In the tense and tender place between form and freedom, tradition and innovation, safety and vulnerability, great things can happen.

A variety in styles may be offered in the manner just described or through a blended worship style that contains—within any one service—characteristics and forms that are at once liturgical, traditional, and contemporary. A blended style of worship honors diversity, encourages inclusivity, and maintains a healthy corporate identity. A church developing a blended worship style must periodically consider its identity. Who are we? What are our gifts? What do we have to offer God? A church that develops a blended

This is the vision of blended worship—a vision that embraces the eclectic approach as a mirror of the diversity of the Body of Christ and as a celebration of our God-given, wonderfully multifaceted human nature.

—Hanan Yaqub

worship style values the building of community and views worship as a corporate event of the community of faith. A church that develops a blended worship style will struggle with the integral and necessary balances—between form and freedom, formality and informality, past and present, heritage and culture—to offer worship that is pleasing to the Holy One, meaningful to the gathered, relevant to the culture, but spiritually separate from the world.

In reality, it is important to note that most worship is blended despite any essential style it may claim. By virtue of its evolutionary nature, worship has dialectically preserved tradition and embraced innovation throughout time. History has proved this. In our efforts to innovate—or remain the same—we must be careful to preserve the delicate balance between form and freedom.

Perhaps the biggest challenge facing a blended worship style is the possibility that the style becomes a mismatched hodgepodge or jumbled mess of styles. Consider this example from a contemporary, yet liturgical, congregation: Meeting in a school auditorium, this worshiping congregation engaged in a very casual style of worship. Their almost lackadaisical approach to worship appeared meaningful to many of the regular worshipers gathered. They seemed unbothered by the constant milling about, people coming and going during the service, children swinging from stair railings, and one paper airplane taken to flight. While I am not personally opposed to informality, humor, and creature comfort, I found the high concentration of these characteristics mixed with the constant stir and motion around me detrimental to worship. While the service contained the usual components and liturgical forms—confession of sin, Apostles Creed, prayers, praise, Scripture lessons from the New Testament and the Psalms, a sermon, and the Eucharist—it rendered much of what was done ineffective, at least in part, due to the abysmal lack of reverence. I witnessed a liturgically-oriented congregation, using the components and following the form of ordered worship, but apparently without the slightest concern for what Evelyn Underhill describes in *Worship* as "liturgical good manners," or a sense of style and restraint.[25] For me, a visitor, the juxtaposition of order and disorder, praise and familiarity, proclamation and apology, struck me as oddly disconcerting and mismatched, something like a bathing suit at church or a business suit at the beach.

Despite its shortcomings, this church's efforts to blend liturgical and contemporary worship deserve praise. Possibly their

The impact of the contemporary meeting the conservative [liturgical or traditional] in worship gives it a creative power. Both enable Christians to sink their roots deeply in the faith and to spread their wings widely in the world. Such worship contributes to the renewal of the church.

—DONALD WILSON STAKE

greatest failure was not maintaining a sense of reverence. By losing their "liturgical good manners" the congregation produced a discomforting and mangled mix of things holy and unholy. They failed primarily in their casual, out-of-control handling of a sacred moment. Underhill writes that "a certain restraint, a sense of style, is characteristic of all good liturgical action: for it exists to express the common worship of the family, not the fervor of the individual soul."[26] Her statement suggests *balance* between form and freedom, formality and informality, for the sake of the common enterprise and not individual taste.

Principles of balance, quality, and integrity—thoughtfully engaged—can help ensure that a contemporary service can be reverent, a traditional service relevant, a liturgical service creative, and a blended service coherent. The characteristics of worship (what worship *is* and what it *is not*) as well as the other principles presented in the preceding chapters of this book apply equally well to any style. Furthermore, each style can and should demonstrate inclusive, relevant, reverent worship of the highest quality and integrity. A blended service need not become a jumbled mess of styles any more than a contemporary service must remove the hymns to be contemporary. A traditional service may easily incorporate liturgical and contemporary expressions while remaining essentially traditional. Oftentimes the crucial matter of planning makes the difference.

Questions to Ponder

1. Is worship that is casual, familiar, informal, and laced heavily with contemporary culture's values acceptable? In what ways is this form acceptable? In what ways is it unacceptable?

2. Is ordered, change-resistant, historic liturgy still effective? How? When?

3. Who decides what is acceptable and unacceptable in worship in your setting? What standard is used for making judgments concerning style and acceptable worship in your church?

4. If a decrease in formality in worship is desired, how can reverence be preserved?

5. If an increase in formality in worship is desired or needed, how can warmth be preserved?

6. Consider the congregational singing opportunities within your church's worship. In a given service, how many hymns are sung? How many gospel songs? How many choruses?

7. What is usually meant by the familiar phrase, "We want to sing the old hymns"? Hymns and gospel songs learned in childhood? Or ancient hymn texts written by such figures as Bernard of Clairvaux (1091–1153)?

8. What changes might be made to a traditionally styled worship service to make it a blend of traditional and contemporary?

9. What changes might be made to a liturgically styled worship service to make it more contemporary?

10. How may a service contain aspects of liturgical, traditional, and contemporary styling yet retain a sense of coherence and continuity?

11. Make a list of suggested guidelines for the purpose of ensuring that any worship service *of any style* remains reverent, relevant, high in quality, and full of integrity.

NOTES

[1] Ken Garfield, "Congregations loosen up the liturgy," *The Charlotte Observer*, 14 September 1996, 1G.

[2] Jeff Sturgeon, "All creatures great and small—and slimy—are blessed," *The Roanoke Times*, 28 August 1995, C1.

[3] Dennis Huspeni, "Churches catch a wave of worship," *The Charlotte Observer*, 19 October 1996, 3G.

[4] Bruce L. Shelley, "Then & Now," *Moody* 96/6 (1996): 24.

[5] Michael Warren, "Culture, Counterculture and the Word," *The Landscape of Praise: Readings in Liturgical Renewal*, ed. Blair Gilmer Meeks (Valley Forge: Trinity Press International, 1996), 282.

[6] This summary of worship's evolutionary character comes from class notes taken in "New Testament 2396: Worship and Ministry in The New Testament," with Professor R. Alan Culpepper, The Southern Baptist Theological Seminary, Louisville KY, Fall 1982.

[7] Ferdinand Hahn, *The Worship of the Early Church*, trans. David E. Green, ed. John Reumann (Philadelphia: Fortress Press, 1973), 1.

[8] R. Alan Culpepper, opinion expressed in class lecture in "New Testament 2396: Worship and Ministry in the New Testament," The Southern Baptist Theological Seminary, Louisville KY, Fall 1982.

[9] Hahn, *Worship of the Early Church*, 104-105.

[10] Culpepper lecture.

[11] Hahn, *Worship of the Early Church*, 52.

[12] Frank C. Senn, "The Spirit of the Liturgy, A Wonderland Revisited," *The Landscape of Praise: Readings in Liturgical Renewal*, ed. Blair Gilmer Meeks (Valley Forge: Trinity Press International, 1996), 18.

[13] Percy Bysshe Shelley, "Mutability," *The Literature of England: An Anthology and a History*, ed. George B. Woods, Homer A. Watt, and George K. Anderson, vol. 2, rev. ed. (New York: Scott, Foresman and Company, 1941), 257.

[14] These are general and incomplete descriptions of liturgical, traditional, and contemporary worship styles. These isolated examples are provided for the sole purpose of illustration and should not be considered exhaustive or rigid.

[15] Robert Webber, quoted by David Duggins, "In Spirit and in Truth," *Moody* 96/6 (1996): 30-31.

[16] Harry Eskew, interviewed by Terri Lackey, "Is Tossing Hymns Chucking History?" *Facts & Trends* 42/9 (1996): 9.

[17] Ibid.

[18] Selected statements on "The Hymn and Theology," from Harry Eskew and Hugh T. McElrath, *Sing with Understanding: An Introduction to Christian Hymnology* (Nashville: Broadman Press, 1980), 59-60.

[19] Thom S. Rainer, "Evangelism and Culture," *The Tie* 64/2 (1996): 7.

[20] Harold M. Daniels, "The Languages of Worship," *Reformed Liturgy & Music* 30/4 (1996): 203.

[21] Ibid.

[22] Frank C. Senn, "Worship and Evangelism," *Reformed Liturgy & Music* 31/1 (1997): 29.

[23] Ibid., 22.

[24] Ibid.

[25] Evelyn Underhill, *Worship* (New York: Crossroad, 1985), 110.

[26] Ibid., 110.

CHAPTER 8

Worship Reform—How?

The Hebrew prophets frequently had much to say about worship. Often theirs was the task of persuading their ancient Hebrew audiences to amend not only their worship practice, but their lifestyles as well. Specific abuses in worship leadership and practice are cited within the prophecies of Joel, Amos, Micah, Zephaniah, Haggai, and Malachi. More often than not, these spokesmen of Israel denounce empty, vain worship, which fails to produce righteousness and ethical living. The theme of balance between outward and inward devotion is woven through the preaching of these ancient figures as each seems to understand how worship and righteous living are tethered in direct relationship.

Save me from the soothing sin
Of the empty cultic deed
And the pious, babbling din
Of the claimed but unlived creed.
Let my actions, Lord, express
What my tongue and lips profess.

—Thomas H. Troeger

A study of the prophets quickly reveals worship reform is no new concept. Rather, it is an ongoing, circular process rooted in early Hebrew worship. Understanding this, the prophets can help present-day worshipers like us realize the need and benefit of ongoing worship reform as they continue to remind us to check worship abuses and to carry our worship beyond the sanctuary into the marketplace.

What follows is a number of suggestions to enable worship leaders and worship planning teams to engage in the ongoing process of worship renewal and reform.

> *Cautious, careful people, always casting about to preserve their reputations . . . can never effect a reform.*
>
> —Susan B. Anthony

Prioritize

Begin by making worship your priority. The church, in most cases, will follow your lead. If your congregation senses worship is not high on your list of ministry priorities, most worshipers will reflect this same attitude about their worship. Others to whom worship is already a high priority may feel frustrated, especially if worship experiences are frequently predictable, lack freshness and creativity, and are routinely similar week after week.

If worship is really a priority, adequate time must be given to its planning and preparation. Worship planning and preparation takes time, lots of it. But to say worship is a priority and not spend time developing it is enigmatic.

Read and Study

Read and study about worship. Then share your new insights with the congregation

> *If our presiding exhibits a lack of care and preparation, we confess that worship is unimportant in the life of the church, instead of its being the very heart and soul of the church's ministry.*
>
> —Yme Woensdregt

through preaching, study groups, newsletter articles, and example. Begin building a bibliography of worship resources, adding to your list as you attend seminars, workshops, and classes on worship.

Many years ago I developed the habit of scanning for worship resources—from bulletins, newspapers, periodicals, newsletters, articles, and so forth. To organize my findings, I build resource files to hold my collection of clippings, articles, workshop notes, etc. Then, when I need to design worship around a particular theme or occasion, I go to my resource file for ideas. What follows in table 6 is a simple listing of my filing system. I share these categories because this organizational system has proved helpful to me through the years, but I urge you to create your own. If it is helpful, I encourage you to add to my lists in the spaces provided.

TABLE 6: MY FILING SYSTEM

Worship Resources

Anthem Literature	Hymns: Solos from the Hymnal	Scripture
Banners	Hymns: Using the Hymnal	Section Headings (Bulletin)
Benedictions	Inclusive Language, Inclusive Worship	Seeker Sensitive Worship
Bibliography	Innovative Worship	Sermon
Bulletins	Invitation, Commitment, Offering	Service Music: Preludes, Offertories, Postludes
Calls to Worship	Keyboard Accompanists	Symbols
Celebrations	Litanies	Welcome
Communion	Modulations	Worship & Church Growth
Congregational Involvement	Music and Worship	Worship & Tradition
Congregational Singing	Prayers (subdivide by type)	Worship Planning
Doxology		Worship (Articles about)
Drama		
Feasts		
Hymnody		
Hymn Descants		
Hymn Introductions		

Special Services

Advent	Homecoming	Rites of Passage
Baptism	Hymn Services	Summer Sunday Nights
Communion	Installation/Commissioning	Stewardship
Creative Worship	Lent	Thanksgiving
Christmas	Maundy Thursday	Vespers
Doctrine	Memorial Day, Grief or Loss, All Saints' Day	Weddings
Drama	Ordination	Word
Epiphany	Pentecost	Other Special Services by Title
Fine Arts Series	Revivals	
Funerals		
Hanging of the Green		
Holy Week		

Pray

Literally bathe the entire worship process—planning, leading, participating, evaluating—in prayer. Pray that God will effectively use your creativity—a gift from the Master Creator. The Apostle Paul admonished the church in Thessalonica to *Rejoice always, pray without ceasing, give thanks in all circumstances; for this is the will of God in Christ Jesus for you* (1 Thess 5:16-18). This is excellent advice for Christians and particularly for worship planners and leaders. Leaders, be in an attitude of prayer as you make any preparation for worship, no matter how small or insignificant it may seem. This attitude suggests an openness and desire for God's leadership through the Holy Spirit. Where such willingness to God's leadership exists, the Holy Spirit will always be present giving guidance.

The poetic strains of Psalm 19:14 make an excellent prayer for both worship leaders and participants: *Let the words of my mouth and the meditation of my heart be acceptable to you, O LORD, my rock and my redeemer.*

Educate

Congregations often have been kept in the dark about what is expected to happen in worship. Parishioners automatically expect—or are automatically expected—to worship. By sharing in the new insights you have gained through study, teaching events, sermons, informal conversations, and by example in worship leadership, your congregation will begin to grow in their worship understanding and practices.

You will recall from my personal testimony shared in the preface of this study guide that I acknowledged my own poverty regarding worship despite a rich heritage within the church. While I do not seek to fault any worship leader from my youth or early adulthood, I am often amazed at my lack of understanding about worship, but even more amazed by the epiphany bringing my poverty into focus. It dawned upon me that I going through the motions where worship was concerned, not realizing the importance of my contribution as a worship leader—or worshiper. I saw how my understanding of worship was shallow, and my contribution to worship, although meaningful, was much less than my best effort. In the years intervening since my self-discovery, I've read of other worship leaders who share similar testimonies. I often wonder why this is so. My pondering leads me to believe that worship leaders must never *assume* congregations fully understand worship until we have engaged them in some ongoing education about worship. To neglect dialogue and teaching about worship, I fear, is to be remiss in an essential ministerial duty. As ministers of the gospel, we have a responsibility to help people understand worship and participate as fully as possible.

This book is designed primarily for group study for any number or composition of groups: worship leaders, worship leader and congregational groups, worship committees, boards of worship, and congregational members desiring to worship more effectively. I encourage you to consider your church's current assortment of educational and study groups: special topic groups, mission study groups, book study groups, Bible study groups, etc. Consider establishing worship study groups. These groups may meet for four weeks, eight weeks, or a quarter before they disband and the study is offered to a new group. Find a design that will fit your people's schedules and tolerances, but by all means, offer opportunities for small groups to make in-depth studies of worship.

Finally, be enthusiastic in your own attitude and participation in worship. Enthusiasm is contagious. Through these efforts you will raise the consciousness level of your congregation about worship and worship participation.

Be a Visionary

Ask yourself, *Where does God want to lead the congregation? What biblical themes need to find expression in the life of our church?* Consider including the church in your planning and vision by listing the Scripture reference and theme interpretation for the upcoming worship service in the church newsletter so worshipers may read and study the passage prior to Sunday's worship. Consider providing a sermon outline in the order of service, and encourage

. . . another key obstacle [to worship] is that churches often fail to teach people how to worship. "We'll teach people how to teach. We'll teach them how to sing. We'll teach them how to work with kids. We'll teach them about almost everything. But we don't teach them a worship concept. . . . We assume that people automatically can do it."

—DAVIS DUGGINS

The primary, essential ingredient is passion. If a liturgical leader does not communicate that she believes that what she is doing is important with all that she is—heart, body, soul and mind—others will also come to understand that worship is simply one more option among a host of others. Passion has to do with commitment.

—YME WOENSDREGT

note-taking and active listening. Consider linking worship themes and sermon topics to Scriptures being studied in the educational program.

Make creative use of the bulletin (i.e., order of service, worship folder, or program) for sharing your vision. Reserve bulletin space for printing and expanding the order of service. Publish the theme interpretation in your church newsletter the week before the corresponding service and again in the bulletin to give worshipers an opportunity to mentally prepare for worship. Consider the Sunday bulletin the *worship folder,* removing announcements from the bulletin to a weekly church newsletter or a removable bulletin insert. The bulletin will then become exclusively worship focused, drawing attention away from other concerns to worship. Announcements and other concerns of the church may be considered at another time. (See chapter 4 for an in-depth discussion of announcements.)

Plan

Use the planned approach to worship preparation. Worship is important enough to spend a good amount of your time and effort in planning it. Planning is our best effort in building worship services and can become another of our offerings to the Giver of Life. God's Voice can and does speak through purposeful worship planning. Both long-range and weekly short-term planning are crucial. Whatever your purpose or theme for the worship service is, you are more likely to succeed in accomplishing that purpose if it is well-planned rather than expecting worship to happen automatically.

Pastors, consider a private planning retreat to choose Scriptures, sermon topics, and themes for an upcoming quarter, trimester, or year. Then work closely with the minister of music to enable her or him to choose music to coordinate with the scriptural themes. When sermon and music go hand in hand, the congregation sees that a true concern for worship has taken place among its staff members.

After the pastor has shared the result of his/her planning, ministers of music can then consider the same retreat idea in planning the hymns, anthems, special music, and service music. It is advantageous if the minister of music will communicate the plans to the accompanists so that the efforts of all musicians are coordinated.

Another approach is to use the common lectionary as a guide for worship planning. The lectionary provides a systematic approach to Bible study as it relates in three-year cycles the biblical story of God's redemptive revelation. If the common lectionary is used as a guide for worship planning and educational study within the life of a congregation, everyone has the opportunity to be on the same page in studying, planning, leading, and participating in the cultic life of the congregation. The Scripture becomes the unifying link between education and worship, worship planning and participation, and private and public devotion, thereby immersing the church in and drawing her through the word.

Planning ahead gives more time for study and pondering, so plan ahead as far as possible. But be careful to stay in tune with week-to-week congregational and pastoral concerns, adjusting your plans to meet these needs. (See chapter 9 for a detailed discussion of planning and practical concerns.)

Use a Team Approach

Some pastors and staff or volunteers with major leadership responsibilities in worship enjoy a team approach to worship planning. The team approach to planning and leadership widens ownership, education, and commitment to worship. The quality of worship leadership exhibited on Sunday reflects the quality of planning behind the scenes. An effective team approach needs trained and dedicated team members, requires trust and respect, shares responsibility, power, and control, and provides planners and leaders with a lot of creative space. These elements lend themselves to the enhancement of worship vitality and renewal.

Paul Westermeyer, in *The Church Musician*, writes about the necessitous team approach to worship planning and leadership by the pastor and minister of music. This insightful author recognizes and discusses the different perspectives held by pastors and music ministers due largely to the differences in their training. Because of divergence in their individual and professional perspectives, a large potential for conflict exists as well as an equally large need for planning and communication between the two in order to avoid what Westermeyer calls the "schizoid condition of much American worship."[1] Westermeyer goes on to explain that both pastor and musician are essential because worship does not happen without leaders. Perhaps in his most convicting statement of the entire text, Westermeyer asserts, "If they lead well and work together, a powerful partnership for the people results. If they do not work together, we have a wicked waste."[2]

Explore the wisdom in a team approach to worship planning and leadership. Try it and stick with it even during times of discouragement. I believe your efforts will make a remarkable difference that your congregation will notice.

Some congregations in recent years have organized worship committees to aid the worship planning process. See chapter 10, "A Team Approach to Planning," for a discussion about worship planning teams, worship committees, and special interest groups.

Emphasize

Pastors, emphasize worship through your preaching. Ministers of music, emphasize worship through music. How? Organize both the spoken and sung messages around a central scriptural theme. Beautifully sculptured services take form from meaningful themes.

If you do not use the common lectionary as a guide, consider sermon series on biblical books, biblical characters, or acts of worship such as praise, prayer, offering, word, and table. Another idea is to follow the Christian year as you plan worship that emphasizes the unfolding biblical story: Advent, Christmas, Epiphany, Lent, Palm Sunday, Holy Week, Maundy Thursday, Good Friday, Easter, Ascension Day, Pentecost, Trinity Sunday, Reformation Sunday, and All Saints' Day.

Pastor Wayne Price, in his book *The Church and the Rites of Passage*, 1989, suggests building services of celebration around life experiences and rites of passage: birth, baptism, graduation, marriage, retirement, and death, as well as transitions in marriage, residence, and career.[3]

Ministers of music can emphasize worship and enhance the congregation's worship experience by helping congregations sing hymns more effectively. Enjoyable, positive learning experiences in this genre may be provided through informal hymn rehearsals. These mini-rehearsals may be scheduled following a fellowship supper, during a Sunday school opening assembly, or during worship preparation time preceding worship. Periodic hymn services organized around a particular topic or theme are not only excellent ways to emphasize hymnody, but provide exceptional worship opportunities. Ministers of music might be wise to consider teaching special seminars or church training classes about selected great hymns of the faith. And certainly, ministers of music who understand and employ meaningful hymn introductions and thoughtful hymn usage in every worship service do much to enhance the congregation's appreciation for and participation in hymn singing.

Endless possibilities exist for creative worship planners. The spark of creativity ignites worship renewal.

Enable

Enable your congregation fully to understand the symbols of worship. As new members join, as people are converted, as children mature and gain adult understandings, the often taken-for-granted symbols of our faith need to be explained again, demonstrated in new ways, and reinvested with fresh meaning. Consider all five human senses—sight, hearing, touch, taste, and smell—as you think of ways to explain and demonstrate the symbols of faith and practice. Explore creative and thoughtful use of the biblical symbols of bread, wine, cross, water, lamb, palm, incense, seeds, fire, wind, light, salt, blood, and church, among others.

The presider [worship leader, minister, liturgist] does not do everything in worship. Rather, the presider functions to unify the assembly as it engages in its own task of worshipping God. The presider enables and facilitates the worship of the one, common Body of Christ. In doing so, the presider calls forth the gifts of other members of the worshipping community.

—YME WOENSDREGT

If we emphasize soul competency and the priesthood of all believers, then we must take seriously worshiper responsibility in worship. As worship leaders, our responsibility enjoins us to enable all who worship—both staff ministers and lay ministers—to worship God in spirit and truth.

At the risk of sounding repetitive, consider the following efforts to enable your congregation to worship more effectively:

1. Use the lectionary passages as a guide for selecting worship themes, choosing Scripture passages for inclusion in worship, and the centralizing force behind all worship planning.

2. Publish lectionary references in a church newsletter so that the congregation may read and study the passages prior to Sunday's worship either through individual study or through family devotional events.

3. Use the lectionary passages in the educational program of the church so that the congregation may study and discuss the passages in small groups prior to worship.

4. Conduct a minister-led Bible study with interested congregational members using Sunday's focal passage during the week preceding worship. Allow

the study group's discussion to influence and broaden worship planning and leadership.

5. Publish hymn numbers, titles, and tune names in the church newsletter so members can sing or read the hymn texts during the week prior to worship. A prerequisite to the effectiveness of this practice, of course, would be for every family of the church to own a personal copy of the hymnal.

The single most important thing we can do to change our experience of public worship is to revitalize our practice of personal worship.

—Marjorie J. Thompson

6. Encourage personal devotion and worship by church members and member families. Offer training seminars on how to develop personal and family devotional practice.

Marjorie J. Thompson, in her book *Soul Feast: An Invitation to the Christian Spiritual Life*, offers worshipers this admonition: "When we begin to steep ourselves in scripture on a regular basis, we hear the Sunday scripture readings differently. Our own daily prayer becomes tilled soil for receiving the seed of God's Word in the liturgy."[4]

Train

Train people to worship by training them to pray, read, testify, sing, and dramatize. Conduct church training classes on a wide array of subjects such as how to pray publicly, the different types of prayers and their purposes, public speaking, banner making, dramatic reading, interpretive movement, liturgical dance, and worship planning. Just as choristers and soloists rehearse

There are three ingredients that must be present in making healthy changes. First, you have to love the people, genuinely be on their side. Second, what you propose has to make sense. Something totally "off the wall" and foreign to a given tradition is not likely to be supported—and probably should not be. Third, you have to make sure that the people understand what you are doing. If those three elements are present, almost anything is possible.

—Paul Westermeyer

musical offerings, laypeople and ministers alike need to rehearse for their roles in worship leadership and participation.

Augment
Change for the sake of change is not especially good, but change for the sake of freshness and vitality is essential. Begin where the people are and augment with sensitivity and care, understanding that creative placement of already familiar forms can add freshness. Add to your worship creative, positive, and thought-provoking experiences.

Evaluate
Finally, constantly evaluate and re-create. This is an ongoing process, not a one-time event. Effective evaluation will allow room for success and failure, and there's always room for additional evaluation.

In a 1990 conference on renewing worship, Thomas Troeger, hymnist and theologian, and Carol Doran, professor of church music, shared the following list of questions to ask and ponder when considering your worship practice.[5] As I have returned again and again to this list in my own study and worship, I relay their questions to you as guides for renewing worship within your congregation.

When Considering Your Worship Ask:
1. What is the nature of our worship?
2. What does our denominational tradition require?
3. What is actually possible?
4. What will edify the congregation?
5. What have we been doing?
6. Do these actions glorify the Giver of Life or the individual presenting them?
7. In what ways do our current worship services balance form and freedom?
8. In what ways would you like to improve the balance of form and freedom?
9. What gifts and aspects does our worship strongly employ?
10. What gifts and aspects does our worship strongly neglect?
11. Does this service add up to an expression of our theology?
12. List all forms of artistic expression currently being used in your worship. What is not working as well as you would like? What would you add or subtract?

> *"I like it" or "I don't like it" are not helpful expressions in evaluating worship . . . . Each of us must take responsibility for our response or suggestion; we must be honest about how we feel and always include some analysis as to why we feel a certain way: I feel this way because. . . .*
>
> —Carol Doran and Thomas H. Troeger

13. When considering materials in worship, hold up the gospel standard. How does each selection measure up?
14. Do the selections reflect the "mind" of the church? How?

In addition to the questions shared by Doran and Troeger, I have developed a critique standard of my own that has been useful in evaluating worship. Organized around five areas, the standard is little more than an inventory of questions and considerations. Feel free to add your own questions to those set forth below.

Arrangement and Presentation of Worship Folder
1. Is the order of service neat?
2. Are there any misspelled words or typographical errors?
3. Does the spacing allow for easy reading?
4. Is the language artistic and creative?
5. Is the order easy to follow?
6. Are the expectations clear?
7. Is the information complete, adequate, and accurate?
8. Who is doing what? Are worship leaders identified by name and title?
9. Who are the music composers/arrangers?
10. What are the hymn titles and tune names?
11. Are there section captions grouping and clarifying what is happening?
12. Is a consistent parallel structure followed in the presentation of names, titles, and captions?
13. Are the church name and the date of the service listed at some point in the worship folder?
14. If I am a visitor, will I know what's going on? Does the worship folder help or hinder my participation in the service?
15. Are large print editions available to those with this need?

Rhythm of Worship

1. Does the service flow?
2. Are there disruptions or breaks in the flow?
3. Is there a logical progression of events or actions?
4. Consider interpolations and transitions between components or sections of the service. How are these handled? Evaluate transitions in terms of language, fluidity, effectiveness, thoughtfulness, and relation to the current worship theme.
5. Are there recognizable patterns in your church's worship?
6. Considering proportion, is any aspect of worship overdone, omitted, too long, or too brief?
7. Is there an overall theme? Is it biblical? Is it obvious? Is it clear? How was it developed?
8. Are there common threads weaving the service together?
9. Is there a balance in form and freedom?
10. Is there evidence of planning and coordination among worship leaders?

Strengths and Weaknesses

List the strengths and weaknesses of the overall service. What did you discover?

Other Important Concerns

1. Is the congregation actively involved? How?
2. Is variety within the order?

Long-term Considerations

Compare orders of worship over a period of six weeks, asking these questions:

1. Surprised? Bored?
2. Is the same format used weekly? Why? How often does it change and to what degree?
3. If the same format is used routinely, what about the service changes from week to week?
4. Is there variety in style, content, and character?

Worship renewal need not be a puzzling experience, but it does suggest a process of growth and maturation for you and your congregation. The process of worship reform is complex and cyclical. For the purposes of discussion and clarification, I have isolated strings woven into the reform process. Yet, in reality, the strings cannot really be isolated, for one string pulls another: prioritizing affects emphasis; educating, enabling, and training are interconnected; vision shapes emphasis; training undergirds enabling; and so forth. As a worship leader, I admonish you to always examine your motives and your actions in the ongoing process of evaluation.

Integrity involves the heart's motives as well as the mind's thought, and whoever would end up with a more truthful understanding of worship must muster as much honesty as he [or she] can in the attitudes he [or she] brings to reflection upon worship.

—PAUL WAITMAN HOON

Questions to Ponder

1. As a part of your private devotional/study time or as a topic for group study, read and study one or more of the following minor prophets: Joel, Amos, Micah, Zephaniah, Haggai, or Malachi. List the worship abuses cited by each prophet studied, noting how he links worship to lifestyle. In what ways does the prophet call for reform? What are the implications for your worshiping congregation?

2. Begin building a worship resource file. What resources would you add to my list provided in "Read and Study"?

3. What study or focus groups exist within your church's program? Consider how a worship study group (or groups) could be added to this schedule.

4. Evaluate your personal participation in worship. What do you do when it's not your time to lead? Do you study your sermon notes during the anthem? Do you sing the hymns? Do you rehearse your next address to the congregation when someone else is speaking? Do you flip through your hymnal during the sermon? Do you allow your mind to wander aimlessly during worship? Do you participate in joint prayers, confessions, and readings? If you sit on the rostrum or in the chancel during worship, what does your posture say about your attitude of worship?

5. What biblical themes need to find expression in the life of your church?

6. What use does your church make of the Sunday bulletin? How does the church newsletter promote worship? How do these two instruments differ?

7. Study the existing worship planning process in your setting. Who plans the worship services of your congregation? How much time and emphasis is given to long-range planning? How much time and emphasis is given weekly to worship planning? In what ways would you like for it to be different?

8. What or who dictates the themes of your worship services? The pastor? The civic calendar? The liturgical calendar? The worship planning team? Scriptural themes? Does your worship seem to routinely lack any theme at all?

9. How is worship emphasized within your church? List the different ways. Is this emphasis adequate or inadequate? Why? What more might you do to emphasize worship?

10. What efforts have been made within the last year to enable the congregation to worship more effectively? What more needs to be done to continue the enabling process?

11. What attempts to train worshipers and worship leaders have been made in the life of your congregation within the past year? Are any of these ongoing? In what areas is additional training needed?

12. In what ways does your present order of worship change from week to week? How does it stay the same? In what areas is freshness needed?

13. In what ways is worship in your church evaluated? By whom is worship evaluated? How often?

14. Consider interviewing a cross-section of your congregation about their worship experience or polling your congregation regarding their worship experience with the use of a questionnaire. Incorporate any recent informal comments and criticisms of vocal parishioners regarding worship. What themes or recurring motifs are voiced, if any?

NOTES

[1] Paul Westermeyer, *The Church Musician* (San Francisco: Harper, 1988), 100-101.

[2] Ibid., 101.

[3] Wayne Price, *The Church and the Rites of Passage* (Nashville: Broadman Press, 1989).

[4] Marjorie J. Thompson, *Soul Feast: An Invitation to the Christian Spiritual Life* (Louisville: Westminster John Knox Press, 1995), 61.

[5] Carol Doran and Thomas H. Troeger, "Renewing Worship," opinion expressed in workshop presentation, Worship and Music Conference, Montreat NC, 24-30 June 1990.

CHAPTER 9

The Planning Process

In chapter 8, numerous ways for implementing worship reform were suggested, among them planning. This chapter will isolate the planning process, examining it more fully. Some practical concerns associated with planning and designing worship services will also be addressed.

Planning is our best effort in building worship services that exalt God. In fact, our planning can become another of our offerings to the Most High in worship. The Breath of God can and does work through purposeful worship planning. Both long-range and weekly short-term planning are crucial. If we plan to exalt the Holy One in a worship service, we are more likely to succeed than if we leave our purpose to chance or assumption.

Long- and Short-term Planning

Long-range planning allows consideration for seasonal emphases, observances of church ordinances, thoughtful selection and adequate learning of music, and a balance of worship themes during the year. Usually a good idea is to start with special calendar emphases, such as the liturgical year, holidays, special offerings, and carefully selected denominational emphases, if any. Still better is to allow the common lectionary of Scripture themes to be the focus of your long-range planning. Planned in three-year cycles, the common lectionary allows major portions of the biblical story to be told and retold in an organized, conceptual manner.

If we are to worship fully, with our whole selves, we must accumulate layers of knowledge about the stories that define us as the people of God.

—Bonnie Jean Lamberth

Used as a long-range planning tool, the common lectionary provides all worship leaders with a scriptural starting point for their individual planning responsibilities. No one must wait on the preacher to provide Scripture passages and topics months in advance. Typically, music must be planned months in advance of a given service to provide adequate time—for selection, ordering, cataloging, pre-rehearsal preparation by director and accompanists, six to eight or more weeks of choral rehearsal time—before presentation. Using the common lectionary as a planning guide, the minister of music is not dependent upon the preacher for texts and topics six months in advance. This tool can relieve pressure and possible tension for both of these important worship leaders.

Weekly or short-term planning, particularly between preacher, minister of music, and any other significant worship leaders, gives the worship leading team opportunity to fine-tune each worship service into a meaningful whole. During week-to-week planning, consideration may be given to timing, transitions within the service, last-minute additions and deletions of details, reminders to laypeople involved in leadership roles, sensitivity to congregational life, and joint prayer time for leaders.

Effective long-range planning builds on a God-given hope that is prayerful and powerful. In prayerful ways—open to God's power—the long-range planning committee genuinely prays, "What is God calling us to do—as [God's] people?"

—Kennon L. Callahan

Above all, week-to-week planning allows worship leaders the chance to see that each service points Godward and allows for the encountered God to reach inward to worshipers. Planning allows worship leaders to check and correct misdirected worship components that may be given undue emphasis, that bring attention only to themselves, or that fail to lead worshipers to an encounter with the Creator.

If you have found yourself opposed to planning for some reason, then consider how the no-planning approach is in itself *a plan not to plan.*

Planning ahead, in contrast, is an effort to allow the God of Wisdom to work through us as we actively engage our talents, our minds, our experiences, and our resources as God's instruments. Planning also gives worship leaders (committees, staffs, and other groups) the opportunity to work together as a team, complementing one another. God works in groups and committees too.

Planning Sheets

A helpful aid to organize your worship planning might be to create a loose-leaf notebook specifically designated for this purpose. Fill the notebook with worship planning sheets. Through the years, I have discovered and used a number of different worship planning or guide sheets, some preprinted with regular service components or the church's usual order of service. But I have found nothing works better for me than a simple sheet of ruled notebook paper.

Set up your planning notebook by labeling the date, time, and purpose of each worship service at the top of the individual sheets of notebook paper. Each worship service gets its own sheet of notebook paper. Include enough sheets for your long-range planning period: three months, six months, a year. Then insert these plan sheets into your notebook chronologically. On the sheets of paper, jot down notes concerning each of the services, leaving nothing to chance or memory. Notes could include any significant facts affecting the services: Scripture references, theme, study notes on the passage, sermon topic or outline, anthem, communion observance, organist away on vacation, presentation of new members, seasonal considerations, et cetera.

As thoughts and inspirations come, add these to the plan sheets. Do not trust yourself to leave inspirational thoughts and creative ideas to memory. In the rush of busy schedules, sometimes these can be lost forever if not jotted down at the point of inspiration. Then, one or two weeks ahead, begin to finalize the service details. This ongoing process of planning and organizing each service can begin weeks or months, even a year, in advance. Steep the process in prayer, keeping your planning open to God's leadership through the Holy Spirit. Where such willingness to God's leadership exists, the Holy Spirit always will be present giving guidance.

Resource Files

To aid further in the study and planning of worship, build a file of worship materials and resources from which to draw as you plan. A sampling from my own filing cabinets is listed in chapter 8, "Worship Reform—How?" Build a filing system that is helpful and logical to you. Always be on the lookout for good resource materials to add to your files. Use your research as a tool to enrich your leadership of God-centered worship. The materials you gather, along with the attitudes you develop, will not be ends unto themselves, but can represent continued education in developing an art—the art of building worship services that exalt the Holy One.

Creative Ideas

The following suggestions are simply that—suggestions. In offering them, I do not mean for them to be absolutes, nor do I mean churches are right to use them and wrong not to use them. Instead, I offer them as ways to organize and clarify the actions of worship when planning worship and designing the worship folder. It is my belief that well-communicated and well-presented information enhances the worship experience.

Section Headings. One way to organize an order of worship is with the use of section headings that group worship components into sections. For example, an order of worship may be organized fairly simply around such headings as Exaltation, Message, and Offering Our Gifts, adapted from a service of worship by a Presbyterian congregation in Charlotte, North Carolina:

Exaltation
- Hymns
- Choruses
- Anthem
- Solo
- Prayers

Message
- Scripture Readings
- Sermon

Offering Our Gifts
- Anthem
- Testimony
- Offering
- Prayer of Dedication

Another grouping of worship components might follow this simple outline used by an Evangelical Lutheran congregation in Roanoke, Virginia: *Gathering, Word, Meal,* and *Sending.*

The following section headings and components are adapted from a service of worship by a Baptist congregation in Tallahassee, Florida, whose worship theme for the day was *I am the good shepherd* from John 10:11. Section headings seem to outline Psalm 23:

> *God's Presence Sustains Us*
> > Prelude
> > Call to Worship
> > Invocation
>
> *God's Praise Feeds Our Spirits*
> > Hymn
> > Duet
> > Scripture Lesson
> > Prayers of the Church
> > The Lord's Prayer
>
> *God's Guidance Fosters Our Growth*
> > Hymn
> > Litany
>
> *God's Word Nourishes Our Souls*
> > Hymn
> > Solo
> > Sermon
>
> *God's Sacrifice Provides Our Salvation*
> > Hymn
> > Offering
>
> *God's Purpose Sustains Our Purpose*
> > Welcome and Church Program Emphasis
> > Commissioning
> > Benediction
> > Postlude

The following headings and order are adapted from a service of worship conducted by a Baptist church in Louisville, Kentucky:

Our Worship Through Praise
    Prelude
    Call to Worship
    Invocation
    Hymn
    Choral Praise
Our Worship Through Prayer
    Call to Prayer
    Personal Meditation
    Pastoral Prayer
Our Worship Through Giving
    Hymn
    Offertory Prayer
    Offering
    Doxology
Our Worship Through Proclamation
    Scripture Lesson
    Anthem
    Sermon
Our Worship Through Dedication
    Invitation to Christian Discipleship
    Hymn
    Benediction
    Postlude

Still other section heading progressions might resemble the following:

Uniting Our Hearts
    Prelude
    Call to Worship
    Hymn
    Invocation
    Welcome
Confessing Our Sin
    Meditation
    Pastoral Prayer
Praising Our God
    Anthem

        Hymn
   Presenting Our Gifts
        Anthem
        Offering
        Prayer of Dedication
   Receiving the Word
        Solo
        Sermon
   Committing Our Lives
        Hymn of Response
        Church Ministry Highlights
   Departing to Serve
        Benediction
        Postlude

The following order is adapted from a Presbyterian service of worship in Charlotte, North Carolina:

   Assemble in God's Name
        Carillon
        Preparation for Worship
        Call to Worship
   Give Praise to God
        Hymn
        Sacrament of Baptism
        Baptismal Hymn
   Ask God's Forgiveness
        Call to Confession
        Prayer of Confession
        Silence for Private Prayer
        Assurance of Forgiveness
        Response of Praise
   Listen for God's Word Read, Sung, and Proclaimed
        Responsorial Psalm (sung)
        New Testament Reading
        Sermon
        Hymn
        Prayers of God's People

        The Lord's Prayer
        Concerns of the Church
        Offering of Tithes and Gifts to God
        Anthem
        Doxology
        Prayer of Dedication
Go in God's Name
        Closing Hymn
        Benediction
        Postlude
        Carillon

Other creative ways of using section headings to organize worship components can be visualized by the following example of a communion service on the theme of "The Community of Faith (Fellowship/Community)."[1] In this case, section headings are actually phrases taken from Milburn Price's hymn text, "Believers All, We Bear the Name."[2] The hymn is used midway in the service, tying together the hymn's message, the worship theme, and section headings:

Believers All, We Bear the Name
        Prelude
        Call to Worship
        Responsive Scripture Reading
        Hymn Medley
        Invocation
Diverse in Gifts, But One in Christ, We Offer Outstretched Hands
        Offering
        Piano Praise
        Dedication of Gifts
        Hymn
As Christians in the World Today, We Hold Fast to the Word
        Pastoral Prayer
        Scripture
        Sermon
Believers All, In Unity We Follow God's Commands
        Scripture
        Anthem
        Sharing the Bread

        Sharing the Cup
Believers All, Our Common Task is Service in His Name
        Invitation
        Hymn of Commitment & Testimony
        Choral Benediction
        Postlude

A similar technique utilizes phrases from an anthem as section headings. The following example outlines a service of communion on the theme "Knowing God."[3] With the exception of the phrase, *Jesus was Known to Them in the Breaking of the Bread* from Luke 24:35, the headings are taken from an anthem used early in the service, "To Know Thee" by Hank Beebe:[4]

To Know Thee is at First to Know Thy Name
        Prelude
        Anthem: "To Know Thee" by Hank Beebe
        Invocation
        Hymn
        Praise Chorus
        Anthem
To Know Thee is to Know What I Should Pray
        Prayer of Confession
        Anthem
        Pastoral Prayer
        Silent Prayers of the People
To Know Thee is to Come to Know the Truth
        Hymn
        Prayer of Dedication
        Offering
Jesus was Known to Them in the Breaking of the Bread
        Scripture Lesson: Luke 24
        Observance of Communion
        Sermon
To Know Thee is to Finally Find My Way
        Invitation
        Hymn of Dedication
        Benediction
        Parting Hymn
        Postlude

Similarly, section headings might also be created from Scripture passages. In each case, the headings should be crafted in parallel structure and in some way capture the movement and flow of worship. Section headings are not a necessity. They are merely an option for creative worship planning that fosters worshiper comprehension and participation.

Creative Labels for Components. There is no need to be creatively cute or catchy with formatting or labels when designing a worship service. The following suggestions are, instead, offered as suggestions for naming worship components in creative and descriptive ways to enhance understanding of the component's real purpose in the worship event.

Instead of *Special Music*, you might say *Worship through Song, Solo Testimony, Testimony in Song, Testimony, Musical Worship, A Musical Offering, Message through Music*, or *Scripture* (if a Scripture passage is being sung).

Another way of phrasing *Silent Prayer* might be *Discipline of Silence, Silent Prayers of the People, The Prayers of the People, Silence, Silent Prayers and Confession, Conversing with God, Our Silent Prayers, Our Common Prayer.*

Consider labeling hymns as to their specific purpose also. Hymns carry a myriad of theological themes, come in varying forms, and can serve diverse functions in worship. Some hymns are actually prayers, others poems of praise, while others, because of their creedal content, are affirmations or testimonies. Each hymn should be carefully examined for its theological

TABLE 7: HYMN LABELS

Hymn Labels

Closing Hymn	Hymn of Invitation
Congregational Benediction	Hymn of Praise
Hymn of Assurance	Hymn of Preparation
Hymn of Benediction	Hymn of Response
Hymn of Blessing	Hymn of Thanksgiving
Hymn of Commitment	Invitation Hymn
Hymn of Confession	Offertory Hymn
Hymn of Consecration	Opening Hymn
Hymn of Decision	Parting Hymn
Hymn of Dedication	Processional Hymn
Hymn of God's Goodness	Recessional Hymn

message and form before being randomly plopped into a worship service. While it is not necessary or even desirable to label the purpose of every hymn, on occasion this may be desired. The following list, not meant to be exhaustive, shows some examples of the many purposes and uses of hymns in worship. [See table 7.] Can you think of others to add to this list?

Common Threads. Organizing a service of worship around a theme is one way of tying a service together into a meaningful whole. Allowing the Scripture to dictate the theme is probably the best argument in favor of using worship themes and the best way to employ them. Aside from openly stating a chosen theme—scriptural or otherwise—there are subtle ways of lacing together the various components of worship. One is to delicately and sensitively weave common threads through the service. In some cases, only the very astute and sensitive will notice. Here are some examples to explain the concept.

Following the presentation of the anthem, a sensitive pastor uses a phrase from the anthem in his/her pastoral prayer. A thoughtful minister of music borrows an appropriate line from the call to worship to introduce the next hymn. The title of the sermon comes from a phrase found in the hymn of decision that follows its delivery. In celebration of All Saint's Day, many lay leaders are enlisted to assist in worship leadership. The organist deliberately plays for the opening voluntary an arrangement of a hymn tune that will be sung later in the service by the congregation. A phrase from the choral introit is included in a litany read by the people. A certain word or motif appears several places in the service. The liturgist chooses language reminiscent of the worship theme in various transitional statements connecting service components.

Thoughtful, sensitive worship planners and leaders find ways to knit services of worship together by weaving common threads through the fabric of worship. Finding and using common threads in worship requires thoughtful planning and study of biblical texts.

Other Practical Concerns

Without a doubt, it is the Information Age. Data is available to consumers at every turn—through television, radio, newspapers, computers, the Internet, mass mailings, electronic billboards, and more. But when looking at some church bulletins or worship folders, it can be difficult to discern much more than a skeletal outline of the order of service. Depending upon your focus, a printed order of service may not be a requirement of worship, but a poor or tasteless one amounts to less than nothing at all. Sometimes the lack of information in the worship folder is simply a product of poor planning or laziness on the part of worship leaders. By all means, attempt worship on some occasions with no printed order of service at all, but when an order is provided, why not do it as well as possible?

Here are examples of things to consider when printing a worship folder. (See also chapter 8, "Worship Reform—How?" for a critique standard regarding the worship folder.)

Hymns. Hymns are referred to by *number*, not by *page*. For example, consider those hymns that span two pages in the hymnal. The hymn *numbered* 224 may actually reside on *pages 250 and 251*. Usually hymnal appendices are listed on pages with page numbers. Hymns, on the other hand, are found on pages with hymn *numbers*.

The hymns we sing are usually comprised of two parts: text and tune. Texts are usually referred to by their first-line titles and gospel songs are frequently known by chorus first-lines. Most worshipers know hymns by these text-related names. Tunes also have names. These tune names are frequently printed in ALL CAPITALS and are found in various locations on the hymn page. Frequently, hymn texts and tunes are composed by different people. Sometimes, however, the same person authors the poetry and composes the tune. Many times a tune is wed to more than one text. Likewise, texts may be sung to more than one tune in the same hymnbook. An excellent way to acknowledge both the text and tune names is to list both in the worship folder. This practice, indirectly at least, educates the congregation to the differences just mentioned, and over time, people will learn to call hymn tunes by their names. The following example from the *Hymnal of the Moravian Church*, 1969, illustrates a sample worship folder listing:[5]

| Hymn No. 184 | "The Lord's My Shepherd" | CRIMOND |
| Hymn No. ___ | "Hymn Title" | TUNE NAME |

In this example, the title of the hymn derives from the first line of the first stanza of the hymn text. The text is a version of Psalm 23 from the *Scottish Psalter* of 1650.

Sometimes an organist or pianist will play a hymn arrangement in a service of worship. On those cases, it is helpful to inform the congregation of what tune is being played and where they may find the text for meditative purposes. The following entries suggest a way to do this:

Category	"Title of Arrangement" (Text found at Hymn No. ____)	Arranger
Offertory	*Variations on DUNDEE* (Text found at Hymn No. 33)	Lambert

Anthems. When listing an anthem in the worship folder, it is appropriate to provide the anthem title plus information concerning the composer, arranger, or source. Several specific examples follow the generic one:

Anthem	*Anthem Title*	Composer or Composer/Arranger or Arranger or Source
Anthem	*Surely the Lord Is in This Place*	Mueller
Anthem	*Spirit, Now Live in Me*	Leech/Arr. Bock
Anthem	*Infant Holy, Infant Lowly*	Arr. John Rutter
Anthem	*Forth He Came at Easter*	Old French Folk Tune

Where space allows, full names of composers and arrangers may also be used. Information concerning the choir, soloist, or instrumentalist can easily be centered beneath the anthem or solo title for an attractive presentation. Consider the following examples: an anthem presented by an adult choir and two soloists, and an anthem presented by an ensemble with harp accompaniment:

| Anthem | *It Is a Precious Thing* Adult Choir David Fitzgerald, baritone Deborah Moore Clark, soprano | Peter/Arr. Dickinson |
| Anthem | *Angels' Carol* Adult Ensemble Beth Dechent, harp | John Rutter |

Listing anthem words in the worship folder may also be desired. This practice provides an immediate help to worshipers whose understanding of the text is enhanced by reading the words silently as the choir sings. In those cases when an anthem is sung in a foreign language, it is critical to understanding to print a translation of the lyrics. To reprint anthem words, however, copyright law requires permission must first be obtained from the publisher. Oftentimes, publishers will grant free permission to print anthem words in church bulletins, if permission is requested in advance, and if a simple phrase of credit follows the quoted text (for example, © *Copyright 1983 Music Publications, Inc. All rights reserved. Used by permission.*). Always write to the publisher in advance, ask permission to print texts, and follow their specific instructions.

Who Are the Worship Leaders? To visitors, it is especially helpful to list in the worship folder who is doing what. Many times, bulletins give no worship leader names or simply list *pastor* for the person who delivers the message. If your church expects no visitors or new members, and the congregation is small enough that everyone knows everyone else by name, failing to list worship leaders in the worship folder might carry little negative consequence. However, listing leader names in the worship folder is a simple matter that provides worshipers with information and offers the church a historical record should this information ever become needed. The following sample entries illustrate a simple way to provide data on who's who:

Sermon	*Sermon Title*	The Rev. Mr. Richard Moore, Pastor
Invocation		Mrs. Nancy J. Teague

Other means could be employed to share leadership information. A section of the worship folder located at the end of the order of worship might be reserved for listing worship leaders and their roles.

Yes, Neatness Counts. When I was in grade school, certain projects, like reports or term papers, often included points for spelling and neatness. Students would frequently argue with teachers who took off points for sloppy work: "But the information is correct. I did the report, so why does it have to be neat?" We are long past the days of receiving numeric grades for our efforts, but you and I both know we are graded daily on the impressions we make, the things we say and do, and the type of work we produce. Yes, it does pay to be neat. Presentation is important. The business world accepts this concept readily, asserting *clothes make the person*. So how does this principle apply to worship? When it comes to worship leadership, the only thing worse than no leadership is sloppy leadership. When it comes to a worship folder, perhaps the only thing worse than no folder at all—when one is needed—is a messy worship folder. Consider the following checklist when evaluating the attractiveness—and effectiveness—of your church's worship folder. Feel free to add other considerations to the checklist:

- typographical errors
- misspelled words
- parallel structure[6]
- spacing
- print size
- readability
- overall appearance

These and other arrangement and presentation considerations are also taken up in chapter 8, "Worship Reform—How?"

Besides the items discussed in this section, what other practical concerns can you think of that deserve attention when planning worship? Make a list of these and discuss them with your study group.

Questions to Ponder

1. Discuss the pros and cons of planning. Discuss the pros and cons of not planning.

2. Discuss the pros and cons of planning, organizing, and writing out in advance public prayers. What other worship components might benefit from being planned in advance?

3. With bulletins from several Sundays in hand, evaluate the effectiveness and attractiveness of your church's worship folder based upon the information suggested in this chapter.

4. What advantages might come from producing and using a professional-looking, attractive worship folder for services in your church?

5. Try this role-playing exercise: Pretend you are a visitor worshiping with your congregation for the first time. Taking nothing for granted, what information in the worship folder would facilitate your worship experience? What was unclear? What else do you need to know?

NOTES

[1] Deborah Moore Clark, "A Service of Communion: The Community of Faith (Fellowship/Community)," *Church Administration* 35/12 (1993): 33.

[2] Milburn Price, "Believers All, We Bear the Name," *The Baptist Hymnal* (Nashville: Convention Press, 1991), 399. The hymn is set to the tune EDGE, also by Milburn Price.

[3] Clark, "A Service of Communion: Knowing [God]," *Church Administration* 35/4 (1993) 39.

[4] Hank Beebe, "To Know Thee," no. JH504, High Street Music, 1989.

[5] Scottish Psalter, "The Lord's My Shepherd," *Hymnal and Liturgies of the Moravian Church* (Elk Grove IL: Walter M. Carqueville, 1969), no. 184. The hymn is set to the tune CRIMOND, melody by Jessie Seymour Irvine, arranged by David Grant.

[6] Parallel structure refers to consistency, uniformity, and agreement of the parts of speech within the construction of sentences, paragraphs, outlines, lists, and so forth. Parallel structure includes, but is not limited to, subject-verb agreement within sentences and tense agreement within sentences and paragraphs. More specific to our topic, the term applies to consistency within a series of captions in a worship folder. For instance, an order of service containing *The* Prelude, *A* Call to worship, and *Hymn* Number 3 would lack parallel structure; whereas, an order of worship using consistently formatted captions such as Prelude, Call to Worship, Hymn Number 3, or *The* Prelude, *The* Call to Worship, *The* Hymn Numbered 3, and so forth, would exhibit parallel structure.

CHAPTER 10

A Team Approach to Planning

Two models illustrating team approaches to worship planning will be examined in this chapter. To be sure, these models do not represent the only ways for teams or groups of people to plan effective worship services, but they do illustrate viable, workable, and effective models, worthy of consideration. Each is very different from the other. The Myers Park model is a church staff worship leadership model, whereas the Oakhurst model is congregational, utilizing worship planning teams of laypeople. No doubt, other excellent models exist beyond these. But insofar as my experience is concerned, I have found these two to be, at once, exceptional and outstanding.

The Myers Park Model

At Myers Park Baptist Church in Charlotte, North Carolina, worship is planned around Scripture selections that follow the Revised Common Lectionary. Most of the Bible study classes within the educational curriculum of the church also follow the lectionary. This practice allows the majority of church members engaged in Bible study to have read and studied Sunday's focal Scripture passage prior to Sunday's worship.[1]

Months in advance of a given service, using the Revised Common Lectionary and various lectionary worship planning workbooks, Minister of Music Noël C. Lovelace begins to select choral pieces that will tie into the lectionary selections. Many of these are reviewed and rehearsed at the annual Labor Day choir retreat.

Each Monday, the entire ministerial staff of eight comes together for enrichment and Bible study. The preacher of the week for the following

Sunday chooses the focal Scripture from the lectionary selections, which the staff then studies by reading, acting out, drawing, and/or discussing.[2] The group explores the meanings of the text in their lives. William L. Dols, Jr., Minister of Education for the church and also editor of *The Bible Workbench* materials used in the weekly study, relates that the Bible study "process is a rich, feeding time for the staff." He attests to the bonding quality of the joint study, saying, "I feel closest to the staff during this time. In this setting, we seem most open to personal sharing."

As a result of their joint study, broad lessons often emerge from the biblical text. But because the study and revelation process is not managed too tightly nor over-controlled, Dols testifies that often the staff members leave the Bible study "with some direction, but no theme for Sunday's worship."

According to Dols, the Myers Park Bible study and worship planning process "asks the preacher not to write the sermon before the Bible study." Dols preaches frequently at Myers Park. Joseph D. Aldrich, Minister of Congregational Care, also preaches occasionally. Joe underscores this thought by asserting, "You can't come to Bible study with preconceived ideas, trying to force something in that's not there. The text is primary in the process."

Immediately following the staff Bible study, three members linger to continue the worship planning process: the preacher, the minister of music, and the liturgist. (The roles of preacher and liturgist alternate among the ministerial staff from week to week.) At this time, these three worship leaders divide and assign worship responsibilities, parceling out various leadership roles among themselves, such as who will lead the call to worship, the prayer of confession, the affirmation of faith, and so forth. Then, these main figures go their separate ways, each working on their respective assignments, choosing or writing liturgy for inclusion in Sunday's worship.

Typically, the preacher of the week (the senior minister or an associate) engages the congregation through the call to worship, which sets the stage for the entire service. He or she also reads the Scripture, delivers the sermon, and offers the closing blessing in worship. The liturgist leads all other portions of the service except the music, which is led by various music leaders: minister of music, organist, choir, vocalists, instrumentalists, and music associates. Sometimes the prayers are split between the preacher and the liturgist. At other times, they are combined and led by either the liturgist or the preacher for the day.

The minister of music selects hymns to fit the biblical theme and the rise and fall of the rhythm of worship.[3] As hymns, hymn responses, and the flow of worship are considered, Lovelace also considers key relationships between the pieces of worship music that will be used. When choosing the hymn that follows the sermon, Lovelace tries to select a hymn encapsulating the message of the homily.

On Wednesday, the worship leaders for the week meet together for a second time. In this meeting, the three leaders share their respective contributions to the planning process, time the service, and adjust any or all parts of the service as needed.

When interviewing Lovelace, Dols, and Aldrich about the Myers Park Bible study/worship planning process, I asked the following questions. Their responses follow.

What problems can occur using this Bible study/worship planning process? Aldrich shared, "If one of the worship leaders comes to the process with pre-set ideas, we're in trouble. If the preacher has exactly in mind what he or she wants to preach, or if the minister of music has chosen a certain anthem and rehearsed it for eight weeks, but it doesn't fit what emerges from the Bible study, things can get out of sync. We all must come into the Bible study open for the process to work."

What changes do you foresee making to the process? Dols responded by sharing that plans are underway to add a phase of yearly long-range planning into the process. "Yearly planning will allow us to calendar special days, choose which lectionary texts and themes will be used, and consider how we might follow some special themes during the seasons of Lent and Advent, for example." Dols added, "This type of yearly planning will also give some guidance to the long-range planning required of the minister of music."

The staff is also studying, according to Aldrich, how to involve laypeople in worship leadership: "Giving lay persons responsibility in worship leadership is not a frequent practice at Myers Park. We are trying to figure out a way to train a core of lay leaders who might rotate leadership responsibilities over a period of time. We have not yet decided on the best approach at this time, however."

What is the best thing that occurs from this study/planning process? Dols responded eagerly that "Worship becomes the mid-wife which delivers the text. The whole worship service—not any one portion—enlivens the text and biblical story. Sometimes multiple themes emerge for the congregation. Worshipers often leave the service remarking what the service meant to them—how it moved them, what significance it had, the conclusions they drew—but each of the shared perspectives may be radically different. In those times, we [the leaders] are warmed by the knowledge worshipers have engaged the biblical story. It is then the story becomes a transformational event in the lives of those who have encountered it."

As a frequent worshiper in the Myers Park congregation, I expressed to Noël Lovelace how impressed I am from my congregational perspective with how the various parts of the services thoughtfully transition and connect. Not only do the various musical components relate thematically, but calls to worship, prayers, confessions, sermons, affirmations, and blessings also integrate effectively, drawing on common threads. Beyond this, however, the transitional statements—the connective language and spoken interpolations between worship components—also seem to mesh meaningfully in theme, tone, or language. After sharing these observations, I posed the following question:

Does any one person control or coordinate the worship planning behind the scenes? To my question Lovelace replied a resounding, "No." He continued by saying, " I am glad to learn the efforts of our coordinated worship planning—based upon Bible study—come across so well. No human force controls it."

The Oakhurst Model

The worship planning model of Oakhurst Baptist Church in Decatur, Georgia, is a classic plan for involving laypeople in worship planning and leadership, using the talents of multiple groups of people within a church community. Implemented by Pastor Lanny Peters, the Oakhurst model is based firmly upon three guiding principles:

1. The Priesthood of Believers
2. Free Church Tradition
3. Primacy of Scripture

The teaching of the priesthood of believers, which originates in Scripture, has been courageously developed through Christian history by reformers such as Martin Luther, John Calvin, Ulrich Swingli, and other Protestant leaders.[4] Walter B. Shurden in *The Doctrine of the Priesthood of Believers* has this to say about the doctrine's biblical roots:

> The doctrine of the priesthood of believers is about curtains coming down. "Jesus cried again with a loud voice and yielded up

his spirit. And behold, the curtain of the temple was torn in two, from top to bottom . . ." (Matt 27:50-51). The curtain was one, but symbolized in the curtain and the Jewish Temple were many separations: people from God, laity from clergy, females from males, Gentiles from Jews, and secular from sacred.[5]

For those like Oakhurst and myself who espouse this liberating belief, each believer and each worshiper functions as a priest or minister, responsible and accountable directly to God. Some refer to this teaching as *soul competency.*

Those churches considered within free-church traditions have typically been Baptists, Methodists, Presbyterians, Moravians, and Churches of Christ, to name a few. The Oakhurst model, without doubt, falls into this free-church category. Peters explained that "Oakhurst is free to make use of the rich heritage of the church in planning worship. We may draw from other traditions for prayers, hymns, and so forth. We have the freedom to wear robes or not to wear robes. We have the freedom to use an ancient confession of faith or write our own or not have a corporate confession at all."

Roman Catholics, Episcopalians, Lutherans, Anglicans, and the Reformed churches that have typically followed set liturgies are not generally considered to be free-church denominations. Current discussion and practice seems to suggest, however, that a new attitude favoring exploration and creativity in worship planning, leadership, and liturgy is occurring within some of these well-established liturgical traditions, opening them to new freedoms in worship not present a generation or two ago.

The third principle guiding worship at Oakhurst is the primacy of Scripture. Peters explained, "The Bible is the ground of our faith and thus the beginning place for worship. That's why we generally use the common lectionary to plan worship at Oakhurst. It helps me avoid preaching on only my favorite texts. But it does not mean we cannot depart from the lectionary as we need to. The lectionary provides a beginning place, a disciplined way to approach Scripture, and a way to allow the Scriptures to form the worship services."

The structure of governance at Oakhurst provides for a standing Worship and Music Committee. This committee functions as an umbrella group, giving feedback and evaluation to staff planning, conducting special projects (like choosing and purchasing new hymnals or making banners), overseeing policy, and being responsible for various worship maintenance matters such as maintaining the sound system, banners, and any other physical properties pertaining to worship. Apart from this standing committee, however, a number of special teams are frequently at work within the Oakhurst church community. These special planning teams, working closely with the pastor and minister of music, "meet to discuss the upcoming lectionary readings and help decide on the themes and format of the services. Any church member who is willing may volunteer for one of these worship planning teams," said Peters.

According to Peters, all worship teams are Bible study groups *first*. Using the common lectionary as a coordinating tool for choosing Scripture around which worship is ultimately planned, each team begins by struggling with the biblical text, asking, how does this text shape worship? Peters testified that "we spend a good amount of time here [in Bible study] *before* planning the order of worship." In this way, the Oakhurst model closely resembles the Myers Park model already presented.

Peters continued by saying, "For the most part, the church follows a three-year calendar of Scripture readings known as a lectionary, which is designed for people to hear a wide variety of Bible passages. It also corresponds to the major festivals of the Christian church year: Advent, Christmas, Epiphany, Lent, Holy Week, Easter, and Pentecost. Occasionally the church diverges from the lectionary to celebrate other events such as Reformation Sunday, Peace Sunday, World Communion Sunday, and Great Day! [a unique occasion at Oakhurst, observed at least twice a year with a special service introducing and welcoming new members, followed by a luncheon in their honor]. Nevertheless, the themes of a service emerge as the Scriptures for the week are read and contemplated."

A good deal of flexibility is built into the process at Oakhurst, so it is somewhat difficult to describe in exact terms how the Oakhurst system functions. Every worship team at Oakhurst is different from every other worship team. Typically, however, teams fall into two categories: seasonal and ad hoc teams.

Seasonal worship teams form to study and plan worship around seasonal emphases such as Advent, Epiphany, Lent, or Easter. An Advent worship team, for example, may form in October and meet through December before completing its work and disbanding.

Ad hoc worship teams are composed of various groups within the congregation. Each group is different, and while some ad hoc teams may be formed from among special groups—like deacons, disabled people, the church's prison ministry team, ethnic groups within the congregation, or women, for example—others are simply eclectic groupings of laypeople with varied talents. At times, the church staff may work alone without lay involvement, forming their own ad hoc worship team. Peters related that "we usually have two or three groups going at one time. But even this schedule changes. From time to time we take breaks. We do not have teams for every season of the year." The ideal group, according to Peters, is comprised of three to five people who commit themselves to one to four study and planning sessions.

Another standing committee called Gift Seekers figures into the Oakhurst creative worship model.[6] This committee—appointed by the congregation to discern the gifts and talents of congregational members—supports Oakhurst's revolving, creative worship process by discovering and recruiting helpers who possess various talents and abilities—bakers, banner makers, poets, artists, and so forth. Once discovered, laypeople are encouraged to use their gifts on future ad hoc worship teams. Artists and creative people work on bulletin cover designs. Someone on every team is enlisted who is sensitive to the needs of children in worship. At Advent, the church has been known to ask different types of families to light the Advent candles in worship: a foster family, a single-parent family, a racially-integrated family, a two-mother family, a group of disabled adults from a local home for the disabled, and the pastor and his family. Conceivably, every kind of family configuration represented within the Oakhurst community may be invited at one time or another by the pastor or worship team to light the Advent candles.

The Gift Seeker Committee is just one way Oakhurst commits itself to discovering people's gifts. From a survey of the congregation, information concerning the gifts, talents, and interests of the Oakhurst membership is stored in a computer program.[7] Peters said, "When involving people in worship planning we want to look first at people's gifts, considering what they do well."

Occasionally, Oakhurst forms Response Groups of ten people each. These groups serve for either a month or a season, offering valuable feedback to the pastor and the worship team regarding worship. Response groups share their insights by answering questionnaires prepared by the pastor and worship teams. The response groups—and anyone worshiping within the congregation—may share their responses to the various worship experiences by writing letters to the Worship and Music Committee, the pastor, or the worship teams.

In interviews with Peters about Oakhurst's worship planning process, the following questions were raised. His responses follow.

Why do you use this particular worship planning process? Peters replied that the process offers a richness and diversity that one person cannot give. The more people are involved in worship planning, the more they are able to appreciate the process. "Our process gives people a chance to be in the kitchen, not just the dining room." Feeling worship is too often dominated by clergy, Peters continued, "At Oakhurst, we believe worship should involve the whole person—head and heart, thoughts and emotions—and provide opportunities both to receive care and to offer one's gifts and abilities for service." The Oakhurst process, based firmly upon belief in the priesthood of all believers, allows laypeople to exercise their responsibility as priests to one another, works as an excellent teaching technique about worship, and helps people build relationships as they work together.

How do staff members relate to the various worship teams? The pastor coordinates worship on a week-to-week basis working with the various special teams. At times, coordinating leadership is delegated to other staff members as well. Anthems and major musical works are routinely chosen by the minister of music. Organ music is selected by the organist. Since Oakhurst follows the lectionary or some general theme for all its worship services, the minister of music is freed to plan music months in advance. Hymns are chosen by various people—the teams, the pastor, or the minister of music, each working in dialogue with the others. Ideally, the hymns, like the anthems, are chosen weeks in advance. Teams may suggest that an oboist or guitarist render a certain piece of music for a service. Sometimes sermons are based upon anthems or major musical works. "At Oakhurst, worship planning is initiated at a lot of different places by a lot of different people," said Peters. "There's a lot of back and forth in the process."

In sum, said Peters, "The system requires a flexible staff, a high level of trust, and people who share similar goals who are committed to diversity."

Who is in charge on Sunday morning? Peters admitted this is a frequently asked question before forming his reply: "For people who are used to one person leading worship every Sunday, Oakhurst's 'cast of thousands' approach may seem confusing. Actually, we at Oakhurst believe every member of the church is a minister of the church, and so worship is led by staff members (pastor, associate minister, minister of music, organist) and by laypeople. We have the same idea about serving the Lord's Supper. Both ordained clergy and laypersons are eligible to serve Communion, because we believe we are all called to be God's ministers."

What problems arise using this system of worship planning? Peters cited three problem areas: a lack of consistency in style, difficulty in controlling service length, and the fact that the staff and congregation must be people who are comfortable with conflict and work within groups. Peters attests to the fact that "we have failures sometimes—but more often, we produce something very powerful. While there are no absolutes using this plan, any risk we take is worth the reward. I would not do it any other way."

How could this approach to worship planning be improved? Peters admitted Oakhurst probably needs to be more committed and consistent about training those who lead in worship. "We offer periodic training classes," says Peters. "For example, one training class focused on how to read Scripture publicly. We need to offer more opportunities for training worship leaders."

What are the strengths of using this plan? Peters cited many:

1. The heavily-involved lay process is *very* Protestant in its practice of the priesthood of all believers.
2. Involvement in Bible study and worship planning makes better worshipers.
3. People get to go back into the kitchen to see for themselves how a service is put together.
4. The pastor, minister of music, and the congregation are all involved in worship planning together, sharing responsibility and accountability.
5. Ideas are affirmed. People are affirmed.
6. The process offers periodic training in music and worship leadership.
7. Because Oakhurst uses a mix of experienced and inexperienced people in the process, there are no prerequisites to becoming involved. Laypeople are educated to the planning process as they are involved.
8. Our children and youth grow up in an environment that allows them to fully participate in worship. They often suggest good ideas.
9. The strength of the worship experience at Oakhurst has a direct and positive impact upon missions. Our people are empowered by worship to do missions.

If you had the opportunity to initiate the process somewhere else, what would you do differently? "First," said Peters, "I would not move to a church that is not open to this process. I could never go back to old ways of doing worship planning." Peters warned against getting worship teams too large. "Ten people is too many on a worship team." The system requires a tremendous amount of coordinating and energy, so Peters advises pastors and staff teams to allow time for breaks when no teams are meeting.

What advice would you give to churches wanting to implement this process? To this final question, Peters replied simply, "Start small, one ad hoc group at a time."

Implications for Prayer Book and Confessional Traditions

Although the Myers Park and Oakhurst worship planning models are targeted at churches traditionally within free-church traditions, leaders within prayer book and confessional traditions may also find helpful insights and commonality within these models. This is particularly true since both models, although quite different in focus, use biblical passages from the Revised Common Lectionary as the foundation of their planning. Use of the Revised Common Lectionary (or Episcopal or Roman Catholic Lectionary) Scripture selections as the basis of worship planning is a practice securely grounded and deeply respected within the various prayer book traditions.

Troy Messenger, Director of Worship at Union Theological Seminary in New York, suggests a model for planning and leading worship that is equally applicable to churches within prayer book, confessional, and free-church traditions.[8] Using musical metaphors to frame his recommendations, Messenger describes worship planning as canon (repetition, form) and improvisation (difference, freedom). Canons are the recognizable patterns in worship, those things that stay the same, helping us find our place. Forming an essential framework or form for worship, the constancy of the canons—particularly within the prayer book traditions—grounds worshipers in the faith, rehearses the collective story, connects each generation of worshipers with those before, reenacts a common story, and gives depth to worship. The depth and breadth of this bulwark, however, can serve as a springboard for doing some things differently in worship. Consider first the metaphor of good jazz.

Worship is a lot like good jazz. This eclectic musical genre, although improvisational, follows a fairly basic formula.[9] First, the musical theme is played by the ensemble. Tempo, meter, and harmonic framework are established. Following the initial musical statement, musicians within the group are given opportunities to render their individualized expressions of the theme through what is known as the "solo" refrain. As the theme is passed around the group, it is changed and modified by the sensitivity and creativity of each musician who is bound by the limits of the jazz form—the tempo, the meter, the harmonic framework. After the improvisational refrains circuit the group, the entire band plays the "out" chorus, consisting of "ecstatic excursions of music within the harmonic framework of the composition."[10]

Using the jazz metaphor to describe worship, Messenger recommends a fourfold formula for improvising worship involving feedback, options, participation, and artistry.

Just as jazz artists are aware of each performer within the ensemble and the responses and interactions with the attending audience, worship leaders may rely upon feedback as a dimension of worship—through planning, through sensitivity to reactions between and among worshipers within the worship event, and through the prayers of the people. Discerning worship leaders will note the responses and reactions of worshipers: What are worshipers saying about worship? What are their complaints? In what do they find meaning? What do the faces of worshipers tell you? What reactions do you sense from worshipers? What are their prayer concerns? For whom and what do they pray?

The jazz formula allows musicians certain options. Soloists may play variations in counterpoint to the musical theme and choose from an assortment of chords that fit the given harmonic framework. Musicians playing background to soloists will play accompaniments in consonance to what is being created by the featured soloist. Worship leaders also have many available options. The incorporation of symbols and the arts into worship invites different expressions and interpretations by artists. Nontraditional worship spaces equipped with moveable chairs, altars, and vestments afford many configurations for seating, engaging, and moving congregations. Lutheran pastor Mark Graham attests to the latitude that exists through hymn selection, variations on the confession, changes to the presentation of the psalmody, and the availability of many new worship materials through various publication services and resource centers.[11]

The ensemble effort of jazz means each musician must participate. Worship is also an ensemble effort demanding participation. When congregations of individuals come together in worship, unique human combinations form worshiping communities. In worship we bring our whole selves—bodies, minds, voices, spirits, senses. And we come together collectively with our varied gifts. We speak in many languages—inclusive and exclusive, non-gendered and gendered, poetry and prose, articulate and simple, rehearsed and extemporaneous. Worship may be led by multiple leaders, male and female, young and old, laity and clergy alike. The more participatory worship becomes, the more improvisational it becomes.

Good jazz is played by skilled artists. Worship, too, involves artistry. In worship we testify to the work and creativity of God, we express God's creativity innate within us, and as we allow the Holy Spirit to work in and through us—changing and completing us—the artistic Spirit of God may create in us masterpieces on human canvas.

Messenger's model of canon and improvisation suggests ways to plan and lead worship with creativity while preserving worship's essential form and structure. The methods described in the Myers Park and Oakhurst models could easily implement the four tenets of Messenger's improvisational process: feedback, options, participation, and artistry.

Other Team Approaches

As a writer, I have had many opportunities to design and publish worship services meant to inspire and assist worship leaders in finding creative ideas for their weekly leadership task. In this capacity, I have often worked alone. And while creating worship services for publication brings me much pleasure, such services are created in a vacuum as I seldom see or hear of the results of my labor. Worship planning for a local church, however, rarely happens in a vacuum, unless a church is staffed by a sole staff member who plans and leads worship for a host of volunteers busy with other church functions and concerns. Or sometimes a pastor, overwhelmed with other responsibilities, defers the planning process to an interested minister of music who assumes the charge. Even in these situations where the planning is done primarily by one person, feedback from the congregation—in some form or another—usually occurs, giving even the most singular planning process a group dimension.

My interest in worship, coupled with my varied experiences as a church staff member, has taught me most worship planning is a team effort of some kind or another, sometimes functional, sometimes not. What follows are several additional ideas for intentional team approaches to worship planning.

Creative Think Tank. Minister of Music Tom Wideman in a 1992 publication of *Worship* offers the idea of the Creative Think Tank.[12] Comprised of laypeople who want to participate in creative thinking and who have specific gifts—such as music, drama, or visual arts, for example—the Creative

Think Tank at Wideman's church meets the first Saturday of every month for the purpose of giving laypeople hands-on experience in planning special worship features. The group aims to accomplish one or two different projects each month that might include an original dramatic reading, a multimedia presentation, a Christian art exhibit, or a special emphasis of some kind. Each Creative Think Tank seeks to involve at least one new person in each Think Tank and in each project. This goal, if realized, keeps the process fresh and, over time, involves more and more members of the congregation in this behind-the-scenes, creative planning effort. Wideman writes of the group, "We look two months in advance at the sermons and/or emphasis and then start 'dreaming.' After we come up with ideas, we begin 'fine tuning' and determining . . . what can be done realistically with the amount of time and resources available. Each person is assigned a project, and we begin."[13] Wideman writes that the Creative Think Tank meets several needs in the congregation he serves:

1. It is a ministry to people who want to use their gifts for God.
2. It is a resource for creative worship.
3. It is a tool that can allow for follow-through.
4. It is a tool for evaluating our effectiveness in helping people worship.[14]

Special Study Groups. Churches whose worship is routinely planned by staff may periodically offer the congregation opportunities for study about worship and experimentation with worship planning. This was the case at a church where I was once a member. During my tenure with this church, several opportunities for study about worship and worship planning were made available to the congregation. I will share two specific examples.

One Sunday school class engaged in a unit of study about worship. This thirteen-week endeavor culminated with the class designing a worship service for which they

Groups may be brought together to give input to the staff who plan worship, without expecting the lay group to work out the nuts and bolts of an order of worship. Some churches have an ongoing group for this purpose, open to anyone who wishes to participate. Others invite people to participate for a month or a season, then rotate the membership of the group, so that eventually everyone in the church will have had a turn.

—Leslie Withers

wrote some original liturgy pieces: a dramatic theme interpretation, call to worship, prayer of confession, and offertory prayer of dedication. Class members used these original components and provided leadership in the service.

A second group engaged in a weeklong study and discussion of worship through an adult Vacation Bible School class. The study group spent a large portion of their meeting time in dialogue, examining and discussing our church's regular worship practice and thinking thoughtfully and creatively about how our practice might be improved. The final night of the class the group—working with a Scripture text and sermon outline provided by the pastor—made practical suggestions for how the Scripture and theme of the message might be developed in a service of worship. These suggestions were shared with the pastor for use in worship planning.

Standing Worship Committee. In recent years, some congregations have put into place standing worship committees with various worship-related functions and responsibilities.[15] A quick survey of several churches from various denominations and cities revealed a number of functions a standing worship committee might perform.[16] A conglomeration of these responsibilities is provided below to lend ideas about possible responsibilities a standing worship committee might assume. In no way is the list meant to be exhaustive, nor is it meant to suggest that any one committee should assume all the responsibilities outlined. You will quickly note that some of the functions overlap, while others are quite distinct. The best advice I can give to a church wishing to form a standing worship committee is for the church first to determine its particular needs for such a committee, study the functions of other worship committees, and then decide for themselves what functions would best serve their particular congregation. Here are some possibilities:

Meeting Schedule
- Meet monthly to evaluate worship.
- Meet at least quarterly with the ministerial staff to provide feedback about the content, quality, variety, spontaneity, and relevance of the worship experiences.

Member Responsibility & Training
- Study worship's biblical basis and principles.

Advisory Functions
- Act as a liaison from the congregation to the staff on worship issues.
- Serve as an advisory body to the staff worship leadership.
- Be a sounding board for proposed changes in worship brought by the staff or other groups in the congregation.
- Encourage the laity to welcome and support alternative worship styles on a periodic basis.
- Provide guidance and insight from the lay perspective regarding worship.
- Increase lay member understanding of the intent of worship.
- Help the ministerial staff develop and implement a new approach to the revitalization of the church's spiritual life through the worship experience.

Physical Properties
- See that sanctuary appointments, worship resources, and supplies are provided and properly cared for.
- Supervise physical aspects of the worship service for proper atmosphere: flowers, banners, decorations, liturgical colors, etc.
- Supervise nature and quality of music in all services, including sound system, audiovisual recording, etc.

Human Resources
- Recruit and train worship assistants: lectors, ushers, communion assistants, acolytes, crucifers, altar guild ministers, etc.
- Supervise the distribution of bulletins and announcements at all worship services.
- Secure pulpit and worship leader supply when necessary.
- Find ways to integrate the various worship experiences and talents brought to the church by its members.

Lord's Supper & Baptismal Services
- Coordinate the administration of the sacraments (communion and baptism) including preparation and cleanup.
- Recommend to Session (ruling elders) which children, with parental approval, should be admitted to the Lord's Table.

Policy
- Determine and recommended policies and procedures for the use of the sanctuary and other places of worship within the church building.
- Approve all wedding music.

Special Projects & Events
- Plan and oversee annual Religious Arts Festival.
- Conduct periodic surveys to discover the congregation's evaluation of worship and their desires for its improvement.
- Develop with the ministerial staff some creative seasonal, familial, and/or age-grouped worship experiences.
- Plan or give input to special worship events: Hanging of the Green, Christmas Eve, Lord's Supper Services, etc.
- Investigate the possibility of establishing a music/arts/drama group that could periodically enhance the dynamism of the church's regular services of worship.

A worship committee may be formed in any number of ways—by appointments, hand-chosen participants, volunteers, elected representatives, and so forth. How your church forms a standing worship committee may depend upon the system of governance employed by your church. As the previous list suggests, standing worship committees may exist for many different reasons depending upon the needs of a given congregation. In any case, the underlying purpose of any worship committee is to help congregations understand and own their worship. Worship committees are not intended to serve as firing squads or as outlets for groups of cranky, dissatisfied people wishing to vent criticism and tear down the efforts of worship leaders. Conversely, worship committees should be staffed with people open to new understandings about worship through quality study and discussion. Gifted people willing to invest and share in the worship process and to claim ownership and responsibility for worship are needed to serve on worship committees. And finally, worship committees need to be led by worship leaders interested in relationships and feedback.

Congregational Dialogues. Following a meeting called for the specific purpose of dialogue about worship between the pastor and congregation, one wise pastor asked his congregation to turn in suggestions for a worship plan for a specific Sunday morning.[17] To further prepare his parishioners for the task, the pastor handed out copies of the text from which he planned to preach, the sermon title, and a projection of what the sermon would likely say. Then he suggested that individuals, families, or groups think through how worship could be done consistently with this theme, and appropriately for the whole congregation. The pastor then used the responses in planning worship for the following week. The process took about two weeks, starting with the congregational dialogue meeting and ending with the designated worship service.

Another approach undertaken by other congregations might be to distribute response forms to interested worshipers prior to the worship experience. Response forms might include questions to guide worshiper thinking, allowing them opportunities immediately *after the service* to respond to the various components of worship. Opportunities to evaluate the overall effectiveness and impact of the worship experience upon them personally might also be provided in such a questionnaire. Some sensitive pastors have been known to distribute response forms that request feedback specifically concerned with the sermon—its clarity, quality, impact, and delivery, to name a few. Care must be taken, however, in asking worshipers to fill out questionnaires and record responses *during* worship, as these exercises could easily interfere with their focus and concentration, adversely affecting their worship.

Possibilities for feedback and dialogue are virtually endless. Worship leaders need first to determine what feedback is important to them and how they will respond to it before offering their congregations productive and positive avenues for responding. It may be wise to realize, however, that feedback from the congregation regarding worship will always come, solicited or not. How it comes back to worship leaders may vary in its method, directness, and tone. Understanding this, it seems healthy and prudent for worship leaders to welcome and respond to open, direct, and honest responses so parishioners can feel heard and respected.

Questions to Ponder

1. Who plans worship in your church?

2. How are Scripture passages selected for inclusion in your church's worship?

3. Does worship in your setting revolve around a theme each week? If so, how is this theme selected? Is the theme biblical—stemming from a focal Scripture passage—or is the theme determined by some other method?

4. If yours is a prayer book tradition, how might the Myers Park and Oakhurst planning models be applicable in your setting?

5. If yours is a free-church tradition, how might Messenger's ideas of canon (repetition, form) and improvisation (difference, freedom) be applicable in your setting?

6. Who leads worship in your setting? How are these leaders chosen?

7. Who controls worship in your church setting? How do you know?

8. Consider the gifts of those you know within your congregation. Make a list of these individuals and their specific gifts.

9. Using your list of people and gifts, share your perceptions with your study group. Consider concrete ways to affirm the gifts of the people you have listed. During the next two weeks, follow up with appropriate affirmations of these people and their gifts.

10. How does a person volunteer to use his or her gifts in worship planning or leadership in your church setting?

11. As you consider how worship is done in your setting, how might you do it differently? As a group, list the promises and costs of doing worship differently.

12. What process for feedback about worship does your church currently employ?

NOTES

[1] The educational curriculum of Myers Park includes six weekday and Sunday Bible study groups that use *The Bible Workbench: A Resource for Living Our Story Through God's Story* as a study resource. Edited by Myers Park's Minister of Education, William L. Dols, Jr., *The Bible Workbench* offers an alternative Bible study that seeks to engage Revised Common Lectionary texts through imaginative and intuitive encounters and dialogue. *The Bible Workbench* is published by The Educational Center, 6357 Clayton Road, Saint Louis MO 63117.

In addition to this resource, the majority of graded Bible study classes from elementary through adult use curriculum materials produced by the United Church Board for Homeland Ministries/United Church Press, 700 Prospect Avenue East, Cleveland OH 44115-1100. These materials include *The Inviting Word*, which uses the Revised Common Lectionary as its biblical guide, and *Imaging the Word*, which is a supplementary source of traditional and contemporary images, music, stories, photography, poetry, drama, liturgies, and Bible commentary that assists in understanding Scripture. *The Inviting Word* is a comprehensive set of curriculum materials for all ages that seeks to connect education, worship, preaching, and service around common Bible Scriptures by encouraging its users to respond personally and uniquely to the biblical story.

Other special interest study classes at Myers Park use various other materials in keeping with the focus of their particular study.

[2] The staff of Myers Park Baptist uses *The Bible Workbench: A Resource for Living Our Story Through God's Story* as its Bible study guide.

[3] For a discussion and diagram of this rhythm, see James A. Berry, *In the Beauty of Holiness: The Worship of God at Myers Park Baptist Church, Charlotte, North Carolina* (Charlotte: Myers Park Baptist Church, 1986).

[4] Walter B. Shurden, *The Doctrine of the Priesthood of Believers* (Nashville: Convention Press, 1987), 9-23.

[5] Ibid., 6.

[6] Once this standing committee achieved its goals, the Gift Seeker Committee at Oakhurst was dissolved as a standing committee. Its function—discovering the gifts, talents, and interests of the congregation—was subsequently absorbed by the standing Worship and Music Committee.

[7] Ideally, a congregational survey should be updated every three to four years. Asking each new member to complete a gift and interest profile at the time of his or her orientation and induction is done by some congregations.

[8] Troy Messenger, "Canon & Improvisation: A Model for Planning & Leading Worship," Lecture at 68th Annual Ministers Conference, University of Richmond VA, 29-31 July 1997. Also, personal interview, 31 July 1997. The ideas presented in Troy Messenger's lecture and personal interview have been expounded by the author.

[9] "Jazz," *Harvard Dictionary of Music*, ed. Willi Apel, 2d ed. (Cambridge: The Belknap Press of Harvard UP, 1972), 440-44.

[10] Ibid., 441.

[11] Mark Graham, letter to the author, 30 June 1997. Also, personal interview, 16 October 1997.

[12] Tom Wideman, "Creative Think Tank," *Worship: Resources for the Church Musician* 3/1 (1992): 13.

[13] Ibid.

[14] Ibid.

[15] A standing worship committee would not be the preferred configuration for a group actively involved in worship planning. This responsibility would better be given to a separate group or groups as discussed earlier in the chapter.

[16] This list of worship committee functions was compiled from a sampling of the following sources with standing worship committees: Grandin Court Baptist, Roanoke VA; Kirkwood Baptist, Kirkwood MO; Myers Park Presbyterian, Charlotte NC; St. Mark Evangelical Lutheran, Roanoke VA; and Sharon Baptist Church, Charlotte NC.

[17] The congregational dialogue described was led by Dr. Paul D. Duke, Pastor of Kirkwood Baptist Church, Kirkwood MO, June 1991. The process was described in his newsletter column to the church "From Your Pastor," *The Kirkwood Kindler* 23/24 (1991): 2.

The Consequences of Authentic Worship

Life and liturgy are inexorably linked. A play on the redundancy of the words "worship service" illustrates this point: worship = service, service = worship. In reality, the two cannot be separated. Life and liturgy are bound. They are tethered. No matter how hard we try to separate them, nor how miserably we fail to connect them, life and liturgy are joined in firm embrace. Paul Waitman Hoon, a former Methodist pastor and professor at Union Theological Seminary in New York, describes this liturgical action as anthropological. Hoon writes, "The congregation's entire life grounds the dynamics of liturgy, and the question of action cannot be dealt with in detachment from that life."[1] For Hoon, "the cultic action of the congregation and their apostolic action in the world are the same action performed under different modes."[2]

Cries of the Twelve Hebrew prophets frequently link abuses in worship to impoverished and unethical living. Amos, the shepherd from the mountains, condemns empty, vain worship and challenges his audience to do what is right. Micah, the small-town artisan and proletarian, denounces empty, unrelated ceremony and unethical living, petitioning his audience for justice, kindness, and humility. Zephaniah, citizen of Jerusalem and a man of royal descent, cries out against indifference, cites numerous worship abuses, and decries wrong living. His prophecies link worship and right living. The postexilic prophet Haggai, a virtual unknown, links liturgy and life. He preaches that liturgy and life cannot be separated, and because of this, spiritual values, priorities, and cultic worship affect the balance of life.

Community

As already stated, individuals and communities worship. Worshiping communities are composed of individuals worshiping side by side. When worship takes place, something remarkable happens. In worship, God gathers up worshiping individuals and transforms them into a new whole—a community—that, with unity of purpose, exists to serve and worship the Holy One. Karl Barth, a significant Protestant theologian of the twentieth century, described the process like this: "In divine service [worship] there takes place that which does not take place anywhere else in the community. In divine service the sabbath intervenes between six working days on the one side and six more on the other. In [worship the community] exchanges its working clothes for its festal attire. [Worship] is now an event as community."³

The Christian community is not a mere phenomenon, however distinguished. It is an event. Otherwise it is not the Christian community.

—Karl Barth

But what does this transformation mean for individuals and congregational communities? What other consequences come from worship?

Edification

The apostle Paul writes frequently about edification or building up. In his letters to the churches at Corinth and Ephesus, in particular, Paul admonishes both congregations to engage in activities that serve to build up the body of Christ, whether in worship, in church life, or in daily living. Of worship, the apostle writes, *What should be done then, my friends? When you come together, each one has a hymn, a lesson, a revelation, a tongue, or an interpretation. Let all things be done for building up* (1 Cor 14:26).

One consequence of worship is the edification of individuals and the community of faith. Through acts of worship, people are built up, made better, affirmed, improved spiritually, and enlightened in moral and religious knowledge. These are the marks of edification. In worship, the church is edified. The edification that comes through worship is so significant that Karl Barth makes this claim: "It is not only in worship that the community is edified and edifies itself. But it is here first that this continually takes place. And if it does not take place here, it does not take place anywhere."⁴

Change

In chapter 2, five scriptural models are examined at length. One model is the story of Abraham and Isaac on Mount Moriah. The passage from Genesis 22:1-19 isolates a significant incident in the lives of Abraham and Isaac. Our reader's vantage allows us to peer into a particular worship event between God and Abraham. Many wonderful things happened in the ancient encounter, but one significant consequence for Abraham as a result of the event was change. Abraham was changed forever following the near-sacrifice of his beloved son Isaac. God taught the patriarch lessons about obedience, surrender, sacrifice, and divine provision. The Parent of Good may also teach us new ways in worship. Just as Abraham left the altar with a new and changed understanding of the God he worshiped, so may we also be changed in worship.

God only knows the inspiration we can find from worship. Harry Emerson Fosdick, minister emeritus of Riverside Church in New York City, wrote:

> Some years ago a roistering group of boys, on jollity bent, passed the chapel at the University of Chicago, and one of them shouted, "Let's look in!" So they burst uproariously into the chapel, straightway became quiet, stayed far longer than they had intended and, as they came out, one boy was heard saying to another, "Strange, isn't it? A place like that does something to you." . . . Isaiah went into the Temple and heard a voice which said, "Whom shall I send and who will go for us?" and the young man went out to his prophethood saying, "Here am I; send me." John Wesley worshipped one day in a little Moravian church in old London, and went out on fire to change the whole climate of English Christianity. Harriet Beecher Stowe sat in a little church in Brunswick, Maine, and deeply moved by the communion service, envisioned the death of Uncle Tom and went out to write her influential book.[5]

Worship effects change in the lives of worshipers. Individuals may be changed and communities of faith may be changed to conduct themselves in ways never before imagined. Baptist pastor W. Rand Forder writes about the revolutionary effect of worship:

> The resultant element in worship is revolution. When worshipers encounter the living God in Jesus Christ, attitudes are changed, behavior is different, relationships are transformed and lives are reborn. . . . An appropriate question after the experience of worship is not, "What did I get out of it?" but, "Who am I becoming through it?"[6]

Churches may be changed from fun and fellowship groups into ministry groups of real caregivers. These spiritual communities may, in turn, transform the civic communities and municipalities that surround them. From the seedbed of worship, individuals and communities may hope to turn the world upside down.

The apostle Paul blessed and charged the churches of Asia Minor with this benediction from which we, too, can find God's imaginative inspiration: *Now to [God] who by the power at work within us is able to accomplish abundantly far more than all we can ask or imagine, to [God] be glory in the church and in Christ Jesus to all generations, forever and ever. Amen* (Eph 3:20).

Calling

A consequence of worship has to do with God's call. Isaiah 6:1-12 illustrates this consequence of worship. In the prophetic passage, the Lord asks, *Whom shall I send, and who will go for us?* (Isa 6:8). God calls Isaiah into service to which Isaiah answers, *Here am I; send me!* (Isa 6:9). In this temple episode Isaiah's worship experience makes him receptive to God's call. Through authentic worship, Isaiah's call to service and his resulting receptivity can also be ours.

Our calling need not be sudden or dramatic, although it may be. More normally, perhaps, our calling may grow out of a sense of awareness of what might be possible given our individual gifts and capacities. The call of God is as individual as each person. And while calling is concerned with large decisions regarding life ministry and vocation, it may also focus on the smaller, but no less important tasks of daily projects and responsibilities. The call of God is part of a daily, ongoing process whose primary concern is dedication of life. Because Isaiah worshiped—because he had praised, confessed, and received the cleansing grace of God's forgiveness—he was able to hear God's call and respond affirmatively. So can we.

Service

Isaiah's worship experience led him to new service as a prophet. The story of Isaiah reveals how the connection between worship and service, liturgy and life, is made in the mind and life of Isaiah. Remembering our equation, *worship = service, service = worship*, there is no course for the true worshiper to follow except service to God. Service is a natural consequence of worship. What is true for individuals is equally true for congregations. Worship breathes life-giving energy into congregations. Worship motivates church communities to serve the world about them. Worship evokes servant action to those in need. Worship musters strength for churches to tackle unusual and challenging ministries. Worship encourages families of faith to keep on when the going gets tough. Worship induces service. Not only is service a consequence of worship, worship *is* service.

For some people religion is attending weekly services. And in preparation for those services, they dress the part, do and say the right things. That's good, for the hours they are in service. But it's actually after a person leaves the meeting house that the rubber of faith meets the road of life. That's when religious radials tend to blow out and faith begins swerving all over the place.

—JOY THOMPSON

Righteous, Ethical Living

The pre-exilic prophet Micah, c. 715–700 BC, denounced unethical living and empty form or ritual in worship. According to Homer Hailey, in *A Commentary on the Minor Prophets*, 1972, Micah's prophecy serves a consolidating purpose:

> Micah took the cardinal teachings of Amos, Hosea, and Isaiah and bound them into one embracing statement which includes all. Amos gave emphasis to the need of justice, "Let justice roll down as waters, and righteousness as a mighty stream." Mercy as shown in the lovingkindness of Jehovah was the great theme of Hosea. Isaiah pleaded with the people to have humble fellowship with God. Micah brings all of these together in his striking declaration, "What doth Jehovah require of thee, but to do justly, and to love kindness, and to walk humbly with thy God" (6:8).[7]

Micah's simple message—the thesis of the prophetic book—proclaims that justice, kindness, and humility are offerings the God of Love desires. Ethical living embodies true worship. Paul Waitman Hoon states this firmly when he writes, "Let it be clear once and for all that the congregation can partake of the action of Christian worship only as they act ethically toward their fellowmen, and that they can partake of the reality of Jesus Christ in worship only as they partake of the reality of the world. If worship is to possess integrity, its action must be held within this truth as in a vise."[8]

Life and liturgy are inexorably linked. They are so bound that worship brings about dramatic consequences in the lives of people and faith communities. Worship transforms individuals into communities, edifying and changing them. Through worship, people and congregations hear God's call and respond in acts of specific and appropriate service. Worship produces righteous, ethical living. Karl Barth sums up the connection between life and liturgy with these words: "Worship and the everyday life of Christians . . . are not two departments which are separate . . . but two concentric circles of which worship is the inner which gives to the outer its content and character . . . ."[9]

Questions to Ponder

1. List the consequences you personally experience as a result of worshiping in your setting. What difference does worship make in your life at the present time? Share your discoveries with your discussion group.

2. As a group, list and discuss how your congregation is affected by worship in your setting. What are the consequences of worship for your community of faith? What difference does worship make in the life of your congregation? What changes does worship effect?

3. In what ways does your congregation function as a community of faith? What are the strengths of your church community? What are the weaknesses? Where is there room for improvement?

4. In what ways does worship in your setting edify or build up the body of Christ? How? In what ways does worship in your setting fail to edify?

5. Who are you becoming through worship?

6. Who is your church becoming through worship?

7. How do you hear God's call on your life? How does worship figure into your sense of calling and your response?

8. How do you serve the Holy One?

9. How does your church service the Holy One? List specific ways.

10. In a brainstorming exercise, list new and specific ways your church might serve God. How might these be effected?

11. What prohibits your church from service? How might these barriers be broken down?

NOTES

[1] Paul Waitman Hoon, "The Nature of Liturgical Action," *The Integrity of Worship: Ecumenical and Pastoral Studies in Liturgical Theology* (Nashville: Abingdon, 1971), 325.

[2] Ibid., 292-93.

[3] Karl Barth, *The Doctrine of Reconciliation*, trans. G. W. Bromiley (Edinburgh: T. & T. Clark, 1958), 697-98, vol. 4, 2 of *Church Dogmatics*.

[4] Ibid., 638.

[5] Harry Emerson Fosdick, *Dear Mr. Brown* (New York: Harper, 1961), 157.

[6] W. Rand Forder, "Worship," *The Religious Herald* 158/31 (1990): 14.

[7] Homer Hailey, *A Commentary on the Minor Prophets* (Grand Rapids: Baker Book House, 1972), 190.

[8] Hoon, "The Nature of Liturgical Action," 347.

[9] Barth, *The Doctrine of Reconciliation*, 640.

Bibliography

Aldrich, Joseph D. Personal interview. 29 April 1997.

Allen, Horace T., Jr. "Liturgy as the Form of Faith." *The Landscape of Praise: Readings in Liturgical Renewal*, ed. Blair Gilmer Meeks. Valley Forge: Trinity Press International, 1996. 7-10.

Anthony, Susan B. *The Last Word: A Treasury of Women's Quotes*, ed. Carolyn Warner. Englewood Cliffs NJ: Prentice, 1992.

Augustine of Hippo, Saint. *Expositions on the Book of Psalms*. LF 6, 178 on Psalm 138:2.

Bailey, Raymond. "The Worshiping Church 4020." Opinion expressed in class lecture at The Southern Baptist Theological Seminary, Louisville KY, Spring 1982.

Bailey, Robert W. *New Ways in Christian Worship*. Nashville: Broadman Press, 1981.

———. "A Theology of Worship." *Search* 13/3 (1983): 17-27.

Baker, Robert G. *Amos: Doing What Is Right: A Study Guide*. Macon GA: Smyth & Helwys Publishing, Inc., 1995.

Bangert, Mark P. *Symbols and Terms of the Church*. Minneapolis: Augsburg Fortress, 1990.

Barth, Karl. *The Doctrine of Reconciliation*, trans. G. W. Bromiley. Edinburgh: T. & T. Clark, 1958. Vol. 4, 2 of *Church Dogmatics*. 13 part-vols. 1932–1967.

Bartow, Charles L "Scripture: Living Literature." *Reformed Liturgy & Music* 29/4 (1990): 187-90.

Batchelder, David B. "Counting the Cost: Assessing What's at Stake in the 'Worship Wars.'" *Reformed Liturgy & Music* 30/2 (1996): 89.

Beebe, Hank. *To Know Thee*, no. JH504. High Street Music, 1989.

Bell, John L. "Hymns Are Heterogeneous." *Reformed Liturgy & Music* 31/1 (1997): 66-67.

Berry, James A. *In the Beauty of Holiness*. Charlotte NC: Myers Park Baptist Church, 1986.

Bolinger, Dwight, and Donald A. Sears. *Aspects of Language*. New York: Harcourt, 1981.

Bowman, Raymond A. "Exegesis." In volume 3 of *The Interpreter's Bible*, ed. George Arthur Buttrick. 12 vols. Nashville: Abingdon Press, 1952. 784-802.

Brown, K. Bradford. *Signs of Life: Mental Touchstones for the Warrior of the Spirit.* London: Lifetomes Press, 1990.

Buttrick, George A. "Exposition." In volume 7 of *The Interpreter's Bible*, ed. George Arthur Buttrick. 12 vols. Nashville: Abingdon Press, 1952. 308-16.

Callahan, Kennon L. *Twelve Keys to an Effective Church: Strategic Planning for Mission.* San Francisco: HarperSanFrancisco, 1983.

Christensen, James L. *Don't Waste Your Time in Worship.* Old Tappan NJ: Fleming H. Revell Company, 1978.

Clark, Deborah Moore. "A Service of Communion: Knowing [God]." *Church Administration* (January 1993): 39.

———. "A Service of Communion: The Community of Faith (Fellowship/Community)." *Church Administration* (September 1993): 33.

Coffin, Henry Sloane. "Exposition." In volume 5 of *The Interpreter's Bible*, ed. George Arthur Buttrick. 12 vols. Nashville: Abingdon Press, 1952. 632-35.

Coleman, L. H. "Genesis 20:1 to 22:24: The Sacrifice of Isaac." *Bible Book Study for Adults: Genesis (Part I)*, 1/1/78-84 (October-November-December 1978).

Culpepper, R. Alan. "New Testament 2396: Worship and Ministry in the New Testament." Opinion expressed in class lecture at The Southern Baptist Theological Seminary, Louisville KY, Fall 1982.

Daniels, Harold M. "The Languages of Worship." *Reformed Liturgy & Music* 30/4 (1996): 199-206.

Detterman, Paul, ed. *Reformed Liturgy & Music.* Louisville KY: Theology & Worship, Congregational Ministries Division of the Presbyterian Church (USA), 1997.

Dillard, Annie. *Holy the Firm.* New York: Harper, 1977.

———. *Pilgrim at Tinker Creek.* New York: HarperPerennial, 1990.

———. *Teaching a Stone to Talk: Expeditions and Encounters.* New York: HarperPerennial, 1982.

Dols, William L. "Critical Background." *The Bible Workbench: A Resource for Living Our Story Through God's Story* 4/3 (1997): 55-56.

———. Personal interview. 29 April 1997.

———. Prayer of Thanksgiving and Intercession. Worship at Myers Park Baptist Church. Charlotte NC, 20 April 1997.

Doran, Carol, and Thomas H. Troeger. *New Hymns for the Lectionary: To Glorify the Maker's Name.* New York: Oxford University Press, 1986.

———. "Renewing Worship." Opinions expressed in workshop presentation at Worship and Music Conference. Montreat NC, 24-30 June 1990.

Duck, Ruth. "Wash, O God, Our Sons and Daughters." *The Myers Park Baptist Church Hymnal.* Charlotte NC: Myers Park Baptist Church, 1995.

Duduit, Michael. "Boomers and the Bible." *The Tie* 62/2 (1994): 10.

Duke, Paul D. "From Your Pastor." *The Kirkwood Kindler* 23/24 (1991): 2.

———. Letter to the author. 7 July 1997.

———. Letter to the author. 4 August 1997.

Duggins, Davis. "The Worship Gap." *Moody* 96/6 (1996): 19-22.

Eskew, Harry, and Hugh T. McElrath. *Sing with Understanding: An Introduction to Christian Hymnology*. Nashville: Broadman Press, 1980.

Forder, W. Rand. "Worship." *The Religious Herald* 158/31 (1990): 14.

Fosdick, Harry Emerson. *Dear Mr. Brown*. New York: Harper, 1961.

Foster, Richard J. *Celebration of Discipline: The Path to Spiritual Growth*. New York: Harper, 1978.

Francisco, Clyde T. "Genesis." *The Broadman Bible Commentary: General Articles, Genesis-Exodus*, ed. Clifton J. Allen. Nashville: Broadman Press, 1969. 187-90.

Gaddy, C. Welton. *The Gift of Worship*. Nashville: Broadman Press, 1992.

Garfield, Ken. "Congregations loosen up the liturgy." *The Charlotte Observer*, 14 September 1996, 1G.

Gloer, Hulitt. "A Temple of Flesh and Blood." 3 March 1991.

Gibble, Kenneth L. "How Wasteful Can Worship Be?" *Christianity Today* 25/21 (1981): 17.

Gaebelein, Frank E. "Heeding the Whole Counsel of God." *Christianity Today* 25/17 (1981): 29.

Graham, Mark. Letter to the author. 30 June 1997.

———. Personal interview. 16 Oct. 1997.

Green, Fred Pratt. "For the Fruit of All Creation." *The Baptist Hymnal*. Nashville: Convention Press, 1991.

Groote, Gerhard [ed. Thomas à Kempis]. *The Imitation of Christ*. Trans. Richard Whitford. Ed. Edward J. Klein. New York: Harper, 1941.

Hahn, Ferdinand. *The Worship of the Early Church*. Trans. David E. Green. Ed. John Reumann. Philadelphia: Fortress Press, 1973.

Hailey, Homer. *A Commentary on the Minor Prophets*. Grand Rapids: Baker Book House, 1972. 186-221.

Hess, Carol Lakey. "The Shaping and Shaking of Congregational Life." *Reformed Liturgy & Music* 25/2 (1991): 65-68.

Hoff, Ron. *"I Can See You Naked": A Fearless Guide to Making Great Presentations*. New York: Andrews and McMeel, 1988.

Hoon, Paul Waitman. *The Integrity of Worship: Ecumenical and Pastoral Studies in Liturgical Theology*. Nashville: Abingdon, 1971.

Hughes, Dennis J. "Editorial Introduction." *Reformed Liturgy & Music* 30/2 (1996): 42.

Hughes, Kent. *Disciplines of a Godly Man*. Quoted by Davis Duggins in "In Spirit and in Truth." *Moody* 96/6 (1996): 28.

Huspeni, Dennis. "Churches catch a wave of worship." *The Charlotte Observer*, 19 October 1996, 3G.

Hustad, Donald P. *Jubilate! Church Music in the Evangelical Tradition*. Carol Stream: Hope Publishing Company, 1981.

Hymnal and Liturgies of the Moravian Church. N.p.: Provincial Synods of the Moravian Church in America, 1969.

"Jazz." *Harvard Dictionary of Music,* 1972 ed.

Jerome, Saint. *Letter 54.* Quoted in John Bartlett, *Familiar Quotations.* Ed. Emily Morison Beck. 15th ed. Boston: Little, 1980. 128.

Jones, Cheslyn, Geoffrey Wainwright, and Edward Yarnold, eds. *The Study of Liturgy.* New York: Oxford UP, 1978.

Jones, W. Paul. "Pastures of the Wilderness: Worship as Historical and Cosmic Gesture." *Weavings* 10/4 (1995): 14.

Julian of Norwich. Quotation appearing in *The Charlotte Observer,* 24 Nov. 1996, C1. No other source information available.

Jüngel, Eberhard. *Karl Barth, A Theological Legacy.* Trans. Garrett E. Paul. Philadelphia: The Westminster Press, 1986.

Kelleher, Margaret Mary. "The Rite of Sprinkling as an Invitation to Worship." *The Landscape of Praise: Readings in Liturgical Renewal,* ed. Blair Gilmer Meeks. Valley Forge: Trinity Press International, 1996. 268-75.

Kelley, Page H. *A Nation in the Making.* Nashville: Convention Press, 1969.

———. "Isaiah." In volume 5 of *The Broadman Bible Commentary: Proverbs-Isaiah.* Ed. Clifton J. Allen. 12 vols. Nashville: Broadman Press, 1969. 208-12.

Kierkegaard, Søren J. *Purity of Heart.* Trans. Douglas Steere. New York: Harper, 1938. 163ff.

Klooster, Fred H. *The Significance of Barth's Theology.* Grand Rapids: Baker Book House, 1961.

Koehnline, Phyllis. "Listening to What We Say and Sing and Pray." *Reformed Liturgy & Music* 29/4 (1990): 215.

Lackey, Terri. "Is Tossing Hymns Chucking History?" *Facts & Trends* 42/9 (1996) 9.

———. "Reaching Boomers and Busters," *Facts & Trends* 40/4 (1994) 6.

Lamberth, Bonnie Jean. "Glorifying and Enjoying God." *Reformed Liturgy & Music* 31/1 (1997): 68.

———. "Musical Hospitality in the House of the Lord." *Reformed Liturgy & Music* 30/4 (1996): 224.

———. "Reclaiming Our Biblical Heritage." *Reformed Liturgy & Music* 31/2 (1997): 142.

Lamm, Wilbur C. Exerpt from *The Guide,* a newsletter published by The First Baptist Church of Columbus GA, documentation incomplete. Dr. Wilbur C. Lamm was a frequent writer for The Sunday School Board of the Southern Baptist Convention in the 1960s.

Lovelace, Noël. Personal interview. 29 January 1997.

Martin, Ralph P. *Carmen christi: Philippians ii.5-11 in Recent Interpretations and in the Setting of Early Christian Worship.* Cambridge: University Press, 1967.

Meeks, Blair Gilmer, ed. *The Landscape of Praise: Readings in Liturgical Renewal.* Valley Forge: Trinity Press International, 1996.

Messenger, Troy. "Canon & Improvisation: A Model for Planning & Leading Worship." Lecture at 68th Annual Ministers Conference. University of Richmond VA, 29-31 July 1997.

———. Personal interview. 31 July 1997.

Mitchell, Robert H. *Ministry and Music.* Philadephia: The Westminster Press, 1978.

Moderow, Karen. "Breaking Through the Sunday Blues." *Moody* 96/6 (1996): 31.

Mollenkott, Virginia Ramey. *The Divine Feminine: The Biblical Imagery of God as Female.* New York: Crossroad, 1994.

Moltmann-Wendel, Elisabeth. *I Am My Body: A Theology of Embodiment.* New York: Continuum, 1995.

Muilenburg, James. "Exegesis." In volume 5 of *The Interpreter's Bible*, ed. George Arthur Buttrick. 12 vols. Nashville: Abingdon Press, 1952. 632-34.

Mullins, Rich. "Awesome God." *Songs for Praise & Worship.* Nashville: Word Music, 1992.

Murray, Shirley Erena. "Community of Christ." *The Myers Park Baptist Church Hymnal.* N.p.: Myers Park Baptist Church, 1995.

Myers Park Baptist Church. Exerpt from the call to worship. Myers Park Baptist Church. Charlotte NC, 22 September 1996.

The Myers Park Baptist Church Hymnal. N.p.: Myers Park Baptist Church, 1995.

Notebaart, James. "A Furore Normanorum, Libera Nos Domine." *The Landscape of Praise: Readings in Liturgical Renewal.* Ed. Blair Gilmer Meeks. Valley Forge: Trinity Press International, 1996. 288-94.

Oates, Wayne E. *Nurturing Silence in a Noisy Heart.* Garden City: Doubleday, 1979.

Peters, Lanny. Telephone interview. 26 April 1995.

———. Telephone interview. 11 September 1997.

Peterson, Wilferd A. *The New Book of the Art of Living.* New York: Simon & Schuster, 1963.

Petty, Troy W. "Worship and Renewal." *The Religious Herald* 155/23 (1982): 12.

Phillips, J. B. *Your God Is Too Small.* New York: Macmillan, 1961.

Price, Milburn. "Believers All, We Bear the Name." *The Baptist Hymnal.* Nashville: Convention Press, 1991.

Price, W. Wayne. *The Church and the Rites of Passage.* Nashville: Broadman Press, 1989.

Rainer, Thom S. "Evangelism and Culture." *The Tie* 64/2 (1996): 6-8.

Reeder, Rachel. "Art of Our Own Making." *The Landscape of Praise: Readings in Liturgical Renewal.* Ed. Blair Gilmer Meeks. Valley Forge: Trinity Press International, 1996. 11-13.

Rinkart, Martin. "Now Thank We All Our God." *The Presbyterian Hymnal: Hymns, Psalms, and Spiritual Songs.* Louisville: Westminster/John Knox Press, 1990.

Robertson, A. T. *A Harmony of the Gospels.* New York: Harper, 1922.

Robinson, Robert. "Come, Thou Fount of Every Blessing." *The Presbyterian Hymnal: Hymns, Psalms, and Spiritual Songs.* Louisville: Westminster/John Knox Press, 1990.

Saliers, Don E. "Liturgy as Art." *The Landscape of Praise: Readings in Liturgical Renewal.* Ed. Blair Gilmer Meeks. Valley Forge: Trinity Press International, 1996. 120-26.

Scott, R. B. Y. and G. G. D. Kilpatrick. In volume 5 of *The Interpreter's Bible: Ecclesiastes, Song of Songs, Isaiah, Jeremiah.* Ed. George Arthur Buttrick. 12 vols. Nashville: Abingdon Press, 1952. 12 vols. 151-164, 204-13.

Scottish Psalter. "The Lord's My Shepherd." *Hymnal and Liturgies of the Moravian Church.* Elk Grove IL: Walter M. Carqueville, 1969.

Searle, Mark. "The Uses of Liturgical Language." *The Landscape of Praise: Readings in Liturgical Renewal.* Ed. Blair Gilmer Meeks. Valley Forge: Trinity Press International, 1996. 105-10.

Segler, Franklin M. *Christian Worship: Its Theology and Practice.* Nashville: Broadman Press, 1967.

Senn, Frank C. "The Spirit of the Liturgy, A Wonderland Revisited." *The Landscape of Praise: Readings in Liturgical Renewal.* Ed. Blair Gilmer Meeks. Valley Forge: Trinity Press International, 1996. 14-21.

———. "Worship and Evangelism." *Reformed Liturgy & Music* 31/1 (1997): 22-30.

Shelley, Bruce L. "Then & Now." *Moody* 96/6 (1996): 23-25.

Shelley, Percy Bysshe. "Mutability." *The Literature of England: An Anthology and a History.* Ed. George B. Woods, Homer A. Watt, and George K. Anderson. Volume 2. Revised edition. New York: Scott, Foresman and Company, 1941. 257.

Shurden, Walter B. *The Doctrine of the Priesthood of Believers.* Nashville: Convention Press, 1987.

Simpson, Cuthbert A., and Walter Russell Bowie. *The Interpreter's Bible: General Articles, Genesis, Exodus.* George Arthur Buttrick, ed. Volume 1. Nashville: Abingdon Press, 1952. 642-46.

Sloyan, Gerard S. "What Is Liturgical Preaching?" *The Landscape of Praise: Readings in Liturgical Renewal.* Ed. Blair Gilmer Meeks. Valley Forge: Trinity Press International, 1996. 228-34.

Sparkman, G. Temp. *Writing Your Own Worship Materials.* Valley Forge: Judson Press, 1980.

Stake, Donald Wilson. "The Liturgical Infection." *Reformed Liturgy & Music* 31/1 (1997): 14-17.

Stauffer, S. Anith. Quoting from *Mystagogical Catecheses* 2/4 in "A Place for Burial, Birth and Bath." *The Landscape of Praise: Readings in Liturgical Renewal.* Ed. Blair Gilmer Meeks. Valley Forge: Trinity Press International, 1996. 136-44.

Stewart, Don H. *Matthew 5-7: Design for Discipleship.* Nashville: Convention Press, 1992.

Strader, Rebecca Sue. "Liturgy: Is 'Relevance' Relevant?" *Reformed Liturgy & Music* 31/1 (1997): 31-35.

Sturgeon, Jeff. "All creatures great and small—and slimy—are blessed." *The Roanoke Times,* 28 August 1995, C1.

Tarwater, John. "The Value of Worship." Southern Baptist Brotherhood Commission Breakfast. 1988.

Taylor, Charles L., Jr., and Howard Thurman. *The Interpreter's Bible: Lamentations, Ezekiel, Daniel, Twelve Prophets.* Ed. George Arthur Buttrick. Volume 6. Nashville: Abingdon Press, 1952. 973-003[?].

Temple, William. *The Hope of a New World.* New York: Macmillan, 1942.

Thompson, Joy. "Churches take lead in service: Part of worship should be putting faith to work." *The Charlotte Observer,* 28 April 1997, 13A.

Thompson, Marjorie J. *Soul Feast: An Invitation to the Christian Spiritual Life.* Louisville: Westminster John Knox Press, 1995.

Tribble, Harold W. *From Adam to Moses.* Nashville: Convention Press, 1934.

Troeger, Thomas H. *New Hymns for the Lectionary: To Glorify the Maker's Name.* New York: Oxford UP, 1986.

———. "Three Parables of Healthy Congregational Song." *Reformed Liturgy & Music* 29/4 (1990): 216.

Tuck, William Powell. "The Lord's Prayer." *Formations* 1/4 (1992): 33-65.

Ugolnik, Anthony. "The Text is Not Enough." *The Landscape of Praise: Readings in Liturgical Renewal.* Ed. Blair Gilmer Meeks. Valley Forge: Trinity Press International, 1996. 211-19.

Underhill, Evelyn. *Worship.* New York: Crossroad, 1985.

Van Dyke, Karmen. "How Shall We Sing the Lord's Song in a Strange Land? The Story of the First Presbyterian Conference on Worship and Music That Included New Songs of Praise." *Reformed Liturgy & Music* 30/2 (1996): 72-75.

Wainwright, Geoffrey. *Doxology: The Praise of God in Worship, Doctrine and Life.* New York: Oxford UP, 1980.

Warren, Michael. "Culture, Counterculture and the Word." *The Landscape of Praise: Readings in Liturgical Renewal.* Ed. Blair Gilmer Meeks. Valley Forge: Trinity Press International, 1996. 279-87.

Webber, Robert. Quoted by David Duggins, "In Spirit and in Truth," *Moody* 96/6 (1996): 26-32.

Westermeyer, Paul. *The Church Musician.* San Francisco: Harper, 1988.

White, James F. "Coming Together in Christ's Name." *The Landscape of Praise: Readings in Liturgical_Renewal.* Ed. Blair Gilmer Meeks. Valley Forge: Trinity Press International, 1996. 152-56.

———. *New Forms of Worship.* Nashville: Abingdon, 1971.

Wideman, Tom. "Creative Think Tank." *Worship: Resources for the Church Musician* 3/1 (1992): 13.

Williams, Samuel F., Jr. "Piece of Mind." *Northminster News* 46/48 (1987): 2; 48/40 (1989): 1; and 52/16 (1993): 1.

Willimon, William H. *What's Right with the Church.* San Francisco: Harper, 1985.

Willis, Charles. Quotation of Bruce Leafblad in "Worship requires top priority." *Facts & Trends* 32/6 (1988): 2.

Withers, Leslie. "Lay leadership in worship produces variety and involvement for all members." *SBC Today* 9/3 (1991): 9.

Woensdregt, Yme. "The Pastor as Liturgist." *Reformed Liturgy & Music* 30/4 (1996): 167-72.

Wren, Brian. "God of Many Names." *Praising a Mystery: 30 New Hymns by Brian Wren.* Carol Stream, Ill.: Hope Publishing Co., 1986.

———. *What Language Shall I Borrow? God-Talk in Worship: A Male Response to Feminist Theology.* New York: Crossroad, 1995.

———. "When Christ Was Lifted from the Earth." *The Baptist Hymnal.* Nashville: Convention Press, 1991.

Wright, G. Ernest. "Exegesis." In volume 2 of *The Interpreter's Bible.* Ed. George Arthur Buttrick. Nashville: Abingdon Press, 1952. 490-92.

Yaqub, Hanan. "A Case for Blended Worship." *Reformed Liturgy & Music* 30/2 (1996): 90.

Young, Robert. *Analytical Concordance to the Bible.* Grand Rapids: Wm. B. Eerdmans Publishing Company, 1970.

APPENDIX 1

Sources and Authors of Sidebar Quotations

Sources are listed in the order quotations are used within the chapters. Each entry is also referenced in the Bibliography.

Preface
Annie Dillard, Pulitzer Prize-winning author. "An Expedition to the Pole," *Teaching a Stone to Talk: Expeditions and Encounters* (New York: HarperPerennial, 1982), 58.

Chapter 1: Why Worship?
Kent Hughes, *Disciplines of a Godly Man*, quoted by Davis Duggins, senior ed., "In Spirit and in Truth," *Moody* 96/6 (1996): 28.

William H. Willimon, Assistant Professor of Liturgy and Worship, Duke Divinity School. *What's Right with the Church* (San Francisco: Harper, 1985), 122.

Robert Robinson (1735–1790), hymnist. "Come, Thou Fount of Every Blessing," *The Presbyterian Hymnal: Hymns, Psalms, and Spiritual Songs* (Louisville: Westminster/John Knox Press, 1990), no. 356.

Martin Rinkart, hymnist, c. 1636. "Now Thank We All Our God," *The Presbyterian Hymnal: Hymns, Psalms, and Spiritual Songs* (Louisville: Westminster/John Knox Press, 1990), no. 555. This version of Rinkart's hymn text is a 1985 adaptation from *Rejoice in the Lord*.

Karl Barth, significant Protestant theologian of the 20th century. *The Doctrine of Reconciliation*, trans. G. W. Bromiley (Edinburgh: T. & T. Clark, 1958), 696, vol. 4, 2 of *Church Dogmatics*.

Evelyn Underhill, poet, novelist, and noted scholar on mysticism of the early 20th century. *Worship* (New York: Crossroad, 1985), 86.

Chapter 2: Scriptural Models for Worship

C. Welton Gaddy, pastor, teacher, and author. *The Gift of Worship* (Nashville: Broadman Press, 1992), 127.

Davis Duggins, senior editor of *Moody*. "The Worship Gap," *Moody* 96/6 (1996): 20.

Julian of Norwich, a 15th-century Christian mystic. *The Charlotte Observer*, 24 November 1996, C1.

Mohandas K. Gandhi (1869–1948), a devout and mystical Hindu who, through passive resistance, fought for the rights and independence of the people of India. No source information available other than author.

Samuel F. Williams, Jr., Pastor, Northminster Baptist Church, Richmond VA. "Piece of Mind," *Northminister News* 46/48 (1987): 2.

William Powell Tuck, former Professor of Christian Preaching at The Southern Baptist Theological Seminary, Louisville KY, 1978–1983. "The Lord's Prayer," *Formations* 1/4 (1992): 36.

Evelyn Underhill, poet, novelist, and noted scholar on mysticism of the early 20th century. *Worship* (New York: Crossroad, 1985), 86.

James Notebaart, director, Office of Catholic Indian Ministry, Minneapolis. "A Furore Normanorum, Libera Nos Domine," *The Landscape of Praise: Readings in Liturgical Renewal*, ed. Blair Gilmer Meeks (Valley Forge: Trinity Press International, 1996), 290.

Karl Barth, significant Protestant theologian of the 20th century. *The Doctrine of Reconciliation*, trans. G. W. Bromiley, vol. 4, 2 of *Church Dogmatics* (Edinburgh: T. & T. Clark, 1958), 639.

Paul Waitman Hoon, professor of pastoral theology, retired, Union Theological Seminary, New York. *The Integrity of Worship: Ecumenical and Pastoral Studies in Liturgical Theology* (Nashville: Abingdon, 1971), 80.

Gerhard Groote (1340–1384), ed. Thomas à Kempis, 15th-century Augustinian monk. *The Imitation of Christ*, trans. Richard Whitford, ed. Edward J. Klein (New York: Harper, 1941), 3.

Don E. Saliers, professor of theology and liturgics and Director of the Masters of Sacred Music Program, Emory University, Atlanta. "Liturgy as Art," *The Landscape of Praise: Readings in Liturgical Renewal*, ed. Blair Gilmer Meeks (Valley Forge: Trinity Press International, 1996), 125.

Evelyn Underhill, *Worship*, 220.

Chapter 3: What Is Worship? Characteristics and Descriptions

Saint Augustine of Hippo, great theologian of the 4th and 5th centuries. *Expositions on the Book of Psalms* (LF 6, 178) on Psalm 138:2.

Annie Dillard, Pulitzer Prize-winning author. *Holy the Firm* (New York: Harper, 1977), 59.

Mark Searle, former associate professor of liturgy, the University of Notre Dame. "The Uses of Liturgical Language," *The Landscape of Praise: Readings in Liturgical Renewal*, ed. Blair Gilmer Meeks (Valley Forge: Trinity Press International, 1996), 110.

Rebecca Sue Strader, co-pastor, Christ Church, Presbyterian, Burlington VT; co-director of the city's Joint Urban Ministry Project, an interfaith crisis ministry. "Liturgy: Is 'Relevance' Relevant?" *Reformed Liturgy & Music* 31/1 (1997): 31.

Don E. Saliers, professor of theology and liturgics and Director of the Masters of Sacred Music Program, Emory University, Atlanta. "Liturgy as Art," *The Landscape of Praise: Readings in Liturgical Renewal*, ed. Blair Gilmer Meeks (Valley Forge: Trinity Press International, 1996), 121-22.

Anthony Ugolnik, professor of English, and priest at Saints Constantine and Helen Russian Orthodox Church, Reading PA. "The Text is Not Enough," *The Landscape of Praise: Readings in Liturgical Renewal*, ed. Blair Gilmer Meeks (Valley Forge: Trinity Press International, 1996), 212.

Samuel F. Williams, Jr., Pastor, Northminster Baptist Church, Richmond VA. "Piece of Mind," *Northminister News* 46/48 (1987): 2.

Bonnie Jean Lamberth, Director of Educational Ministries at Starmount Presbyterian Church, Greensboro NC. "Glorifying and Enjoying God," *Reformed Liturgy & Music* 31/1 (1997): 68.

Richard J. Foster, professor of Spiritual Formation, Azusa Pacific University. *Celebration of Discipline: The Path to Spiritual Growth* (New York: Harper, 1978), 147.

Evelyn Underhill, poet, novelist, and noted scholar on mysticism of the early 20th century. *Worship* (New York: Crossroad, 1985), 86.

Richard J. Foster, *Celebration*, 148.

Paul D. Duke, Pastor, First Baptist Church, Ann Arbor MI. Unpublished letter to the author, 7 July 1997.

Rebecca Sue Strader, "Liturgy: Is 'Relevance' Relevant?" 35.

Anthony Ugolnik, "The Text is Not Enough," 217.

Shirley Erena Murray, hymn writer, 1985. Stanza one of *Community of Christ,* from *The Myers Park Baptist Church Hymnal* (Myers Park Baptist Church, 1995), no. 278. Set to the tune LEONI, a Hebrew melody adapted by Thomas Olivers and Meyer Lyon, 1770.

Evelyn Underhill, *Worship,* 3.

Chapter 4: Worship Is Not . . .

Rachel Reeder, editor, Washington, DC. "Art of Our Own Making," *The Landscape of Praise: Readings in Liturgical Renewal*, ed. Blair Gilmer Meeks (Valley Forge: Trinity Press International, 1996), 11.

Yme Woensdregt, member of the pastoral team at First Presbyterian Church, Regina, Saskatchewan. "The Pastor as Liturgist," *Reformed Liturgy & Music* 30/4 (1996): 169.

James L. Christensen, *Don't Waste Your Time in Worship* (Old Tappan NJ: Fleming H. Revell Company, 1978), 13-14.

W. Paul Jones, professor emeritus of theology, Family Brother of the Trappist Order, and Roman Catholic priest. "Pastures of the Wilderness: Worship as Historical and Cosmic Gesture," *Weavings* 10/4 (1995): 14.

Yme Woensdregt, "The Pastor as Liturgist," 167.

Gerard S. Sloyan, professor emeritus of religion at Temple University, currently teaching at the Catholic University of America, Washington, DC. "What Is Liturgical Preaching?" *The Landscape of Praise: Readings in Liturgical Renewal*, ed. Blair Gilmer Meeks (Valley Forge: Trinity Press International, 1996), 228.

Don E. Saliers, professor of theology and liturgics and Director of the Masters of Sacred Music Program, Emory University, Atlanta. "Liturgy as Art," *The Landscape of Praise: Readings in Liturgical Renewal*, ed. Blair Gilmer Meeks (Valley Forge: Trinity Press International, 1996), 120.

Chapter 5: Components of Christian Worship

Evelyn Underhill, poet, novelist, and noted scholar on mysticism of the early 20th century. *Worship* (New York: Crossroad, 1985), 86.

K. Bradford Brown, *Signs of Life: Mental Touchstones for the Warrior of the Spirit* (London: Lifetomes Press, 1990), 140.

Geoffrey Wainwright, a Methodist minister and theologian. *Doxology: The Praise of God in Worship, Doctrine and Life* (New York: Oxford UP, 1980), 200.

Frank C. Senn, pastor of Immanuel Lutheran Church, Evanston IL, president of The Liturgical Conference. "Worship and Evangelism," *Reformed Liturgy & Music* 31/1 (1997): 28.

Charles L. Bartow, Professor of Homiletics, San Francisco Theological Seminary. "Scripture: Living Literature," *Reformed Liturgy & Music* 29/4 (1990): 187.

Charles L. Bartow, "Scripture: Living Literature," 189.

John L. Bell, minister and hymn writer. "Hymns Are Heterogeneous," *Reformed Liturgy & Music* 31/1 (1997): 66.

Charles L. Bartow, "Scripture: Living Literature," 188.

Franklin M. Segler, former professor at Southwestern Baptist Theological Seminary, Ft. Worth TX. *Christian Worship: Its Theology and Practice* (Nashville: Broadman Press, 1967), 111.

Paul D. Duke, Pastor, First Baptist Church, Ann Arbor MI. Unpublished letter to the author, 4 August 1997.

Paul D. Duke, Numbers 6:24-26 using non-gendered language for God.

Deborah Moore Clark, Jude 1:24-25 using non-gendered language for God.

Donald P. Hustad, semi-retired seminary professor of church music and organ at The Southern Baptist Theological Seminary, Louisville KY. *Jubilate! Church Music in the Evangelical Tradition* (Carol Stream: Hope Publishing Company, 1981), 175.

Chapter 6: Inclusive Language, Inclusive Worship

Rebecca Sue Strader, co-pastor, Christ Church, Presbyterian, Burlington VT, co-director of the city's Joint Urban Ministry Project, an interfaith crisis ministry. "Liturgy: Is 'Relevance' Relevant?" *Reformed Liturgy & Music* 31/1 (1997): 34.

Brian Wren, hymn poet and theologian. Stanza one of *God of Many Names*, from *Praising a Mystery: 30 New Hymns by Brian Wren* (Carol Stream IL: Hope Publishing Co., 1986), hymn no. 8.

Harold M. Daniels, retired, former Associate for Worship and Edito,. *The Book of Common Worship* (1993). "The Languages of Worship," *Reformed Liturgy & Music* 30/4 (1996): 200.

Brian Wren, *What Language Shall I Borrow? God-Talk in Worship: A Male Response to Feminist Theology* (New York: Crossroad: 1995), 108.

Brian Wren, *What Language?* 109.

J. B. Phillips (1906–1982), a Church of England clergyman and author of 17 books and a translation of the New Testament in modern English. *Your God Is Too Small* (New York: Macmillan, 1961), 21-22.

Brian Wren, *What Language?* 132.

Virginia Ramey Mollenkott, feminist. *The Divine Feminine: The Biblical Imagery of God as Female* (New York: Crossroad, 1994), 61.

Virginia Ramey Mollekott, *The Divine Feminine*, 89.

Rebecca Sue Strader, "Liturgy: Is 'Relevance' Relevant?" 34.

Phyllis Koehnline, Pastor of Evanshire Presbyterian Church, Skokie IL. "Listening to What We Say and Sing and Pray," *Reformed Liturgy & Music* 29/4 (1990): 215.

Elisabeth Moltmann-Wendel, a theologian and writer living in Tübingen, Germany. *I Am My Body: A Theology of Embodiment* (New York: Continuum, 1995), 56.

Carol Lakey Hess, Assistant Professor of Pastoral Leadership & Education at Union Theological Seminary, Richmond VA. "The Shaping and Shaking of Congregational Life," *Reformed Liturgy & Music* 25/2 (1991): 68.

Chapter 7: A Matter of Style

Carol Lakey Hess, Assistant Professor of Pastoral Leadrship & Education at Union Theological Seminary, Richmond VA. "The Shaping and Shaking of Congregational Life," *Reformed Liturgy & Music* 25/2 (1991): 68.

Yme Woensdregt, member of the pastoral team at First Presbyterian Church, Regina, Saskatchewan. "The Pastor as Liturgist," *Reformed Liturgy & Music* 30/4 (1996): 169-70.

Margaret Mary Kelleher, associate profressor, Department of Religion and Religious Education, the Catholic University of America, Washington, DC. "The Rite of Sprinkling as an Invitation to Worship," *The Landscape of Praise: Readings in Liturgical Renewal*, ed. Blair Gilmer Meeks (Valley Forge: Trinity Press International, 1996), 268.

Thomas H. Troeger, hymn poet and liturgist. *The Scantest Touch of Grace Can Heal*, from *New Hymns for the Lectionary: To Glorify the Maker's Name* (New York: Oxford, 1986), no. 24, 50-51.

Fred Pratt Green, hymn poet. *For the Fruit of All Creation*, from *The Baptist Hymnal* (Nashville: Convention Press, 1991), no. 643.

Ruth Duck, hymn poet. *Wash, O God, Our Sons and Daughters*, from *The Myers Park Baptist Church Hymnal* (Charlotte NC: Myers Park Baptist Church, 1995), no. 348.

Brian Wren, hymn poet and theologian. *When Christ Was Lifted from the Earth*, from *The Baptist Hymnal* (Nashville: Convention Press, 1991), no. 562.

Thomas H. Troeger, "Three Parables of Healthy Congregational Song," *Reformed Liturgy & Music* 29/4 (1990): 216.

Karmen Van Dyke, organist and Presbyterian elder. "How Shall We Sing the Lord's Song in a Strange Land? The Story of the First Presbyterian Conference on Worship and Music That Included New Songs of Praise," *Reformed Liturgy & Music* 30/2 (1996): 74.

Frank C. Senn, pastor of Immanuel Lutheran Church, Evanston IL, president of The Liturgical Conference. "Worship and Evangelism," *Reformed Liturgy & Music* 31/1 (1997): 30.

Bonnie Jean Lamberth, Director of Educational Ministries, Starmount Presbyterian Church, Greensboro NC. "Musical Hospitality in the House of the Lord," *Reformed Liturgy & Music* 30/4 (1996): 224.

David B. Batchelder, Presbyterian pastor. "Counting the Cost: Assessing What's at Stake in the 'Worship Wars,'" *Reformed Liturgy & Music* 30/2 (1996): 89.

Frank C. Senn, "Worship and Evangelism," 24.

Dennis J. Hughes, editor of *Reformed Liturgy & Music*. "Editorial Introduction," *Reformed Liturgy & Music* 30/2 (1996): 42.

Hanan Yaqub, Minister of Worship and Music at Trinity United Presbyterian Church, Santa Ana CA. "A Case for Blended Worship," *Reformed Liturgy & Music* 30/2 (1996): 90.

Donald Wilson Stake, author and pastor of the Union Presbyterian Church, Schenectady NY. "The Liturgical Infection," *Reformed Liturgy & Music* 31/1 (1997): 15.

Chapter 8: Worship Reform—How?

Thomas H. Troeger, hymn poet and liturgist. Stanza 2 of *As a Chalice Cast of Gold*, from *New Hymns for the Lectionary: To Glorify the Maker's Name* (New York: Oxford UP, 1986), 6-7.

Susan B. Anthony (1820–1906), strategist and organizer behind the 19th-century women's suffrage movement. *The Last Word: A Treasury of Women's Quotes*, ed. Carolyn Warner (Englewood Cliffs NJ: Prentice Hall, 1992), 11.

Yme Woensdregt, member of the pastoral team at First Presbyterian Church, Regina, Saskatchewan. "The Pastor as Liturgist," *Reformed Liturgy & Music* 30/4 (1996): 171.

Davis Duggins, senior editor of *Moody*. Quoting pastor Charles Cooper in "The Worship Gap," *Moody* 96/6 (l996): 22.

Yme Woensdregt, "The Pastor as Liturgist," 168.

Yme Woensdregt, "The Pastor as Liturgist," 171.

Marjorie J. Thompson, an ordained minister of the Presbyterian Church (USA) who teaches at Vanderbilt Divinity School. *Soul Feast: An Invitation to the Christian Spiritual Life* (Louisville: Westminster John Knox Press, 1995), 61.

Paul Westermeyer, chair of the Department of Music at Elmhurst College and cantor at Ascension Lutheran in Riverside IL. *The Church Musician* (San Francisco: Harper, 1988), 69.

Carol Doran, composer and lecturer, and Thomas H. Troeger, hymn poet and liturgist. "Renewing Worship." Opinion expressed in a workshop presentation at Worship and Music Conference, Montreat NC, 24-30 June 1990.

Paul Waitman Hoon, professor of pastoral theology, retired, Union Theological Seminary, New York. *The Integrity of Worship* (Nashville: Abingdon, 1971), 23.

Chapter 9: The Planning Process

Bonnie Jean Lamberth, Director of Educational Ministries, Starmount Presbyterian, Greensboro NC. "Reclaiming Our Biblical Heritage," *Reformed Liturgy & Music* 31/2 (1997): 142.

Kennon L. Callahan, founder and senior consultant of The National Institute for Church Planning and Consultation. *Twelve Keys to an Effective Church: Strategic Planning for Mission* (San Francisco: HarperSanFrancisco, 1983), xx.

Chapter 10: A Team Approach to Planning

Leslie Withers, lay member of Oakhurst Baptist Church in Decatur GA. "Lay leadership in worship produces variety and involvement for all members," *SBC Today* 9/3 (1991): 9.

Chapter 11: The Consequences of Authentic Worship

Karl Barth, significant Protestant theologian of the 20th century. *The Doctrine of Reconciliation,* trans. G. W. Bromiley, vol. 4, 2 of *Church Dogmatics* (Edinburgh: T. & T. Clark, 1958), 696.

Joy Thompson, editorial writer for the Long Beach Press-Telegram, Long Beach CA. "Churches, take lead in service: Part of worship should be putting faith to work," *The Charlotte Observer,* 28 April 1997, 13A.

APPENDIX 2

Recommended Reading

The following six entries, duplicated from the Bibliography, include a brief annotation describing the focus of each book or periodical. This short list represents a recommended reading list for people wanting more. It is intended for those who wish to dig deeper into the subjects discussed in this study guide.

Detterman, Paul, ed. *Reformed Liturgy & Music.* Louisville KY: Theology & Worship, Congregational Ministries Division of the Presbyterian Church (USA), 1997.

A quarterly journal seeking to develop an understanding of Reformed piety, corporate worship, and the role of music in the life of the church through the contributions of many writers. Available by subscription from RL&M Administration Office, 100 Witherspoon Street, Room 2616A, Louisville KY 40202-1396.

Meeks, Blair Gilmer, ed. *The Landscape of Praise: Readings in Liturgical Renewal.* Valley Forge: Trinity Press International, 1996.

A collection of essays penned by a diverse group of writers representing a wide span of traditions and experience. The volume is designed for worshipers, students of liturgy, and any others who delight in praising God.

Mollenkott, Virginia Ramey. *The Divine Feminine: The Biblical Imagery of God as Female.* New York: Crossroad, 1994.

An excellent resource book useful for personal reflection and study as well as group discussion. Mollenkott defines the problem presented by patriarchal language and unearths the many feminine images for God found within the Scriptures.

Segler, Franklin M. *Christian Worship: Its Theology and Practice.* Nashville: Broadman Press, 1967.

A practical, easy-to-read, and concise primer on the meaning of worship providing guidelines for planning and leading worship, especially in evangelical churches within free-church traditions. The volume is designed for worshipers and worship leaders alike.

Underhill, Evelyn. *Worship.* New York: Crossroad, 1985.

Difficult to read in terms of style, organization, and depth, Underhill's Worship *is nevertheless worth the effort to those committed to a serious study of the theology of worship, particularly part 1. Her consistent use of non-personal metaphors naming God engages the imaginative reader as it captures a sense the Otherness of God.* Worship *is a remarkably deep and insightful book.*

Wren, Brian. *What Language Shall I Borrow? God-Talk in Worship: A Male Response to Feminist Theology.* New York: Crossroad, 1995.

An excellent resource for anyone interested in the issue of inclusive God-language and why it matters. The book focuses on questions of language and theological implications.

www.ingramcontent.com/pod-product-compliance
Lightning Source LLC
Chambersburg PA
CBHW062157080426
42734CB00010B/1725